City and Village in Iran

Settlement and Economy
in the Kirman Basin

City and Village
in Iran: SETTLEMENT
AND ECONOMY IN THE
KIRMAN BASIN

PAUL WARD ENGLISH

THE UNIVERSITY OF WISCONSIN PRESS
Madison, Milwaukee, and London   1966

Published by

THE UNIVERSITY OF WISCONSIN PRESS

Madison, Milwaukee, and London

U.S.A.: Box 1379, Madison, Wisconsin 53701

U.K.: 26–28 Hallam Street, London, W. 1

Copyright © 1966 by

the Regents of the University of Wisconsin

Printed in the United States of America by

North Central Publishing Co., St. Paul, Minnesota

Library of Congress Catalog Card Number 66–22856

To Pat and Paul II, who made
this task worthwhile, and to
Elisabeth Ann, who might have
read it.

Preface

The material presented in this book was collected during eighteen
months of field work in 1961–62. Two months were spent in
library research in England, two in travel from London overland to
Iran, three in preparatory work in Tehran, Yazd, and Isfahan, and the
remainder in Kirman and its villages — the actual field area. In the cities,
data were collected, officials were contacted, and library sources were
examined. Two secondary resources proved valuable: the First National
Iranian Census of 1956[1] and a local housing and population survey by
the Malaria Eradication Bureau in Kirman. Village questionnaires from
the 1956 Census provided information on village location, facilities, land
ownership, water supply, and economic activities. Individual household
questionnaires (in the form of 17,000 IBM cards) described each individual in the Mahan region in terms of location by village, age, sex, marital
status, place of birth, citizenship, religion, literacy, education, occupation,
employment status, household industries, and housing. Additional information on agriculture, ownership and cultivation of land, number and
types of domestic animals, and characteristics of household industries,
collected but not tabulated by the Department of Public Statistics (because of doubtful reliability), was copied from the original household
questionnaires.

With exceptions, the Iranian Census appears to be accurate. Data
on mountain villages tend to be erratic, because of deficiencies in collection techniques, lack of accurate knowledge of hamlet location, and the
fact that the Census was conducted in November when mountain people
move to the plains. Data on domestic animals, particularly herd animals,
were difficult to check systematically in the field and are of doubtful
reliability.

The 1961 population and housing survey of the Kuhi Jupar settlements by the Malaria Eradication Bureau in Kirman provided a comparative check on Census data, though information was not complete for large towns and cities. Where available, malaria data are accurate. Spraying teams penetrate even the most remote regions and their colored markings are seen on every peasant's house. Their field maps provided a reliable index of the location of small mountain hamlets.

The first step in field research was to establish a base in the town of Mahan from which villages selected for study could be reached by jeep or donkey. We (my wife and I) rented a house centrally located near the Shah Ni'matullah Vali Shrine and established communications with local political and social leaders, the *bakhshdar* (district head), the *shahrdar* (mayor), and the *kadkhuda* (superintendent of villages), through letters from officials in Kirman City. During the first two months in Mahan we completed a general survey of the area by traveling to each of its forty-two villages and hamlets. Comparative information on population, ownership of land and water, cropping patterns and rotations, specialized crafts, artisans, and herding was collected for each village. Before visiting a village we examined the Census IBM cards and malaria data so that any unusual features such as high or low household/water-supply ratio, large number of craftsmen, or high animal population could be investigated. In each village we selected interviewees on the basis of economic activity. If a village had farmers, shepherds, and weavers, representatives of each occupational group were interviewed in proportion to their importance in the village economy. Members of approximately 10–15% of all households were interviewed.

On the basis of this general survey and our increasingly intimate knowledge of the area and its people, categories of settlements (e.g. city, regional subcenter, large alluvial fan village) were determined. We then selected representative settlements within each category for detailed study and mapping. Two young Iranian schoolteachers were trained to map the houses, gardens, and fields of these "typical" settlements with Brunton compasses. One man mapped the area while the other collected data on land ownership, weaving contracts, cropping patterns, and herding arrangements. Temporary residence was established in each of these settlements, so that by living there we could gain a more detailed knowledge of its particular problems. Information was solicited from the villagers themselves, from village emigrants living in Mahan and Kirman, and from absentee owners and carpet contractors. In small settlements all or nearly all households were interviewed. In Mahan and Jupar approximately 20–25% of the households were examined closely; in Kirman, only about 5%.

Maps in this book are based on field work and other sources. The topographic base map of the Kirman Basin derives from Army Map Service 1942 revisions of older British India Survey maps (1:253,440)[2] and 1956 aerial photographs (1:60,000). The latter provided details on settlement location, irrigation networks, field patterns, and landscape features. Two bases were used for Kirman City maps: the Sahab Geographical and Drafting Institute's 1960 Street Map of Kirman (c. 1:-10,000)[3] and 1956 aerial photographs at scales of 1:6,000 and 1:12,500. Maps of smaller places were plane-tabled in the field with a Brunton compass. Elevations are referred to bench marks on the Army Map Service 1:1,000,000 and 1:253,440 sheets for the area. All figures were drafted by Michael E. Bonine, a graduate student at the University of Texas. All photographs in this study were taken in the field. The transliteration system used throughout is adapted from that of the Royal Asiatic Society; diacritical marks are omitted for ease of reading.

The field research for this study (NAS–NRC Foreign Field Research Program Report No. 28) was supported by the Foreign Field Research Program, administered by the Division of Earth Sciences, National Academy of Sciences–National Research Council, and sponsored by the Geography Branch, Office of Naval Research, Contract Nonr–2300(09), NR 389-105. In addition the Ford Foundation provided a grant for field mapping, and the Universities of Wisconsin and Texas supported library work and writing. In particular, I am indebted to Professors Andrew H. Clark and Frederick J. Simoons for constant encouragement, stimulation, and criticism. Suggestions for improving the manuscript were made by Carleton S. Coon, George J. Jennings, John F. Kolars, Robert C. Mayfield, and Robert J. Miller. In Iran many individuals gave of their time and knowledge: Arthur Goss, Jr., and his wife Betty, Theodore A. Wertime, Mrs. Farangis Yeganegi and Dr. Farhang Mehr of Tehran; Shah Jamshid and Hormuz Surushian, Jamshid Faruhar, Manuchehr Baghkhani, Hushang Masudi, and Farmandar Muhammad Zia'i of Kirman; and my wife Patricia, who assisted in every stage of research and writing. Many other Iranian and American officials, scholars, merchants, and farmers contributed — for which I am very grateful.

East Lansing, Michigan   PAUL WARD ENGLISH
January 31, 1966

Contents

LIST OF ILLUSTRATIONS   xiii

LIST OF TABLES   xv

INTRODUCTION   xvii

1   KIRMAN'S PHYSICAL ENVIRONMENT   3
   Climate   *7*
   Vegetation   *12*
   Soils   *14*

2   HISTORICAL DEVELOPMENT OF SETTLEMENT
     IN KIRMAN   18
   Pre-Sassanian Settlement in Kirman   *18*
   Organized Settlement in Kirman in
     Sassanian Times   *20*
   Islam in Kirman, 641–1850   *23*
   Growth under British Influence,
     1850–1925   *27*

3   THE PATTERN AND MORPHOLOGY OF
     SETTLEMENT   30
   The Settlement Pattern   *30*
   The Urban Center   *39*
   Alluvial Fan Towns and Villages   *49*
   Mountain Villages and Hamlets   *60*

4   TERRITORIAL SOCIOECONOMIC STRUCTURE   65
   Regional Patterns   *65*
   Economic Structure of Kirman City   *69*
   The Regional Subcenters: Mahan and Jupar   *79*

Large Agricultural-Weaving Villages   *83*
Small Villages and Hamlets   *85*

5   URBAN DOMINANCE AND THE REGIONAL
      ECONOMY   87

Maintenance of Urban Dominance   *88*
Impact of Urban Dominance on Rural
Settlements   *94*

6   STABILITY AND CHANGE IN KIRMAN   98
Social Change   *99*
Economic Change   *101*

7   CONCLUSIONS   111

APPENDIX A: Agriculture in Kirman: Crops,
Tools, and Techniques   117

APPENDIX B: Weaving a Kirman Carpet   125

APPENDIX C: Animal Husbandry in Kirman   128

APPENDIX D: Qanats in Kirman   135

APPENDIX E: Land Ownership in Kirman   141

APPENDIX F: Detailed Occupational Structure
of Settlements in Kirman   147

NOTES   155

BIBLIOGRAPHY   181

INDEX   192

Illustrations

Plates, following page 76

1 A   Kirman City from the summit of Qal'ehi Ardashir
1 B   A landlord's house in Kirman City
2 A   A view of upper Mahan
2 B   The Shah Ni'matullah Vali Shrine of Mahan
3 A   A village at the foot of the Kuhi Jupar
3 B   A village street scene
4 A   A mountain village in the Kuhi Jupar
4 B   Summer and winter homes of mountain villagers
5 A   A watercourse in Kirman City
5 B   Village women carrying water
6 A   The coppersmiths' section of the Vakil Bazaar
6 B   A religious leader at the Friday-prayer mosque
7 A   A water mill near Mahan
7 B   The carpenter of Langar repairing tools
8 A   Inspecting the carpet weaver's work
8 B   Weaving a Kirman carpet
9 A   A trip to the market and Friday religious services
9 B   "Taxis" carrying villagers to Kirman City
10 A   Threshing wheat with a *garjin*
10 B   Winnowing and sifting grain in Qanaghistan
11 A   Harvesting potatoes at Muhiabad
11 B   Dividing the harvest
12 A   Sheep and goats in the Kuhi Jupar
12 B   Fuel collectors near Daristan

Figures

1   Topography of Iran   4
2   Topography of the Kirman Basin   6

3	Climates of the Iranian Plateau	8
4	Temperature Ranges at Kirman	11
5	Soils of the Kirman Basin	15
6	Diagram of a Typical Qanat	31
7	Qanats of the Kirman Basin	32
8	Settlements in the Kirman Basin	33
9	Qanats of the Mahan Region	34
10	Settlement Pattern of Mahan	36
11	Nineteenth-Century Kirman	40
12	Modern Kirman	47
13	Integration of the Zoroastrian Quarter	48
14	Linear Settlement Patterns	51
15	Land Use in Sehkunj	52
16	Historical Development of Sehkunj	55
17	Toujigun — A Mountain Hamlet	63

Tables

1	Climatic Data for Kirman City	7
2	Monthly Precipitation (Inches) at Kirman, Iran, 1957–61	10
3	Construction of Buildings, Kirman City, 1956	43
4	Generalized Occupational Structure of Kirman City	70
5	Generalized Occupational Structures of Mahan and Jupar	79
6	Generalized Occupational Structures of the Large Agricultural-Weaving Villages	84
7	Generalized Occupational Structures of the Small Villages and Hamlets	85
8	Land in Crops in Selected Villages of the Kirman Basin	118
9	Location and Ownership of Cattle, Mahan Bakhsh, 1956	129
10	Location and Size of Cattle Holdings, Mahan Bakhsh, 1956	130
11	Location and Ownership of Donkeys, Mahan Bakhsh, 1956	130
12	Location and Size of Donkey Holdings, Mahan Bakhsh, 1956	131
13	Location and Ownership of Sheep, Mahan Bakhsh, 1956	132
14	Location and Size of Sheep Holdings, Mahan Bakhsh, 1956	133
15	Location and Ownership of Goats, Mahan Bakhsh, 1956	134

16   Location and Size of Goat Holdings,
     Mahan Bakhsh, 1956   134

17   Construction Costs of the Javadieh Qanat   139

18   Ownership of Land and Water,
     Mahan Bakhsh   142

19   Some Changes of Ownership in
     Mahan Bakhsh, 1956–62   145

Introduction

It is customary for writers to divide Middle Eastern society into three sectors — city, village, and tribe — each rooted in a separate social environment, each exploiting a different physical environment.[1] Invariably, such authors preface their discussions by warning readers that one must *not* view these segments as discrete economic realms, and cite examples to illustrate the mutual interdependence of each sphere: city dwellers depend on village-grown crops; villagers receive basic commodities, such as salt, sugar, and cloth, from the city; tribesmen supply wool and milk products to marketplaces in return for grain. Having delivered this warning, these writers proceed to discuss each segment as a self-contained system: cities are viewed as islands in a barren land, linked by networks of roads and caravan trails, and occupied by traders and processors who share in "urban" as opposed to "folk" culture; villages are isolated, self-sufficient, inward-looking peasant communities with few external relations; tribes are ethnic and/or political groups who migrate periodically in prescribed patterns. This tripartite view of the Middle East may be an acceptable classroom generalization, but it is unsuitable as a framework for scholarship.[2]

That the generalization has influenced scholarship on the Middle East is witnessed by numerous monographs using a city,[3] a village,[4] or a tribe[5] as the unit of study. In each case the internal structure and organization of the segment under consideration are of paramount concern; external social and economic relationships and the integration of the single community (whether city, village, or tribe) into a larger regional unit are deemphasized or omitted. This bias is particularly prevalent in village studies in which devout insistence on a clear division between "urban" and "rural" communities and the failure to view each settlement

xvii

as part of a larger pattern have caused some perplexing inconsistencies.[6] In Sweet's study of Tell Ṭoqaan, for example, a long and detailed examination of the *internal* structure and organization of the village leads the author to the puzzling conclusion that the "villagers" are "urbanized."[7] Alberts' village of Davarabad, south of Tehran, has nearly as many adult males working in secondary and tertiary activities as in agriculture.[8] In Gulick's village of Al-Munṣif, more villagers work in larger centers than in the village itself, and very few work in agriculture.[9] It is difficult to see, therefore, how the prototype "peasant society" is useful as a conceptual tool in the Middle East.

In the present work a "geographical" approach is used: the region, *not* a single community, is the unit of study.[10] The distribution and diversity of settlements and their functional integration in a complex regional organization are of paramount concern.[11] Spatial patterns of forms of livelihood, occupational structures, dwellings, and water supply systems within a single settlement and throughout the region reveal certain regular associations which combine to form the matrix of the Persian cultural landscape.[12] Analysis of these patterns and associations identifies and separates exceptions from the general rule, thereby lessening the dangers of generalization.

In many cases these spatial patterns vary regularly throughout the region. Individual exceptions reflect local adaptations designed to exploit a particular facet of the resource base or, alternatively, are vestigial remains of past events. But uniformity is the dominant characteristic of the pattern — and uniformity within this area is expectable. The region after all is small and contiguous. Moreover, it is occupied by a single people (Farsi-speaking, Muslim Iranians) possessed of a relatively homogeneous culture and technology. Above and beyond this, however, there is strong evidence that the rural settlements of this region are dominated by the city; that village morphology, economic structure, and territorial organization are products of centralized urban control of rural resources.

The existence of this regional organization of human activity is a major theme of this study. It identifies the Persian landscape as a product of a feudal rather than folk society.[13] Villages are not isolated from the city or from one another. There are strong patterns of interrelatedness between every village and the city, and weaker social and economic ties among villages. The peasantry produces a large enough food surplus to support the heterogeneous occupational structures found in large population centers. Transportation and communication systems link all settlements into the larger pattern. Essentially the same cohesive social and economic region commonly found in more humid areas is found here, descriptions of isolated peasant villages, subsistence economies, and scattered oases notwithstanding.

The field area (the Kirman Basin) provides an excellent laboratory for testing this regional approach. Kirman's physical environment (Chapter 1) presents many of the same problems to permanent settlers as other Middle Eastern areas. It lies in a mountain-ringed basin, has little rainfall, scanty vegetation, and poor soils. All crops must be irrigated and protected from blowing sand; grazing resources have deteriorated, and the fuel problem is acute. The growth of settlement in Kirman (Chapter 2) is at least partly explained by this marginal environment. Kirman was not settled until the third century, when a Sassanian king established a defensive outpost there. Communal clan settlements, often used to explain communal traits in Middle Eastern villages, probably never existed in Kirman;[14] and if one thinks of the number of cities established by urban societies as military camps, fortified monasteries (*ribat*s), and princely towns distributed throughout the Middle East, Kirman may be representative in this regard as well.[15]

Settlements in the Kirman Basin (Chapter 3) range in size and complexity from a major city to mountain hamlets, and include regional sub-centers, large villages, and small villages.[16] There is enough settlement diversity to test the urban-rural hypothesis discussed above. Water is the principal prerequisite for permanent settlement; the *qanat* system which supplies water has shaped the settlement pattern. The economic structures of settlements in Kirman (Chapter 4) vary, but agriculturalists are a majority only in the smallest, most remote villages and hamlets.[17] Most of the people are weavers, merchants, professionals, and unskilled laborers. The organization of economic activity in all settlements is dominated by city dwellers.[18]

This concept of urban dominance (Chapter 5) is a key to understanding settlement and economy in Kirman and explains some of the perplexities produced by village studies elsewhere in the Middle East. The persistent control of hinterland resources by urbanites presumes constant communication between the two "spheres." It explains the urbanized peasantry of the region; they are the logical product of centuries of intimate contact with the city.[19] The underdeveloped nature of small settlements (one reason why they have all been called villages) is also explained by the system of contracts which drains rural economic vitality and concentrates wealth

in the city. In addition, urban dominance clarifies the nature and importance of change (Chapter 6) in Kirman's society and economy. It provides
a different vantage point from which the "stability in change" phenomenon described by Gulick and Alberts can be viewed.[20] In Kirman, modernization has not altered the fundamental organization of economic
activity, despite the ubiquity of Western technology and material goods.

Finally, this study of settlement and economy in Kirman raises questions. *What is the nature of settlement in the Middle East?* Is the cohesive,
hierarchical pattern of settlement found in more humid regions also characteristic in the Middle East, as the data from Kirman suggest? Are
dry-land settlements really scattered, independent units or has the clear
division between desert and sown, the apparent isolation of "oasis type"
settlements on barren landscapes, deceived students of the area into
viewing them as isolates rather than as elements in a rational complex?
Whatever the reason, regional settlement patterns in arid areas are rarely
mentioned in the literature. Secondly, *What is the nature of Middle Eastern social and economic organization?* Can society be divided into "rural"
and "urban" spheres or is there an urban-rural continuum where the
idealized "peasant society" plays a minor role? It is logical to assume that
the great cities of the Middle East were supported for centuries by a
hinterland isolated from urban influence or that an organized system
of control existed? Thirdly, *What is the nature of change in the Middle
East?* What has been the impact on Iranian society and economy of the
technological revolution which is sweeping this part of the world? Are
the Iranians assimilating elements of change or are they modifying them
to fit traditional patterns? What is the "culture core" of Iranian society,
and has it altered under the pressures of Westernization? These questions
are discussed tentatively in the concluding chapter — tentatively, because
the Kirman Basin is after all a very small part of the Middle East, and
comparative studies are too fragmented at present to allow for proven
generalizations. If more studies by anthropologists, economic historians,
geographers, and other social scientists accumulate, this condition will
pass.

City and Village in Iran

Settlement and Economy
in the Kirman Basin

Chapter 1

Kirman's Physical Environment

The heartland of Iran is a high plateau bordered by the Elburz Mountains in the north, the highlands of eastern Iran and Afghanistan in the east, and the Zagros ranges in the west and south (Fig. 1).[1] Several intermontane basins lie on the margins of this plateau; its center is dominated by two of the most forbidding deserts in the world, the Great Kavir (Dashti Kavir) and the Southern Lut (Dashti Lut). Iranian civilization developed in cities located on the inner flanks of the Zagros and Elburz between the mountains and the central deserts. Important trade routes connected these cities. In the north the great silk road passed westward through Mashhad, Damghan, Tehran, and Qazvin before crossing the Zagros into Mesopotamia. The ancient Indian highway ran from Tehran and Qazvin in the north through Qumm, Kashan, Isfahan, Yazd, and Kirman to centers on the Indian subcontinent.

These plateau cities were populated by Persian-speaking Iranians and persistently remained so, whereas numerous invasions modified the ethnic composition and language of outlying sectors of Iran. To be sure, some localized regional characteristics did develop within each intermontane basin around major cities such as Isfahan, Yazd, and Kirman,[2] but these differences were never of primary importance. Constant communication existed between the cities in this arc of settlement; smaller towns such as Anar and Na'in functioned as connecting points (roughly eighty miles apart) between them.

Kirman City is located at the southern end of this arc of settlement.[3] It became the capital of Kirman Province in the tenth century when a local governor moved his capital eastward from Sirjan to escape the growing power of the Buwayhid dynasty of Fars.[4] Subsequently, Kirman

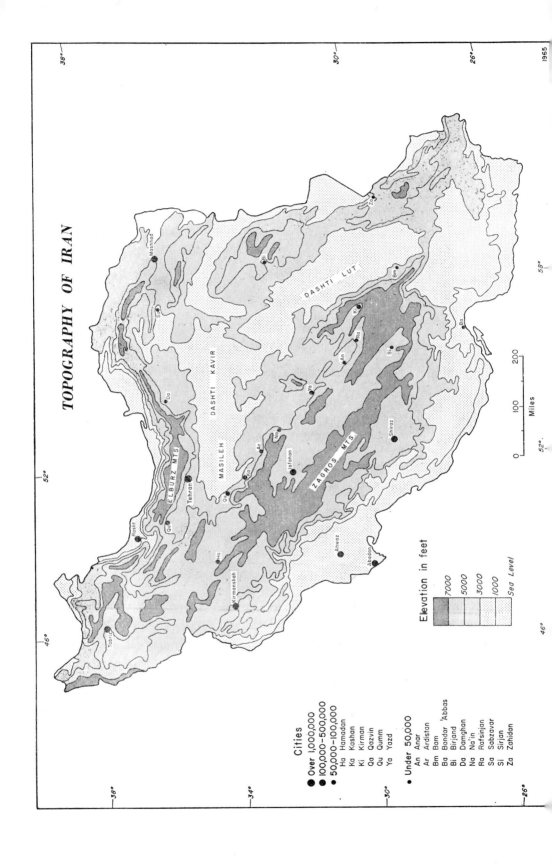

TOPOGRAPHY OF IRAN

ELBURZ MTS

DASHTI KAVIR

MASILEH

DASHTI LUT

ZAGROS MTS

Moshhad
Sa
Da
Bi
Ki
Ra
An
Ya
Si
Bm
Za
Ba
Rasht
Tabriz
Go
Tehran
Qu
Ka
Ar
No
Isfahan
Ha
Kirmanshah
Shiraz
Ahwaz
Abadan

Cities

Over 1,000,000 ●

100,000–500,000 ●

50,000–100,000 ·

Ha Hamadan
Ka Kashan
Ki Kirman
Qa Qazvin
Qu Qumm
Ya Yazd

Under 50,000 •

An Anar
Ar Ardistan
Bm Bam
Ba Bandar Abbas
Bi Birjand
Da Damghan
Na Na'in
Ra Rafsinjan
Sa Sabzavar
Si Sirjan
Za Zahidan

Elevation in feet

7000
5000
3000
1000
Sea Level

0   100   200
Miles

1965

38°   30°   26°   58°   52°   46°   52°   46°   26°   38°   34°   30°

City became the major cultural, economic, and administrative center of southern Iran, serving both Kirman Province and Iranian Baluchistan.[5] At present the city has a population of more than 60,000 and lies on the major north-south highway connecting Tehran and points west with the Indian subcontinent.

The site of Kirman City is similar to that of other Iranian plateau cities. It is located in the mountain-ringed Kirman Basin at an elevation of approximately 5,680 feet. The center of the basin is a sand dune plain roughly twenty miles in diameter (Fig. 2). Kirman lies on the northern edge of this plain where several isolated crags, the basis for defense in ancient times, rise to heights of more than 7,000 feet. The plain is bounded on all sides by coarse alluvial fans which rise steeply to the surrounding mountain massifs. The break in slope between mountains and alluvial fans is sharp; it lies at an elevation of 7,500 feet in the northwest and 7,000 feet in the southeast, because the entire region tilts gently to the south.

The mountain massifs are formed of sandstones and shales overlain by dark limestones.[6] They are interrupted by passes through which routes of travel and trade enter and leave the basin. East of the city the mountains are almost continuous, with peaks such as Kuh Paiyeh and Kuhi Sehkunj reaching heights of more than 12,000 feet. These separate the Kirman Basin from the barren Dashti Lut to the east.[7] The western and southern mountains form three discrete ranges — Kuhi Badaman, Kuhi Dukhtar, and Kuhi Jupar — bordered by four passes. The Kuhi Badaman range in the northwest reaches a maximum elevation of more than 10,000 feet. Between this massif and Kuhi Darmanu in the northeast, a minor trade route runs northward to the ancient weaving center of Ravar, eighty miles north of Kirman City on the edge of the Dashti Lut. Kuhi Dukhtar (8,300 feet) in the southwest is a less imposing upland. In the gap between it and Kuhi Badaman, the major north-south highway from Isfahan and Yazd enters the basin at the town of Baghin (see Fig. 5, p. 15). The third massif, Kuhi Jupar, south of Kirman City, is most striking. Its snow-capped peaks rise to elevations of 11,000–13,000 feet. On the eastern side of this range the north-south highway leaves the basin at Mahan and continues eastward to Bam, Zahidan, and the Iran-Pakistan border.

Fig. 1 (*facing page*). Adapted from Bartholomew's 1:4,000,000 map of the Middle East.

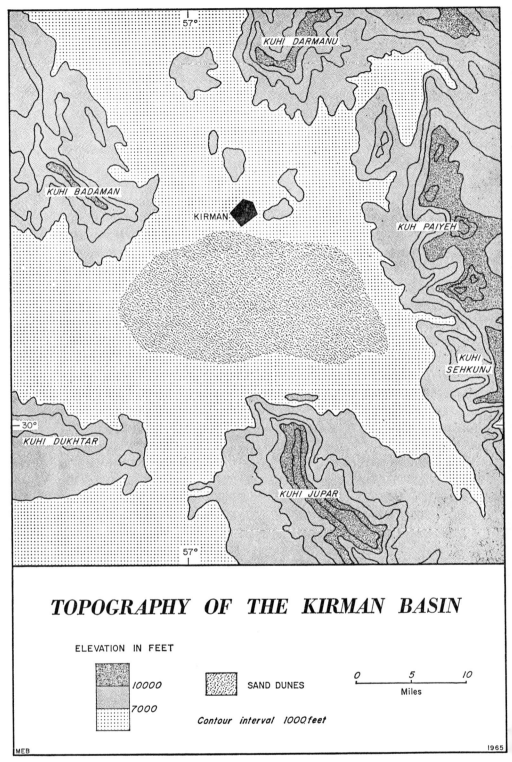

Fig. 2. Data from American Map Service Sheets H–40J, H–40I and 1956 aerial photographs (1:60,000).

CLIMATE

The Central Plateau of Iran is a region of steppes and deserts.[8] High pressure systems centered over Central Asia dominate the climate of the plateau in winter, except when infrequent low pressure systems from the Mediterranean Basin penetrate the Zagros to bring winter rain. In summer the Central Plateau is influenced by a low pressure system extending from the Arabian Peninsula through Persia to Sind. Spring and fall are short variable intervals between long, cold winters and equally long, hot summers. Because large scale pressure patterns are dominant in central Iran, Kirman's climate is representative of a large region. Figure 3 presents temperature and precipitation data for seven stations on the margins of the Central Plateau: Tehran, Isfahan, Yazd, Kirman, Zahidan, Birjand, and Sabzavar. Five of these seven stations (excepting Yazd and Zahidan) have average annual temperatures of 61–62°F. The variation in precipitation is somewhat greater; Yazd is the driest station, with 2.8 inches; Birjand the wettest, with 11.1.

Low rainfall is the most important climatic obstacle to sedentary agri-

TABLE 1
Climatic Data for Kirman City

	Mean temp. °F	Mean maximum temp. °F	Mean minimum temp. °F	Mean temp. range °F	Precipitation in inches	Relative humidity %
Jan.	42.4	55.0	29.8	25.2	1.42	57
Feb.	47.0	60.4	33.6	26.8	.87	51
March	52.6	64.6	40.6	24.0	1.81	43
April	61.8	75.7	47.9	27.8	.87	41
May	69.4	84.7	54.1	30.6	.79	32
June	77.4	93.0	61.8	31.2	.08	20
July	80.0	95.7	64.3	31.4	.27	19
Aug.	77.1	94.6	59.6	35.0	. . .	21
Sept.	72.0	89.8	54.2	35.6	.16	23
Oct.	61.6	80.1	43.1	37.0	.12	31
Nov.	50.9	67.1	34.7	32.4	.31	48
Dec.	43.7	56.8	30.6	26.2	1.26	54
YEAR	61.3	76.4	46.1	30.3	7.96	36

Source: Temperature and precipitation data are based on Iranian Meteorological Department records for an 11-year period, 1951–61. Relative humidity figures are based on records for a 6-year period, 1955–61. Comparative data for earlier periods may be found in G. Stratil-Sauer, "Beobachtungen zur Sommerwitterung einer südpersichen Höhenstation (Ra'in)," *Gerlands Beiträge zur Geophysik*, 41 (1941): 193–225; Philip H. T. Beckett and E. D. Gordon, "The Climate of Kerman, South Persia," *Quarterly Journal of the Royal Meteorological Society*, 82 (1956): 503–14.

CLIMATES OF THE IRANIAN PLATEAU

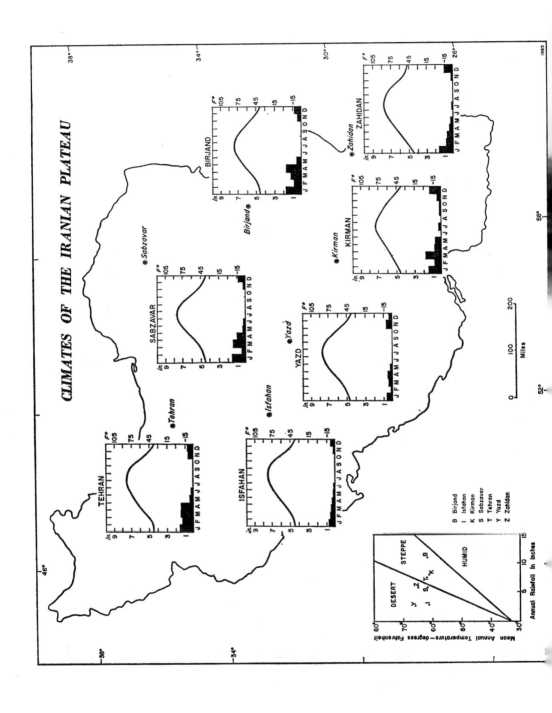

culture in Kirman. Settlements are located where water can be brought to the surface, because all crops must be irrigated.[9] Between 1951 and 1961 the mean annual rainfall at Kirman amounted to less than eight inches (Table 1). Most of this rain fell during the winter and spring months, when cyclonic storms from the Mediterranean penetrated Iran bringing cold front showers to Kirman. Except for infrequent summer thunderstorms and rare monsoon rains, these winter cyclones produce all of Kirman's precipitation.[10] But this rainfall is not an unmixed blessing. Cold front rains in winter and thundershowers in summer often cause considerable damage. Short, intense showers wash whole villages away; adobe houses absorb water and collapse. Perhaps most critical, subterranean irrigation tunnels (*qanats*) are destroyed by torrents of water which flood wadis and pour into the qanat shafts; and when a qanat is destroyed, agricultural activity in the settlement must halt until repairs are completed (see Appendix D, and Fig. 6, p. 31). In April 1962 cold front rains devastated Tehran, Kirman, Shiraz, and Kirmanshah. Nearly five inches of rain fell in less than four days. Hundreds of qanats and more than seven thousand homes were destroyed in these cities.

Furthermore, annual rainfall in Kirman is variable (Table 2). In 1957, for example, Kirman received more than 12 inches of rain (153% of the 1951–61 average); but one year later, in 1958, less than 3 inches (34% of the average) fell in Kirman. In 1960 more than one-third of the year's precipitation fell in March, yet in 1959 less than one-tenth fell in that month. This variability causes considerable hardship to shepherds and farmers in mountainous areas. If the winter rains are late or fail to come, sheep and goats grow thin and die; flock owners and shepherds alike suffer. Farmers in these mountain villages are also vulnerable to rainfall variability. Their qanats are too shallow to penetrate the permanent water table (if such exists) and in drought years these qanats dry up, leaving the wheat and barley crops to wilt in the fields. Settlements at lower elevations generally have more reliable sources of water so that drought affects them more indirectly, through loss of animals and depletion of natural pastures. The people of Kirman have either too little rainfall or rainfall that is delivered too intensely. Unfortunately one or the other condition obtains in most years.

Fig. 3 (*facing page*). Data based on six-year temperature and precipitation averages (1956–61) from the records of the Iranian Meteorological Department.

TABLE 2
Monthly Precipitation (Inches) At Kirman, Iran, 1957–61

	1957	1958	1959	1960	1961	Mean no. rainy days
Jan.	4.05	1.06	1.02	.87	.55	5.2
Feb.	.47	.24	.12	.88	.47	2.6
March	1.22	.63	.19	3.60	1.22	5.0
April	2.44	.08	.26	1.77	1.00	7.4
May	1.02	.24	1.71	.63	.69	4.4
June	.31	. . . .	. . . .	. . . .	. . . .	.4
July	. . . .	. . . .	. . . .	.75	. . . .	.6
Aug.	.02	. . . .	. . . .	. . . .	. . . .	. . .
Sept.	. . . .	. . . .	. . . .	1.41	.11	.4
Oct.	.04	.04	. . . .	. . . .	. . . .	.4
Nov.	1.30	.06	.63	. . . .	.39	3.2
Dec.	1.34	.35	1.14	. . . .	.23	2.0
YEAR	12.21	2.70	5.07	9.91	4.66	31.6

Data for 1957–59 are taken from the *Meteorological Yearbook of Iran* for 1957, 1958, and 1959. Data for 1960 and 1961 are based on unpublished monthly weather summaries for Kirman. Any day with a rainfall of 1.0 mm. (0.039 inches) or more is considered to be a rainy day.

Temperatures in Kirman present fewer problems to sedentary agriculturalists than rainfall, but they too play a role in settlement and economy. Summers are long and hot; July is the warmest month, with an average temperature of about 80°F (Table 1). Winters are also long and are cold enough to require domestic heating, particularly in the mountains. The coldest months are December and January, both of which have average temperatures between 40 and 50°F. Spring and fall are short, cool, delightful seasons.

The annual range of temperature is about 30°F; absolute maximum and minimum temperatures differ by as much as 100°F.[11] Diurnal temperature ranges are also high, and variations of more than 40°F between day and night are common (Fig. 4). Usually the smallest and largest diurnal ranges occur in winter. They are smallest when depressions move into southern Iran and increase humidity and cloud cover (Fig. 4, Jan. 22, 23); they are largest when cold, katabatic winds sweep down from the Kuhi Jupar range onto the plain (Fig. 4, Jan. 3, 26). Because these mountain winds bring freak frosts in April and May, and the winters are so cold, dates and citrus fruit are not grown in Kirman.

Winds at Kirman change regularly throughout the year with the large-scale pressure systems. In winter and spring cyclonic depressions crossing

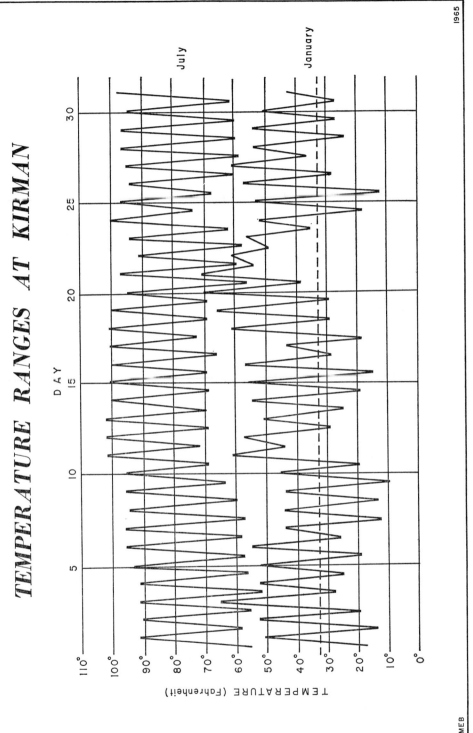

Fig. 4. Data from monthly temperature records (1961) of the Iranian Meteorological Department.

the Central Plateau north of Kirman produce veering wind shifts and strong south and southwesterly winds; intervals between cyclones are marked by weak north and northeasterly winds. From May to December calms prevail about 75% of the time, because of the sheltering effects of surrounding mountains. But nearly every afternoon strong gusts of wind and dust devils blow down the two broad open valleys which enter the basin at Baghin in the west and at Ikhtiarabad and Zangiabad in the north (see Fig. 8, p. 33). These winds are powerful and the sand they bear may frost windshields, remove the paint from automobile fenders, and inundate orchards. Under their influence, sand dunes on the central plain of Kirman have migrated to its southern and southeastern margins, obliterating the old Kirman-Jupar road and covering the northernmost fields of Mahan with sand.

This climatic information applies to the Kirman plain. In nearby mountains, temperatures are lower and precipitation is greater. Fragmentary data for the mountain hamlet of Char-Khanu in the Kuhi Badaman (7,000 feet) and the alluvial fan town of Jupar (6,500 feet) indicate a 16°F daily mean difference in temperature between these two locations.[12] These colder temperatures are reflected in a noticeably shorter growing season in the mountains (see Appendix A), a greater consumption of fuel in winter, and the migration of flocks to the plain during the months of December and January.

VEGETATION

The vegetation of Kirman is sparse.[13] Nothing larger than a bush grows wild in the basin, though at higher elevations one occasionally finds groves of stunted trees in isolated mountain valleys. Except for oasis-like patches of cultivated land near villages, barren sand, gravel, and stone cover large areas. Aridity, summer drought, and high summer temperatures have limited the native vegetation to hardy xerophytic species. Adaptations to these severe environmental conditions vary: dwarf tamarisk, wild rose, and scrub oak have deep and extensive root systems; laurel, oleander, sagebrush, and camelthorn have thick, shiny leaves or spiny thorns that reduce moisture loss by evaporation and transpiration.

The vegetation of Kirman exhibits the expected variation in species and density as elevation changes. In the low foothills a sparse "camelthorn association" is found. Here the manna-producing camelthorn (*Alhagi camelorum*) and other milk-producing vetches (*Hedysarum alhagi, Astragalus gossypinus, A. echidnaeformis*) are found. Wormwoods and other thistle shrubs (*Artemisia absinthium*), sagebrush (*Artemisia* sp.?), and a variety of sages (*Salvia* spp.?) are located in scattered wadis. The common rue (*Ruta graveolens*) and a sagelike plant (locally called *khur*) grow as weeds in and around the cultivated fields.

In mountain valleys at elevations of 7,500–9,000 feet, the camelthorn association gives way to an open, parklike scrub. Vegetation is thicker here because summer temperatures are lower, rainfall is higher, and the land has been less completely scoured by fuel collectors and grazing flocks of sheep and goats. But mature trees are found only in isolated wadis or along watercourses. To achieve maturity, a wild tree must literally have religious or sacred significance.[14] These mountain valleys are used as summer pastures for flocks owned by plains dwellers, and supply the fuel wood and charcoal burned in towns at lower elevations. Dwarf tamarisk (*Tamarisk gallica, T. mannifera*) is the major forage plant here, but it is not tapped for manna in Kirman as it is in Yazd and Mashhad.[15] Upland varieties of Astragalus (*A. geminanus*) produce gum tragacanth, used locally as a shampoo. Many shrubs and thistles, notably species of the wild rose family, also supply forage and fuel. Wild almond, pistachio, and stunted oak trees (*Quercus persica*) are rare, however, because their wood is prized for toolmaking, fuel, and other industrial uses. At higher elevations (over 9,000 feet) the open scrub vegetation is succeeded by a thin cover of mats and thorn cushions, the only plants capable of surviving cold winters on very thin soils.

Man's role in altering the vegetation of Kirman has been critical.[16] Accessible areas on the plains and in the low foothills have been stripped of natural vegetation. Sheep and goats (and other domestic animals in the immediate vicinity of settlements) have destroyed pastures, and fuel collectors have uprooted trees and shrubs. Thus, woody plants and natural forage plants have been removed, leaving thistles, thorn cushions, and small herbs behind. According to Bobek, the natural vegetation of the mountain massifs around the Kirman Basin was "Bergmandel-Pistazien-Baumflur."[17] One rarely finds a wild almond or pistachio tree in these mountains now.

In recent years several factors have accelerated destruction of the remaining vegetation (see Chapter 6). Population has increased and settlement has advanced deeper into the mountain valleys. Trucks and jeeps are now used for fuel collection. In the immediate hinterlands of Kirman City, Zarand, and Shahdad alone, 173,000 goats and 120,000 sheep are grazed on natural pastures.[18] These animals are now grazing in more restricted areas, further depleting the carrying capacity of the land.

In addition to supplying fuel and forage, a number of specific plants are collected by villagers or are allowed to grow wild in the village fields and along watercourses.[19] Most of these plants are used as dyes in the carpet weaving industry; indigo (*Indigofera* spp.?), madder (*Rubia tinctorum*), weld (*Reseda luteola*), and henna (*Lawsonia inermis*) are the most important dye producers. Still other wild plants are valued for magical and medicinal qualities: specifically the common rue (*Ruta graveolens*), pennyroyal (*Mentha pulegium*), mandrake (*Mandragora officinarum*), Job's-tears (*Coix lacryma-jobi*), hound's tongue (*Cynoglossum officinale*), wild mustard (*Brassica alba, B. nigra*), chicory (*Cichorium intybus*), fennel (*Foeniculum vulgare*), and fenugreek (*Trigonella foenumgraecum*). Medicinal plants grown in the household gardens of Kirman include leek (*Allium porrum*), castor-oil (*Ricinus communis*), and coriander (*Coriandrum sativum*). Camelthorn and gum tragacanth, cummin (*Cuminum cyminum*), caraway (*Carum carui*), several species of asafoetida (*Ferula alliacea, F. persica*), and sesame (*Sesamum indicum*) are collected and cultivated as spices.

SOILS

The soils of the Kirman Basin also reflect its dry climate and the impact of man.[20] In this arid environment, mechanical weathering dominates; chemical and biological weathering proceed slowly. Most soils are thin, poorly developed, and unstructured. These skeletal soils vary with local parent material, whereas alluvial soils are graded in size and texture by elevation and location. Only cultivated soils have depth and maturity, reflecting their centuries of human use.[21]

Skeletal soils are found in the mountain massifs surrounding the Kirman Basin (Fig. 5). Slopes in these uplands are nearly devoid of soil; many are bare rock outcrops with piles of unsorted talus at their base. Where soils are found in the mountains, they are thin (2-6 inches) and are held in place by xerophytic mats and camelthorn. Cretaceous limestone is the parent material at higher elevations (above 9,000 feet), interbedded shales and sandstones at lower elevations. Soils located on the latter are better developed because sandstones and shales weather more rapidly than limestone in Kirman's climate.

Alluvial fans form a band around the margins of the Kirman Basin (Fig. 5). Where the slope between mountains and plain is steep, the band

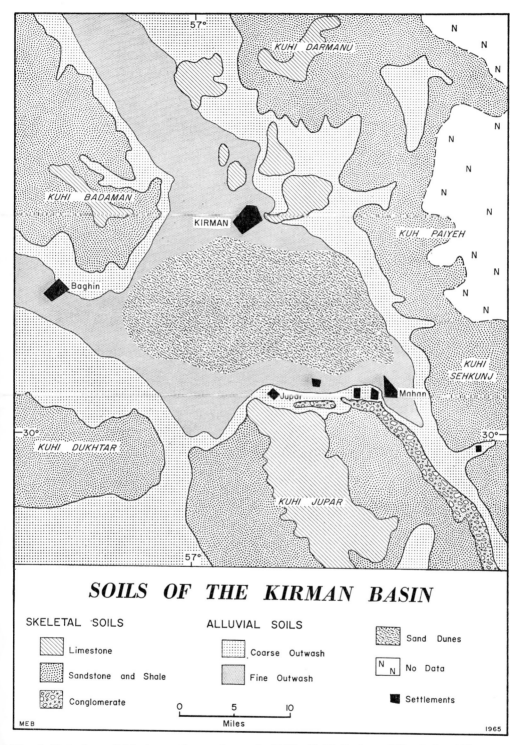

SOILS OF THE KIRMAN BASIN

SKELETAL SOILS

Limestone

Sandstone and Shale

Conglomerate

ALLUVIAL SOILS

Coarse Outwash

Fine Outwash

Sand Dunes

No Data

Settlements

0   5   10
Miles

MEB

1965

Fig. 5. Data from field observation and map in Philip H. T. Beckett, "The Soils of Kerman, South Persia," *Journal of Soil Science*, 9 (1958): 21.

is narrow. Where broad valleys enter the basin in the north and west, wider alluvial zones are found. These soils are graded by location on the slopes of the piedmont fans. The tops of the slopes are covered with rock debris and gravel. At lower elevations, coarse alluvium gives way to fine outwash alluvium, light-textured sandy loams, and clays. Farther out on the plain, alluvial soils are replaced by sand dunes and saline soils. Every large settlement in the basin (Kirman City, Baghin, Mahan, and Jupar) is located in the alluvial zone between the talus slopes and the sand dune plain.

Cultivated alluvial soils in Kirman differ strongly from natural alluvium. They are found on the lower margins of the fans, bordered upslope by coarse gravels and downslope by fine sand (Fig. 5). They are usually low in nitrogen, but vary in this depending on the location and use of each individual field.[22] Soils in the central section of a village are cultivated in vegetables, forage crops, and tree crops, and are heavily fertilized. Manure, night soil, and chemical compounds are applied (unless the owner is impoverished) whenever yields begin to decline. These soils are fine-grained dark loams, high in organic matter and nitrogen. But soils in the large winter grainfields below the village are less fertile, lighter in color, lower in nitrogen and humus content, and coarser in texture. These fields are cultivated once every three or four years; the rotation varies from village to village. Thus, soils closest to the village are most fertile, whereas those farther away produce lower yields; adjustments in land tenure contracts recognize this fact.

The cultivated soils of Kirman often have salt accumulations in their lower levels, but whether this is caused by deposition or soil processes is uncertain.[23] In most alluvial fan villages, slopes are sufficiently steep to allow for natural drainage. White salt crusts are sometimes seen on the sides of water channels, but surface salt rime is usually confined to outwash plains below the village. In the mountain valleys, however, salt accumulation has frequently caused abandonment of settlements. Villages located on small, poorly drained patches of alluvium are bothered most by salt accumulation. Significantly, the place names of many of these hamlets include the word "salt" (*shur*): Shurabad (Salt Village), Qal'ehi Shur (Salt Castle), Shurdar (Door of Salt) and Mazra'eh Shur (Salt Fields) are examples (see Fig. 10, p. 36). All are located on alluvial terraces in the valleys of the Kuhi Jupar; Qal'ehi Shur and Shurdar have been abandoned whereas Mazra'eh Shur has been built on the ruins of an earlier abandoned village.

One final soil problem needs to be mentioned. As noted earlier, the Kirman plain is occupied by shifting sand dunes which are encroaching on the northernmost fields of Mahan, Langar, and Qanaghistan (see Fig. 8, p. 33). Over the years these dunes have been noted by many travelers. In 1952 Beckett mentioned that sand was blowing onto cultivated land, forcing it out of cultivation.[24] A half-century earlier, however, Sir Percy Sykes reported that gardens were "dominating the sand" and that encroachment was not a problem.[25] This apparent disagreement stems from the fact that both processes — encroachment of sand on cultivated land and extension of cultivation onto the plain — are occurring in different parts of the Kirman Basin. At the foot of the Kuhi Jupar, wind erosion is occurring in the upwind (western) settlements, and gardens are being built farther onto the plain. The newly constructed village of Javadieh is an example of this advance. Here topsoil has been carried away by the wind, and cultivated land inside the walled gardens lies several feet higher than the surrounding land, posing a problem of lifting irrigation water to this higher surface.[26] But in the central and eastern settlements at the base of the Kuhi Jupar (e.g. Qanaghistan, Langar, and Mahan) the outer margins of the grainfields have been covered by sand dunes, and no new gardens have been built. Walled gardens in exposed locations in this section of the basin are partially submerged in sand, and the interiors of the gardens lie several feet lower than surrounding land. Irrigation channels to these gardens are deep and must be continuously cleared of sand.

In summary, Kirman's physical environment presents many problems to permanent settlers in the region. Modern Iranians must combat drought, variable rainfall, extreme temperatures, scanty vegetation, rugged terrain, blowing sand, and poor soils, with a limited technology operating within the framework of a feudal society. Even under the best of conditions this environment would be classified as marginal. Yet the Iranians have occupied it for centuries and during these centuries have adjusted their technology and in some cases found new solutions to the problems of permanent settlement in Kirman. The historical development of this region, then, is a story that needs to be told.

Chapter 2

Historical Development of Settlement in Kirman

A settled population existed in Kirman Province as early as the fifth millennium B.C.,[1] living by irrigated and nonirrigated agriculture and various forms of herding. Many of these ancient settlements were destroyed during the Indo-Iranian invasions of the second millennium B.C., when powerful tribes of mounted nomads conquered the Central Plateau of Iran.[2] Centuries later when these nomads themselves settled, a new water supply system, the qanat, was available. The pre-Indo-Iranian settlement pattern therefore bears little relation to the later pattern; but it does provide a comparison, which emphasizes the critical role of water supply in the nature and growth of settlement in Kirman.

The principal factors in the location of pre-Indo-Iranian settlements were water availability and defense. Lacking advanced irrigation techniques, these early settlements were located where natural supplies of irrigation water were accessible at or near the surface: in river valleys, at the mouths of wadis, and in some well-watered mountain valleys. The largest settlements in Kirman Province existed in the river valleys. In the Halil Rud valley of Jiruft and at Bampur, permanent settlement is evidenced by extensive ruins with finely glazed pottery, alabaster, and bronze ware.[3] More numerous but smaller sites are found where piedmont fans meet the plain, as evidenced by surface mounds which rise as much as one hundred feet above the surrounding landscape. Sir Aurel Stein excavated one such village at a place called Talli Iblis (Devil's Mound), near the town of Mashiz southwest of Kirman City.[4]

Talli Iblis is located between piedmont and plain at the mouth of an

18

ancient channel of the Lalehzar River (Rudi Lalehzar).[5] The cultivated fields were located above the village and irrigated by simple diversion channels from the Lalehzar River. The village was built on a mound thirty-seven feet high and more than a hundred yards in diameter. It was walled, and all of its early inhabitants lived within the walls. Talli Iblis was abandoned during the Indo-Iranian invasions and never reoccupied. Smaller settlements also existed in the mountain valleys in early times. The village excavated by Sykes at Khinaman in the Kuhi Badaman mountains west of Kirman City was small and unwalled.[6] It was situated on an alluvial terrace watered by a natural spring. Unfortunately, bronze and ceramic objects from Khinaman have never been clearly dated.[7]

The importance of defense in these early settlements is reflected in their morphology, if not in their sites. With the exception of mountain hamlets such as Khinaman, all known settlements were walled. The fortress (*qal'eh*) formed the core of the settlement; most houses were single-storied mud affairs located within the village walls. Wells supplied domestic water to the qal'eh. The fields were irrigated by intermittent streams or permanent springs. This type of settlement apparently originated in Iran and then spread throughout the Middle East and into Central Asia.[8]

The critical difference between the pre- and post-Indo-Iranian settlement patterns lies in the use of the alluvial fans. In both periods the largest towns were located at low elevations on the plains or in river valleys, where wells could supply domestic water to the qal'eh in times of crisis. But the earliest settlers could not exploit the alluvial fans; their technology was too primitive to cope with the problems of water supply. The ground water table was too deep for wells, and the wadis were too deeply incised in the fans for simple diversion channels. Also, the alluvial fans may well have been forested then, which would have made them less attractive to agriculturalists.[9]

By the sixth century B.C., when the Indo-Iranians began to settle as agriculturalists, to worship one god (Ahura Mazda), and to conquer the Old World under the leadership of Cyrus and Darius, qanat technology was known on the Central Plateau and was used in the Achaemenian capital city, Istakhr (Persepolis).[10] Three centuries later, when the Parthians invaded Iran from the northeast, qanats were in widespread use on the Central Plateau.[11] These gently sloping infiltration channels opened the alluvial fans to settlement and established the foundation of modern plateau settlement patterns.

But permanent settlement did not develop in the Kirman Basin during Achaemenian and Parthian times. Kirman was remote from the centers of change in Iran and off the major trade routes, an isolated district in a frontier province with no major cultural, commercial, or administrative center. The climate of Kirman was dry, with hot summers and cold winters. There was little to recommend the area to agricultural settlers when compared with wetter areas to the north and west. Unirrigated farming could not be practiced in the region, though grazing resources were available for the flocks. The population of the basin was probably composed of mobile tribes which used the area intermittently for pastures.[12] Where the Indo-Iranians did settle permanently in other parts of Iran, their villages were occupied by tribal or clan groupings.[13] Resources were owned and organized on a communal basis; the rights of each individual derived from the higher right of the community. The communal characteristics of modern Iranian villages date from this period. That there are fewer evidences of communalism in Kirman (and Yazd as well)[14] is probably because the region was not settled until much later in history, early in Sassanian times (third century A.D.).

ORGANIZED SETTLEMENT IN KIRMAN
IN SASSANIAN TIMES

In Sassanian times (224–641 A.D.) Persian society was unified by a strong government which controlled all parts of the Central Plateau, even remote Kirman. The Sassanians attempted to model their administration on the earlier Achaemenian principle of centralization. The king was surrounded by seven vassal families who combined to form a feudal landholding aristocracy.[15] These vassals served as governors (satraps), collecting taxes, controlling trade, and administering justice in the provinces. Royal officers retained control of the armed forces, and retired military officers were settled as minor landlords in the provinces.[16] Provincial aristocracies composed of these elements appeared, and miniature courts modeled on the capital were reproduced in each large city. A critical division of society developed between the city-dwelling vassals and lords and the rural cultivators, laborers, and serfs.[17]

But the Sassanians were unable to achieve centralization because they inherited a powerful feudal nobility from the Parthians. The feudal structure was a prominent feature of Sassanian social and economic life. Great feudal families ruled the provinces, with minor lords holding cities and towns, some small free landowners cultivating their holdings, and bondsmen working for both large and small landlords.[18] The principal unit of economic production was the feudal estate; free landowners constituted only a small minority of the agriculturalists. Beneath the feudal nobility came the priest caste, warriors, bureaucrats, and finally the commoner group composed of peasants, artisans, and traders.[19] Each class had a state-appointed leader responsible for the behavior of his group and tax collection from it.

A special group, the village headmen (*dihqan*s), bridged the gap between the urban upper class and rural commoners. These men owned family lands, were hereditary local administrators in the provinces, and represented the feudal aristocracy in local affairs.[20] Their knowledge of remote areas made it possible for them to collect taxes, levy labor services, and provide men for military service from the villages. In many ways the dihqans were the cement which held the various sectors of Sassanian society together.

Agriculture was the primary source of revenue in Sassanian Iran. As a result, the expenses of maintaining royal courts, elaborate fire-temples, the Zoroastrian clergy, and continuous wars with Rome and later Byzantium fell heavily on the peasant population. Peasant life was dominated by predatory tax collectors, labor services, and compulsory military service. Some relief from these continuous levies occurred during the reign of Anushiravan the Just (531–578 A.D.). By his order the land tax was based on a survey, and the dates of tax collection were fixed.[21] This system reformed traditional practices of assessing taxes on produce at various rates and dates as government needs demanded. Improvements in irrigation and agriculture (including the spread of qanats) were effected under Anushiravan, but most of the benefits from these works probably accrued to the feudal landlords and dihqans rather than to the cultivators.

Other major changes occurred in Sassanian Iran, and increasing urbanization was one of the most important. The growth of arts and crafts, the expansion of overseas trade with China, India, and Africa, and the civilizing influences of Mesopotamia on Persian leaders in the third and fourth centuries were major stimuli to the growth of urban centers.[22] New cities were founded and others enlarged by the Sassanian kings. Kirman was one of these new Sassanian cities. In founding it the Sassanians created in the Kirman Basin its first regionally organized settlement pattern.

Kirman City was established as a defensive outpost of the Sassanian Empire by order of the founder of the Sassanian dynasty, Ardashir I (d.

240 A.D.).[23] At this time the major urban center in southeastern Iran was Sirjan, located one hundred miles west of the basin.[24] The site of Kirman was chosen for defensive reasons; its immediate function was to buffer tribal incursions from Baluchistan. The city was built on the northern edge of the Kirman plain, where gently sloping land was available for cultivation and wells could supply water to the city. Most important, two small crags (Qal'ehi Ardashir and Qal'ehi Dukhtar) rose at this spot to elevations a thousand feet above the plain. Fortresses were constructed on both heights; the heart of the city lay on the eastern margins of the modern city between these fortresses (see Fig. 11, p. 40). The palace and military quarters were the major structures in the city, though later a temple honoring Anahita was built.[25]

Three centuries after the establishment of Kirman City, the nearby town of Mahan was built at the foot of the Kuhi Jupar by the Sassanian financier Azar Mahan (531–578).[26] This expansion of settlement from the plain onto the alluvial fans appears to have been stimulated by population pressure on existing resources. According to local tradition, the alluvial fans (including the site of Mahan) were forested at this time.[27] Charcoal burners, fuel collectors, and herdsmen established semipermanent hamlets on the alluvial fans to supplement declining fuel and grazing resources on the plain. As these forests were cleared, powerful political and commercial leaders, Azar Mahan among them, financed the construction of qanats on the alluvial fans, and permanent agricultural settlements were established. These settlements supplied food to the urban population, increased the cultivated area in the basin to accommodate landless peasants, and provided herding and fuel-collecting bases to supply the city.

The impact of this Sassanian process of settlement on the territorial organization of modern Kirman is clear. The present functionally integrated settlement pattern was initiated by this well-equipped feudal society which, as it grew, extended its capital, labor, and technology outward to the alluvial fans and later into the mountains. During the preliminary stages, artisans, well diggers, architects, and laborers were probably imported from the old capital city of Sirjan to construct qanats, wells, houses, and defenses. In this way an urban society was transplanted from other centers of Sassanian power into the basin. Later settlements were founded when this urban society expanded and not, as has previously been believed, through a concentration of small clan villages.

This settlement process explains the paucity of communal traits in the villages of Kirman as compared with other areas of Iran.[28] The under-lying communalism in land tenure and land ownership in the Middle East, where feudal landlordism has been the governing economic system for so long, has always been puzzling. Some have interpreted communal institutions such as pasture rights and periodic redistribution of the cultivated land as evidence of a pristine communism presumably developed when tribal groups settled permanently on the land.[29] According to this view, the tribal group itself has disappeared, but clan institutions persist. In Kirman, if the settlement history presented above is correct, the few communal institutions which do exist in the villages (e.g. pasture rights) developed in the feudalism of the Sassanian period. Under this system, each individual was responsible to the landlord, and equal and common obligations may have given rise to equal rights, the hallmark of communal villages.

ISLAM IN KIRMAN, 641–1850

The Arabs swept over the Zagros Mountains in the seventh century, and a decade after the battle of Nihavand (641 A.D.) the Persian Empire was controlled by Muslim armies. Despite their own long cultural tradition, the Persians rapidly accepted the new religion, concepts, and modes of expression of this alien culture and were integrated into the Islamic community. The speed of the Arab conquest has never been satisfactorily explained, but it was at least partially caused by the decay of Persian royalty and clergy, growing discontent in the empire, and the spiritual and military vitality of the Arab invaders.

Islamization of the Persian population proceeded most rapidly in highly urbanized Persian Iraq and in the large administrative centers of the plateau, in the northeastern province of Khurasan, and on the hot, tropical coasts of the Persian Gulf. In the plateau cities and in Persian Iraq, social pressures and economic sanctions persuaded individuals and families to convert to Islam. One of the most powerful sanctions was the poll tax (*jizya*), which was levied on all non-Moslems. Previously, only the lowest classes of the population paid this poll tax, and considerable social stigma was attached to its payment.[30] Social degradation of this type was the specific cause for the conversion of many land-owners in Isfahan to Islam.[31] In Khurasan and on the southern coasts, conversion was rapid because Arab colonization and intermarriage were considerable.

In the more remote areas of Iran, however, the Arab conquest had little initial impact. Sassanian resistance on a national scale ended with the unsuccessful revolt of Sinbad (d. 755), a merchant of Nayshapur; but in the mountain strongholds of Tabaristan in northern Iran a Zoroastrian dynasty retained power until the eleventh century.[32] In Yazd and Kirman, Zoroastrianism also maintained a firm hold on the population. As late as the ninth century, nearly 200 years after the Arab conquest, the Zoroastrian clergy still had mounted retainers and controlled territory near Kirman City and Sirjan.[33]

Thus in Iraq and most urban centers, the secular bureaucracy quickly accepted the Arabs as masters, adopted the new faith, and maintained their administrative power.[34] But in rural areas where the bureaucracy was not directly supervised by Arabs, conditions varied. Some areas were allowed to remain Zoroastrian in return for a fixed tribute paid annually to the Arabs.[35] In other areas, local administrators (*dihqans*) were confirmed in their power to collect taxes and administer justice only after they converted to Islam.[36] Since the Arabs settled principally in large urban centers, Islamic influence spread erratically into rural areas of Persia as one or another tribal chief, local landlord, or dihqan came under the control of the Arabs. In Kirman this process continued for centuries.

In terms of land ownership and settlement, the conquest period is confusing. In theory, four categories of land ownership existed in Islamic law: (1) crown lands conquered by force, one-fifth of which were set aside for the Prophet and his successors; (2) community land composed of all unowned, cultivated land, which belonged to all Muslims in common and was administered by the religious leader (*imam*) of the community; (3) private property owned by Muslims or non-Muslims which was acquired by purchase, reclamation, or conquest; and (4) community land occupied by the original owners.[37] This system attempted to differentiate between land owned by Arab Muslims and land owned by non-Muslims, but was upset by large-scale conversion to Islam. In practice, the Persian landowning class retained most of their lands and their privileged position as well, but each family now operated under the protection of some powerful Arab-Muslim.

During the seventh and eighth centuries conditions in Kirman were very unsettled. Parts of the province were conquered by the Arabs in 633, but on the death of Caliph 'Umar I in 644 widespread revolts broke out. At least one Arab army perished in the attempt to reassert control over this area, a deed finally accomplished in 718 by Caliph 'Umar II.[38]

His governor, Ghazban ibn Qab'siri, was fiercely religious; within seven years, the fire-temples of the Zoroastrians in Kirman were destroyed and the bulk of the population converted to Islam.[39]

But many sects continued to flourish in Kirman, because the region was an area of dissidence beyond the pale of continuously effective governmental rule. The Kharijite movement, for example, gained temporary control of the provinces of Fars and Kirman.[40] These visionaries roamed the countryside in armed bands. They were noted for their extreme fanaticism, the speed of their cavalry, and their guerrilla tactics. They would mobilize unexpectedly, sweep down and pillage undefended towns, and retire to the mountains to escape pursuit by government troops. The Kharijites were finally crushed in 698–699 by the Arab general Muhallab.[41]

During early Abbasid times (post 750) the largest city in southeastern Iran was Sirjan. Kirman City at that time was not on a major trade route. The caravan route across the Dashti Lut passed through Shahdad (Khabis) and Mahan en route to Sirjan, but bypassed Kirman City. The major north-south highway ran through Sirjan, Jiruft, and Bam or from Sirjan to Ra'in to Bam.[42] Despite this, an eighth-century history of the Makkran noted that Kirman City (called by the Arabs Bardsir) was growing in size and had become famous for the shawls and arms manufactured there. Kirman did not, however, become the leading city of the southeastern region until the tenth century, when the Samanid governor of Kirman Province, Abu 'Ali ibn Ilyas, moved his capital from Sirjan to Kirman, because it lay farther to the west and was less exposed to attack from the Buwayhids of Fars.[43] Forty years later the Buwayhids did conquer Kirman, but by this time Kirman City was permanently established as the major cultural and administrative center of the province.

The Arab geographer Muqaddasi described Kirman City as a small but heavily defended town at this time.[44] Three major fortresses dominated the city, whose plan differed markedly from that of the modern city. The highest of the fortifications lay outside the city walls on Qal'ehi Ardashir. When Abu 'Ali ibn Ilyas was governor of Kirman, he reputedly built a well on this crag and slept there. A second fortress, on the top of Qal'ehi Dukhtar, formed part of the city walls, which were encircled by a moat. The third fortress, the citadel (*arg*) was located in the town next to the great mosque. The town had four major gates and many gardens watered by qanats and wells. Muqaddasi also mentioned the town of Mahan, noting that it was populated by Arabs. The center of Mahan was a walled fortress surrounded by a moat; the land outside this, for a day's march, was covered with gardens. Qanaghistan, also founded in Sassanian times, was evidently considered an integral part of Mahan.[45]

In the eleventh century the province of Kirman came under the control of the Seljuq Turks and remained so until the invasion of the Ghuzz Turks in 1187. Disturbances and tribal warfare were associated with both invasion periods in Kirman, but according to Yaqut the area was prosperous under Seljuq rule.[46] Kirman escaped the Mongol invasion in 1220 because of its remoteness, and was governed by a local dynasty founded by Qutlugh Beg in 1222 which lasted under Mongol suzerainty until 1307. It was during this period that Marco Polo passed through Kirman City en route to Cathay and commented on the swords, daggers, and other weapons made there.[47] He visited the town during the reign of Turkhan Khatun (d. 1282), the daughter of Qutlugh Beg. This remarkable woman built many villages and qanats in the Kirman region, and her reign was one of peace and prosperity. A beautiful green dome (the Qubbai Sabz) erected over her tomb was one of the sights of the city until it was destroyed by an earthquake in 1896.[48]

At the end of the fourteenth century Timur (1335–1405) conducted his Persian campaigns. Kirman, which had been bypassed by the Mongols, was conquered. Constant campaigning by the various armies devastated the countryside, and heavy demands were made on the population. In addition to periodic tax levies, the people were forced to furnish firewood, fodder, and other goods to the ruler's armies.[49] It was at this time that Shah Ni'matullah Vali, the Sufi saint, took up residence at Mahan (1406), where he lived until his death in 1431. His fame as a poet and prophet contributed substantially to the growth of Mahan, which became a pilgrimage center for mystics of the Middle East and India.[50]

The Safavid era (1502–1732) was a time of growth and prosperity for Kirman. The city became an important commercial center on the Indo-Iranian highway. Shawls and embroidery were the most important craft industries; carpet weaving first appeared during the reign of Shah 'Abbas (1587–1629).[51] The shawls of Kirman were the finest produced anywhere in Iran, because the Kashmir goats and sheep of the province produced high quality wool and down. In the seventeenth century the British and Dutch East India companies established factories at Kirman to export raw wools and shawls. Even before their appearance, however, Kirman was sending these products to India and to other parts of Iran.[52]

The city became a transshipment point for European goods and an important link in the chain of trading centers connecting Iran and India. But this commercial growth was aborted by a succession of disasters in the eighteenth century.

In 1720 and again in 1722, Kirman City was conquered by Ghalzai tribesmen from Afghanistan. Fifteen years later, Nadir Shah laid siege to Qandahar and requisitioned baggage animals and the entire grain reserves of Kirman Province for his army; for seven years thereafter the region was in a state of famine.[53] In 1747 the Afghans again attacked Kirman and razed the northern section of the city, the old Zoroastrian quarter (see Fig. 11, p. 40). Still later in the century, after a series of battles between two rival dynasties, the Zands and Qajars, Lutf 'Ali Khan, leader of the Zands, took refuge in Kirman City. The city and the Zand leader were captured in 1794. For three months Qajar soldiers pillaged the province; twenty thousand men were sold into slavery and an equal number blinded.[54]

This oppression continued into the first half of the nineteenth century; insecurity and decay were widespread. Provincial governorships were awarded to members of the ruling family, who exploited them as private domains. The Qajars usually appointed the harshest rulers to Kirman Province as a continued punishment for its earlier support of the Zand dynasty. Throughout the period villages were abandoned, qanats fell into disrepair, and population declined. Travelers were struck with the insecurity of life and property in Qajar Iran and particularly by the oppression of the agricultural classes by government representatives.[55] It was not until the last half of the nineteenth century that the political and economic fortunes of Kirman improved.

GROWTH UNDER BRITISH INFLUENCE, 1850–1925

After 1850 conditions in Kirman eased with the growth of Indo-Iranian trade. This was stimulated by British, Indian (Shikarpur Hindus and Parsis), and native Zoroastrian merchants, who controlled the commerce of the city — except for the carpet trade, which was in the hands of Tabrizi Turks.[56] Kirman's location on the Indo-Iranian highway, its connections with the coastal port of Bandar 'Abbas, and insecurity along alternative routes because of the Indian-Afghan wars contributed to a major economic change in the city. Carpets, shawls, and some gums (tragacanth and asafoetida) were exported in exchange for tea, sugar, printed cloth, candles, metal goods, and spices, which local Kirmani merchants distributed to settlements in the basin and to Shahdad, Sirjan, and Bam.[57]

Kirman City had grown to be a mile long (north to south) and three-quarters of a mile wide.[58] The city walls were in good condition, a reliable index of prosperity, and were pierced by six gates (see Fig. 11, p. 40). In 1865 Kirman's population was estimated at thirty to forty thousand.[59] The city had 28 caravanserais, 12 used for trade and 16 for travelers, 120 shawl-weaving establishments, and 32 baths.[60]

Political conditions had favored this growth. Two governors, Muhammad Isma'il Khan Vakil-ul-mulk (1859–66) and Murtazi Quli Khan (1867–78), were exceptionally fine rulers who established new villages, qanats, mosques, baths, mills, and caravanserais. Muhammad Isma'il Khan, for instance, built Kousar Riz during his reign and also constructed the Vakilabad qanat of Mahan (see Fig. 9, p. 34).[61] Population grew steadily in this atmosphere. Part of the increase was absorbed by an expansion of the cultivated area, notably in the opening of the mountain valleys to settlement. A greater proportion, however, was absorbed by the rapid growth of carpet weaving after the turn of the century.

In the nineteenth century the major craft of Kirman was the manufacture of fine shawls from the down of the Kashmir goat. In 1871 there were only six carpet-weaving establishments in the city, and fewer than thirty looms.[62] Eleven years later Stack noted several hundred carpet-weaving factories in and about Kirman City, the largest of which employed about thirty weavers.[63] By 1900 Sykes found over one thousand looms in Kirman City alone, each supervised by a master weaver with two or three young children doing the actual weaving.[64]

Even at the end of the nineteenth century the now-famous Kirmani carpets were virtually unknown in Europe. Kirman's shawls, however, were in considerable demand in the Western world by ladies of the Victorian era. The largest were more than twelve feet long, took fifteen months to complete, and were marketed in Europe through the Istanbul market.[65] The industry began to decline late in the century because of competition from the looms of Kashmir, and the Kirmanis began to export wool to Amritsar.[66] When styles changed in the twentieth century and imitation cashmere shawls (notably Paisley) became popular, the shawl-making industry disappeared in Kirman.

The decline of shawls coincided with the rapid expansion of carpet weaving in Kirman. This expansion was stimulated by the enterprise of a group of Tabrizi carpet merchants who developed a world market for Persian carpets. Initially, this group collected carpets and rugs from marketplaces in every Persian city and forwarded them to Istanbul for exchange. When the supply of used carpets dwindled as British, American, and French buyers bought Persian carpets in Istanbul, the merchants of Tabriz began weaving carpets specifically designed for the European market.

This modernized large-scale industry soon spread from Tabriz to Kirman and other Persian cities. Kirman had the best wool in Persia and trained craftsmen (ex-shawl weavers) to weave carpets.[67] European firms established offices in Kirman City, and the industry came under their control. Carpet weaving reached a peak in Kirman City in the 1920's, when an estimated five thousand looms were in operation and weaving was the single major activity of the city (see Appendix B). Most of the Kirmani carpets were exported to America.

In the twentieth century, then, carpet weaving became the major industry in Kirman. The expansion in Kirman City spread to villages located nearby. Outside the city, the largest weaving centers were Mahan and Jupar on the slopes of the Kuhi Jupar, and Chatrud, a small town northwest of Kirman City. The weaving industry spurred a population increase particularly in settlements located on trade routes and encouraged an expansion of population without requiring an attendant increase in the water supply. Carpet weaving further intensified existing economic relationships between the city and surrounding villages.

Chapter 3

The Pattern and Morphology
of Settlement

THE SETTLEMENT PATTERN

The pattern of settlement in Kirman has been shaped by environmental conditions, by historical development, and perhaps most important, by water supply systems. The aridity makes irrigation essential, and water supply is an overriding consideration in the location of settlements. Permanent settlements were rare in the region until a technology (qanats) was developed to solve this problem. Because every permanent settlement in Kirman has at least one qanat and all large settlements have several, they are located at sites compatible with the opportunities and limitations offered by this water supply system.

Qanats are gently sloping tunnels dug horizontally into an alluvial fan until the water table is pierced (Fig. 6). Water filters into the tunnel, runs down its gradual slope, and emerges on the surface as a stream.[1] The location and construction of a qanat are rigidly governed by slope, the distribution of subterranean aquifers, rainfall catchment basins, and elevation (see Appendix D). These factors therefore are principal considerations (though defense was important for Kirman City) in the location of initial settlement in qanat-watered regions.[2] Once permanent settlement is established, other forces such as custom, water law, and ownership influence the location of new settlements. But one rule holds true in all qanat-watered regions: because water flows by gravity in qanats, the lower the elevation of a settlement and the greater its catchment basin, the greater the amount of water that can be brought to the surface near it, the greater the amount of land that can be irrigated around it, and thus the greater its population.

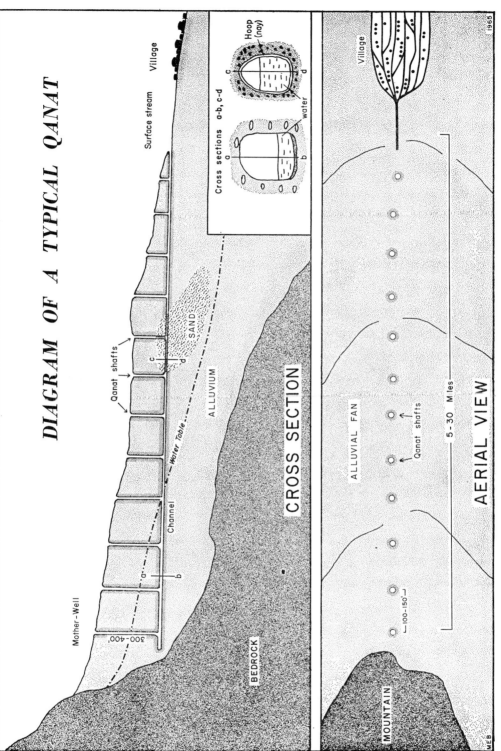

Fig. 6. Data from field observation.

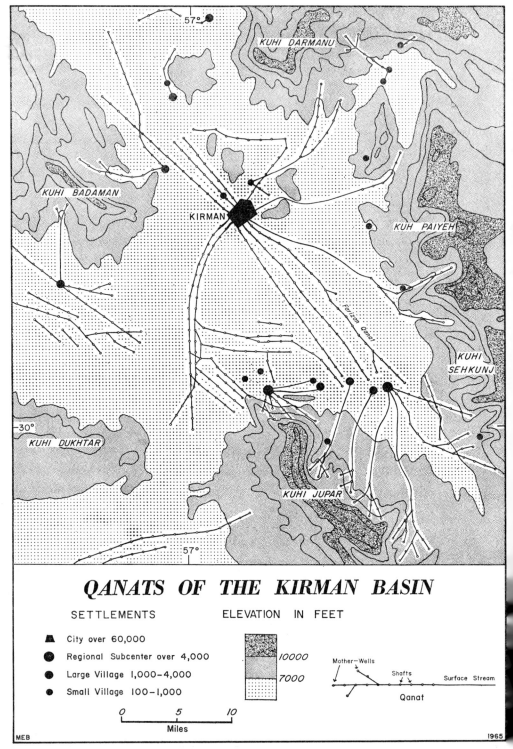

QANATS OF THE KIRMAN BASIN

SETTLEMENTS   ELEVATION IN FEET

▲ City over 60,000
● Regional Subcenter over 4,000
● Large Village 1,000–4,000
● Small Village 100–1,000

10000
7000

Mother—Wells
Shafts
Surface Stream
Qanat

0   5   10
Miles

MEB   1965

Labels on map: KUHI DARMANU, KUHI BADAMAN, KIRMAN, KUH PAIYEH, Farizan Qanat, KUHI SEHKUNJ, KUHI DUKHTAR, KUHI JUPAR, 57°, 30°

Fig. 7. Data from 1956 aerial photographs (1:60,000) and field observation.

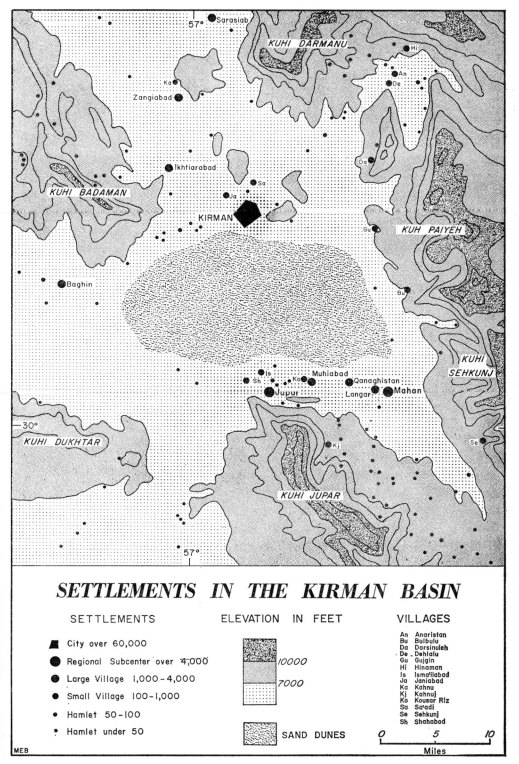

Fig. 8. Data from 1956 aerial photographs (1:60,000) and field observation.

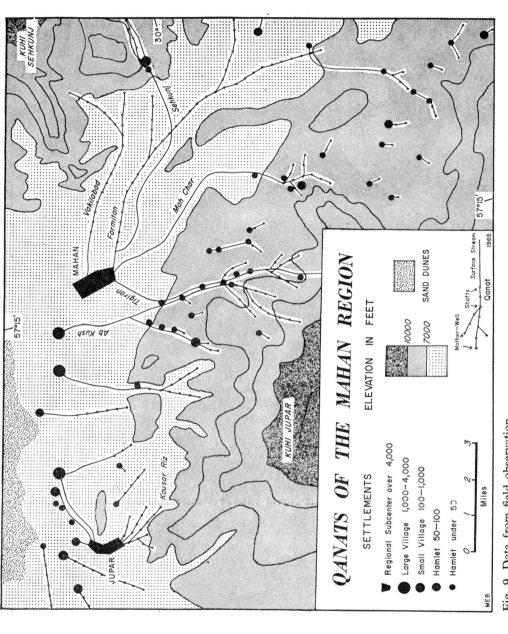

Fig. 9. Data from field observation.

For example Kirman City, with a population of more than 60,000, is located on the northern edge of the Kirman plain at an elevation of 5,680 feet, a low point in the basin. Qanats focus inward on the city. Short qanats (less than five miles in length) originating beneath the alluvial fans at the foot of Kuhi Darmanu in the north and Kuh Paiyeh in the east carry water to the city (Fig. 7). Long qanats cross the central plain from the alluvial fans of the Kuhi Jupar some twenty-five to thirty miles away. The mother wells of these qanats are several hundred feet deep;[3] their tunnels begin beneath the fields of Jupar and Mahan. The most famous long qanat in the basin is the Farizan qanat, which runs twenty-nine miles to the city of Kirman from that section of the Kirman–Bam road opposite the town of Mahan. The exact number of qanats that currently carry water to the city is uncertain.[4] They have been built, repaired, and abandoned over the centuries so that their tunnels now honeycomb the plain and the margins of the city.

The high density of qanat tunnels in the catchment basin of Kirman City presents practical as well as legal barriers to the construction of new, competing tunnels. At the northern margin of the cultivated fields of Mahan, beneath which the tunnels of the long qanats from Kirman City are located, more than five hundred vertical shafts exist in an area less than two square miles.[5] Since law prohibits the sinking of new qanat shafts or deep wells within one kilometer of existing shafts, much of the Kirman plain is closed to any new construction.[6] For this reason there are no other large settlements on the Kirman plain.

All other large settlements in the Kirman Basin are located high on the alluvial fans, beyond the catchment basin drained by Kirman City qanats (Fig. 8). The largest of these are Mahan (over 6,000 people) and Jupar (over 4,000 people); both are located at elevations seven to eight hundred feet higher than Kirman City. Qanats are the only source of water in these towns. Wells cannot be used because the water table lies three to four hundred feet beneath the surface. The qanats of Mahan and Jupar tap smaller catchment basins than do those of Kirman City and deliver less water, because they are located at higher elevations and draw water from smaller alluvial deposits. Most of these qanats are short and their water travels long distances in surface streams from the mountains to the alluvial fans, as Figure 9 shows.

Settlements in the mountain valleys of the Kuhi Jupar are even smaller than those on the alluvial fans (Fig. 10). The largest, Kahnuj, has a population of 175, but most mountain settlements house only two or three

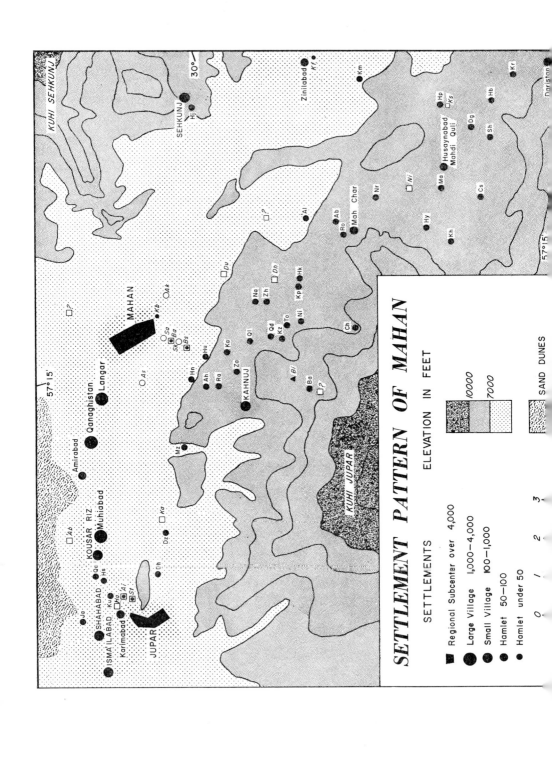

SETTLEMENT PATTERN OF MAHAN

SETTLEMENTS

■ Regional Subcenter over 4,000

● Large Village 1,000—4,000

● Small Village 100—1,000

● Hamlet 50—100

• Hamlet under 50

ELEVATION IN FEET

10000

7000

SAND DUNES

0 1 2 3

KUHI SEHKUNJ

KUHI JUPAR

SEHKUNJ

MAHAN

KAHNUJ

JUPAR

ISMA'ILABAD

SHAHABAD

Karimabad

KOUSAR RIZ

Muhiabad

Amirabad

Qanaghistan

Langar

Husaynabad

Mahdi Quli

Zinilabad

Dariston

Mah Char

Hamlet under 50 ━━━

Ab	Abgarm
Ah	Ahmadabad Dogu
Al	Aliabad
Ba	Baharistan Kush
Ch	Chashmeh Kush
Cs	Chashmeh Shaghin
Dg	Dareh Gaz
Dh	Deh Hunari
Dz	Dagh Razin
Hb	Hanak Bala
Hj	Hujatabad
Hk	Hasanabad Kupang
Hn	Hasanabad
Hp	Hanak Pa'yin
Hs	Husaynabad Akhlaqi
Hu	Husaynabad Mahan
Hy	Husaynabad
Ja	Javadieh
Ka	Karimabad
Kh	Khankistan
Km	Karimabad Sar Dar
Kp	Kupang
Kr	Karimabad Haji 'Ali
Ku	Kuhan Chinar
Kz	Kazimabad
Ma	Mahciabad
Mz	Mazra'eh Shur
Na	Nazimabad
Nr	Narrakan
Ni	Ni'matabad Toujigun
Qa	Qadirabad
Qd	Qudratabad
Ql	Qalatu
Ra	Rahimabad
Ro	Roughanu
Sh	Shurabad
To	Toujigun
Za	Zarkuh
Zh	Zahrud

□ **Abandoned Place**

Ab	Abdullahabad
Dh	Dareh Hasani
Du	Dum Dahaneh Zahrud
Ha	Hakimabad
Ka	Karimabad
Ni	Ni'matabad
?	Unnamed Ruin

◉ **Walled Garden**

Ai	Aishabad
Ba	Bagh Sayyid Husayn
Bs	Bagh Shahzadeh
St	Sayyid Taghi

○ **Mill**

Ak	Asiab Kaleh
As	Asiab 'Abd ul-Hasan
Sa	Sar Asiab Sayyid Husayn
Sk	Sar Asiab Khirandish

● **Teahouse**

Kb	Kafeh Bala Mahan
Kf	Kafeh Sehkunj

▲ **Shrine**

Bi	Eibigrami

□ **Caravanserai**

Ks	Karavansirai Sang

Fig. 10. Data from field observation.

families, who subsist by a combination of agriculture, herding, charcoal burning, and fuel collecting. Larger settlements on the alluvial fans have prior rights to most of the watershed of the Kuhi Jupar range; the qanats which supply water to mountain hamlets, therefore, can tap only local alluvial deposits in tributary valleys. Most of these qanats are less than a kilometer in length, with mother wells reaching a maximum depth of forty to fifty feet. They produce only ten to fifteen *qasab*s of water, not enough to irrigate one-tenth of an acre every twenty-four hours.[7] Further, the shallowness of mountain qanats and their limited aquifers cause annual and seasonal fluctuations in the flow of qanat water. For this reason, mountain settlements are less permanent than their counterparts on the alluvial fans and are periodically abandoned when their water supply fails.

In the Kirman Basin, then, the settlement pattern exhibits a progressive correlation of age, size, elevation, and water rights. The settlement at the lowest elevation (Kirman City) is older, larger, and has prior water rights to the largest catchment area in the basin. As one moves to higher elevations, the alluvial fan settlements (e.g. Mahan, Jupar, and Baghin) have fewer people, were established more recently, and have smaller water hinterlands. This sequence recurs in the mountain valleys where small qanats of recently built (nineteenth-century) hamlets such as Chashmeh Kush, Dagh Razin, and Daristan tap small alluvial deposits. The water hinterlands form a series of progessively smaller arcs; the qanats of each higher settlement begin where those of the next lower settlement end. After this rational, water-oriented settlement pattern became established in the Kirman Basin, a body of custom and law developed to regulate the water supply system. Its original purpose was to protect qanat owners in a risky but essential investment in permanent agricultural settlement. Its principal effect, however, has been to reinforce and maintain the existing settlement pattern and thus retard change.

Water law in Iran is based on Islamic law (*shari'a*) and custom.[8] The earliest known codification of this law is the *Kitābi Qanī* (*Book of Qanats*), which was in existence in the eleventh century.[9] The principal way in which Islamic water law has shaped settlement location in Kirman is through the laws of *harim* ("borders"), which state that ownership of property involves rights over its borders. Thus it is illegal for anyone to dig a well or qanat near an existing qanat, if it can be assumed or proved that loss might result.[10] Because knowledge of tunnel patterns and subterranean geology is limited in the Kirman region, in effect this law prohibits the construction of new channels or deep wells where wet sections of qanats exist. It is, therefore, a stabilizing influence on the settlement pattern.

The Structure and Organization of Kirman City around 1900

At the turn of the century three institutions formed the core of Kirman City: the Friday-prayer mosque, the bazaar, and the citadel (Fig. 11). The central mosque, Masjidi Jami', was located near the eastern wall of Kirman opposite the entrance to the Vakil Bazaar. It was built in the fourteenth century and has been the Kirmani's place of communal prayer on Friday ever since.[11] In the immediate vicinity of the Masjidi Jami' were a number of public baths (*hammam*) in which Muslim religious ablutions could be performed. The most elaborate and finest baths were beside the mosque and in the bazaar; the most famous of these, the Bath of Ibrahim Khan, was built early in the nineteenth century.

The seat of government in Kirman, the citadel (*arg*), was located near the western wall of the city and was ringed by walls to protect government leaders from external attacks and internal uprisings. The political and commercial elite of Kirman lived within its walls or as close to them as possible, for safety in times of chaos and to maintain contact with other civic and commercial leaders in the city.

Between mosque and citadel lay the commercial district of Kirman, the Vakil Bazaar, whose main avenue ran some six hundred yards, making it the longest "straight" bazaar in Persia. In its covered stalls, crowded lanes, and surrounding caravanserais most of the wholesale and retail trade of the city was conducted. At the center of the bazaar a complex of buildings including a bath, a mosque, and a caravanserai was constructed in the nineteenth century by Vakil ul-Mulk, a ruler of Kirman. West of this section, in an area constructed by Ganj 'Ali Khan in the seventeenth century, were a square, several caravanserais, and a number of water reservoirs to supply water to the baths.

Because the Vakil Bazaar was linear, it did not exhibit the concentric hierarchy of crafts and trades found in other Middle Eastern bazaars. Also, since many sections of the bazaar were built and rebuilt at different periods, prestigious craftsmen such as cloth and textile sellers, carpet merchants, jewelers, coppersmiths, and tailors tended to move periodically to the more modern sections. Each trade or craft, however, was still localized in one section of the bazaar. Around the two major squares in the

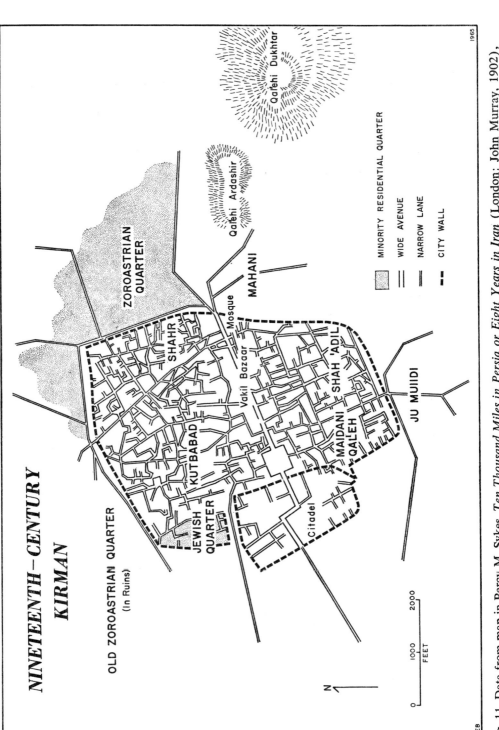

Fig. 11. Data from map in Percy M. Sykes, *Ten Thousand Miles in Persia or Eight Years in Iran* (London: John Murray, 1902),

Vakil Bazaar, the jewelers, cloth sellers, coppersmiths, some of the lesser carpet merchants, shoemakers, and book sellers were located. Merchants in the export trade in wool, carpets, pistachios, almonds, and other products — essentially all the important wholesalers — were not in the bazaar proper, but in the offices and rooms of the caravanserais situated on its margins. These caravanserais were walled on all sides by rooms and offices facing inward to an open-skied courtyard. Wind towers (*badgirs*) rose thirty to forty feet above these buildings to catch the breeze and cool the offices below.[12]

The remainder of Kirman City was subdivided into five residential quarters, Kutbabad, Shahr, Shah 'Adil, Maidani Qal'eh, and the Jewish Quarter.[13] These quarters were separated one from the other by major avenues which extended outward from the bazaar to the margins of the city; each quarter had its own gate in the city walls. Beyond the walls lived the Zoroastrians, a persecuted minority in these days, and the more humble elements of the city's population in Ju Muiidi and Mahani, two of the poorest sections of Kirman.

The Muslim residential districts of Kirman had many characteristics found in other nineteenth-century Islamic towns. Except for a few broad commercial avenues, the streets and lanes in the quarters formed a maze of dark, twisting passageways, alleys, and cul-de-sacs. Most were not more than twelve feet in breadth, just enough to allow two laden donkeys to pass one another. These passages enabled the citizens of Kirman to reach their houses and they were arteries beneath which qanat water was distributed. They were often enclosed by the high outer walls of household compounds and covered with arches to prevent these walls from collapsing. Those lanes used as water distributaries were cobbled. Small openings every twenty to thirty yards provided access to the conduits below; reservoirs (*ambars*) were spaced at intervals along their course. Unfortunately, this water was frequently contaminated by materials brushed or kicked into the channel. For the bulk of the population, these conduits are still the major source of domestic water.

Household compounds covered most of the area in the Muslim residential quarters, but a number of neighborhood crafts and trades which escaped localization in the bazaar, as well as small shrines, mosques, and baths, were also located there. Among those dispersed throughout the city were the bakers, confectioners, vegetable and fruit dealers, grocers, carpenters, blacksmiths, potters, and charcoal sellers. The small shops of these tradesmen were often on little squares formed by the intersection of two or three lanes.

The pronounced irregularity of street patterns in Kirman City was in striking contrast with the rigid general plan which placed the mosque, bazaar, and citadel in the center of the city and then segregated the population within quarters on the basis of occupation, ethnic affiliation, or religion. Several factors contributed to this maze of twisting alleys. First, the religious focus in urban organization tended to decrease political and civic interest in the city. Even now, the Kirmanis have little civic pride and there is no record of any past city planning commissions or organizations.[14] Segregation into occupational and religious quarters created a collection of small communities within the larger whole.

Second, Islamic law was vague about encroachments on the public way. Each property owner had rights which extended in all directions from his dwelling (the laws of *harim* once again), As a result, newly constructed walls tended to move farther into the lane or street, narrowing the right of way. Unless such construction flagrantly blocked passage, legal obscurity and the laxity of civil administrators allowed it to stand. This process continues even today. In one street in modern Kirman, ancient paving blocks have been removed from the roadbed and used to build the walls of neighboring compounds. In another, a deep ditch has been dug in the street to supply clay for the building of a wall. As a result of these forces the residential quarters in Kirman are chaotic; there is no pattern to the lanes, and they are cluttered with arches, projecting walls, and overhanging buildings.

The Jewish Quarter of nineteenth-century Kirman, originally populated by an offshoot of the Yazd community which migrated eastward from Baghdad in ancient times,[15] was even more irregular than the Muslim residential quarters. The lanes of the Jewish Quarter were extremely narrow, rarely more than five feet wide. The compound walls on either side were ten to twelve feet high, with jagged glass and stone set in the top to discourage entry. The entrances to the houses were guarded by massive oaken doors strengthened by metal studs. One had to stoop to enter the low portals. These details of structure within the Jewish Quarter were designed to prevent mounted horsemen from effectively attacking its residents. All facilities necessary to Jewish social and religious life were inside the quarter: baths and schools, a butcher shop, and two synagogues located at the heart of the quarter. The synagogues bore no external symbols, so they were difficult to locate.

The Jews remain today the most depressed segment of the Kirmani population. A second influx of Jews migrated to Kirman at the turn of the century, attracted by the rapidly expanding weaving industry. These men became small shopkeepers and traders and gained the reputation of being the shrewdest and most grasping of the petty dealers in the bazaar. Their habit of discarding waste in the lanes made their quarter the most pungent in Kirman City and led to the local epithet "people of the dirty street." The humble condition of the Kirman Jews is in striking contrast to that of the powerful Jewish community in Tehran.[16]

The town houses in the residential quarters of old Kirman were low-built, one-story structures. They were made of fragile, perishable local materials, mostly baked or sun-dried bricks shaped in molds and smoothed by hand. The exteriors of these buildings were faced with a mud plaster bound with straw. All houses were surrounded by high mud walls. The basic unit of the house was either a square room with a

TABLE 3
Construction of Buildings, Kirman City, 1956

Dominant material	No. of units	% of total
Baked brick	445	4
Baked and sun-dried brick	8,597	68
Sun-dried brick	3,188	25
Mud	115	1
Wood	2	. .
Other	3	. .
Not reported	247	2
TOTAL	12,597	100

Source: Government of Iran, *Census District Statistics of the First National Census of Iran, Aban 1335 (November 1956).* Vol. 17, Part 1 (Tehran: Department of Public Statistics, Ministry of Interior, Government of Iran, 1960), p. 51. See comparative figures for Shiraz in John I. Clarke, *The Iranian City of Shiraz* (Durham: Department of Geography, University of Durham, 1963), p. 21.

spherical dome, a rectangular room with an elliptical dome, two spherical domes centered on an arch, or an open-ended barrel vault (*iwan*).[17] Flat roofs are still rare in Kirman (Plate 1A).

The basic plan of the Kirmani town house was derived from the pre-Islamic peristyle house patterned after the Greek columned courtyard. In the truest peristyle form, all four sides of the courtyard were lined with rooms facing inward on a patio. In modified form, three sides of the courtyard were enclosed, giving the house a U-shaped plan (Plate 1B). The central section of the building was a large veranda flanked by guest rooms. Lateral galleries extended at right angles from this base to form the two sections of the house, the men's quarter (*birun*) and the women's quarter (*andarun*).[18] This architectural principle is consistent with Islamic religious and social attitudes which demand privacy for women. Its model is still seen in the mosques and shrines of the city, where separate praying areas are constructed for men and women.

The more elaborate upper class homes were adorned with columns, plaster ornaments, and stained glass windows. These surrounded the courtyard. Functional structures such as stables, servant quarters, toilet facilities, and storage rooms were masked from view. Lower class homes, however, could not approximate this idealized prototype. In 1956, for example, only 56% of the dwellings in Kirman City were owned by their occupants; the remaining 44% were single-roomed houses occupied by beggars, hawkers, seasonal laborers, and the unemployed.[19] In all cases compound walls remained, but weaving, cooking, storage, animal shelter, and entertaining were accomplished in one room, ten or twelve feet square.[20] A separate women's quarter was made by hanging a curtain at one end.

The outskirts of the residential quarters in Kirman were less cluttered than the centers, and large areas of land near the walls were unused or in ruins. Since land values were lower on these margins, walled orchards, mortuaries, and cemeteries were located there. These facilities, particularly the cemeteries, acted as a collar on the city during the recent period of growth and have been transferred to locations outside the town; new streets and residential sections occupy their place.

The Zoroastrian Quarter and two partially ruined quarters called Mahani and Ju Muiidi lay outside the city walls in 1900 (Fig. 11). In earlier times, the Zoroastrian Quarter had been northwest of Kirman City, but the area was destroyed by the Afghans in 1747, and by 1900 the Zoroastrians had moved to the eastern side of the city. The same "ghetto" characteristics were found in this quarter as in that of the Jews. The streets were narrow, doorways were low, and entry was discouraged by large oak and iron gates. To assure a water supply during times of persecution, each household had its own well powered by a blindfolded cow or donkey, which walked in an endless circle turning two wooden wheels to raise water.[21] Such wells were less common in the Muslim residential quarters, or even in the Jewish Quarter, where persecution was less of a problem.

The location of the Zoroastrian Quarter both before and after the

Afghan invasion of 1747 was outside the city walls, remote from the center of social and commercial activity. This was symbolic of the marginal place of Zoroastrians in Kirmani life in 1900.[22] They were forced to wear somber clothing and were not permitted to wear stockings. They were not allowed to ride horses; if a Zoroastrian riding a donkey passed a Muslim townsman he was forced to dismount. Zoroastrians could not wear glasses, and perhaps strangest of all, in the desert climate of Kirman, they could not carry umbrellas.[23] They were forced to pay the hated *jizya* or poll tax, and by law their houses had to be low enough so that a passing Muslim could touch the roof. As a result, all buildings in the Zoroastrian Quarter were simple, low-built, unpretentious structures. Yet despite these restrictions, the Zoroastrian Quarter was the cleanest and most orderly section of Kirman City. The community was regulated by a council of social and religious leaders, and all disputes concerning land, water, and housing were decided by the head of the council after both sides of the case were heard.[24] In effect, the Zoroastrians lived apart from the Muslims of Kirman and governed themselves. This type of segregation contributed to the lack of rational urban organization in Kirman.

Changing Morphology: Kirman City in 1960

By 1960 the structure and organization of Kirman City had been altered by the impact of the West and associated forces of modernization (Fig. 12).[25] The underlying stimuli for change were the increased security of cities after nomadic groups came under government control; rising urban population with improved medical and health facilities, better transportation facilities, increased religious tolerance; and the power of the central government to impose on old urban areas new city plans adapted to modern transportation mediums.

In the 1930's wide avenues were constructed in Kirman City by order of the central government. The pattern of these new avenues was radial, with major streets running out of the city along the four compass directions. The plan was arbitrarily designed to fit a preconceived concept of street alignment in a "modern" city. Only three avenues connected with major trade routes; the fourth ran eastward from the city and ended at its outskirts. This street, needless to say, was built out of a sense of symmetry or symbolism rather than for any functional purpose.

Local opposition to this new street plan was considerable. Religious leaders opposed violation of cemeteries, and landlords and homeowners feared that their houses would be razed. A compromise was effected in the execution of the plan. The religious leaders were unable to retain their cemeteries but saved their shrines. The hub of the city was built on a cemetery beside one of the important shrines of Kirman, but the shrine itself survived and the street running east from the circle bends northward to avoid it (Fig. 12). Nor do the northern and southern avenues run in true compass direction; they follow the course of the old city walls to avoid razing buildings. The westward-running avenue is most nearly straight, but even this bends at the citadel to avoid destruction of government buildings. This street is now the major east-west axis of Kirman City; it runs roughly parallel to, but several hundred yards north of, the old axis composed of the Friday-prayer mosque, the bazaar, and the citadel. Because of this new plan, the city's center of gravity has shifted. The focal point of the modern city is located on the site of the eastern gate of the old city.

Increased urban population stimulated by declining death rates and urban migration was another impetus for change. Kirman City expanded beyond the confines of the ruined city walls. The expansion was greatest on the eastern, southern, and western margins of the city. The Mahani quarter was reoccupied and expanded to encircle Qal'ehi Ardashir and Qal'ehi Dukhtar (Plate 1A). There was no similar expansion into the old Zoroastrian Quarter in the north and northwest.[26] In the western section of Kirman City, new government buildings were constructed on the site of the old citadel. Many powerful landlords and merchants owned this land, a major factor in site selection. Throughout the city, these newly settled areas are less cluttered, less densely populated, better ventilated, and have wider streets and lanes than the older quarters. A hallmark of the Islamic city — the labyrinth of twisted alleys — is being replaced by regular street patterns which can be used by automobiles and trucks.

The expansion of Kirman City and the shift of its center away from the bazaar encouraged various industries and shops to move out of the old commercial district onto the new avenues. A completely Western phenomenon, the department store, now competes with the single-product stalls of the past. New enterprises such as automobile repair shops, gas stations, travel bureaus, photography shops, ice factories, weaving factories, and government offices are concentrated on the wide avenues. The bazaar is still the center of import-export commerce, but industrial and commercial activity is dispersing throughout the city.

Finally, segregation of Jews and Zoroastrians has decreased in a

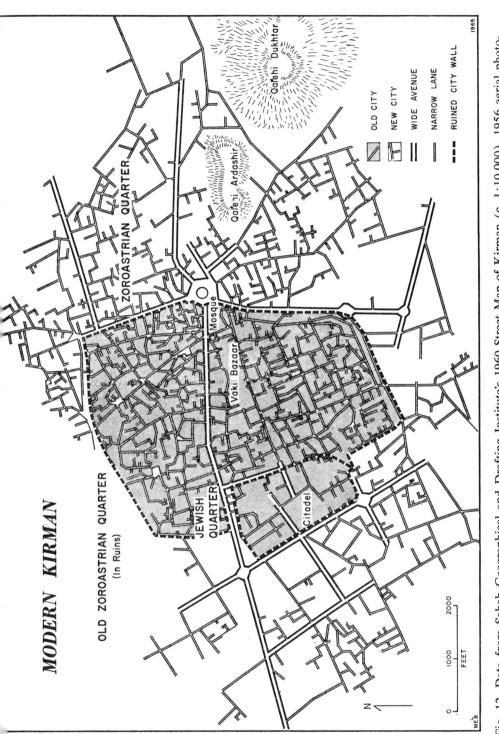

Fig. 12. Data from Sahab Geographical and Drafting Institute's 1960 Street Map of Kirman (c. 1:10,000), 1956 aerial photographs (1:6,000 and 1:12,500), and field observation.

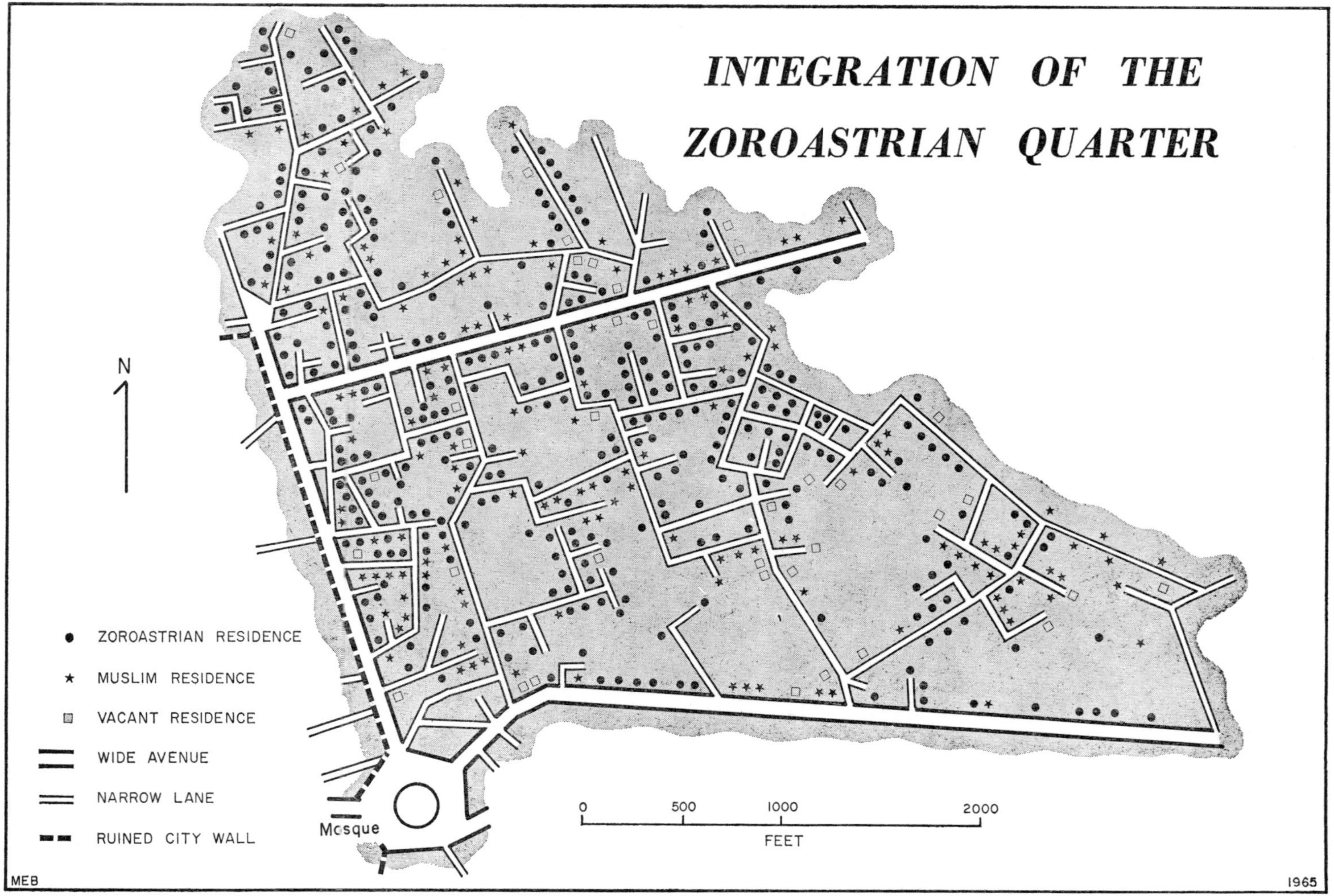

INTEGRATION OF THE ZOROASTRIAN QUARTER

1965

N

	ZOROASTRIAN RESIDENCE
●	ZOROASTRIAN RESIDENCE
★	MUSLIM RESIDENCE
▣	VACANT RESIDENCE
‖	WIDE AVENUE
‖	NARROW LANE
▬ ▬	RUINED CITY WALL

Mosque

0   500   1000   FEET   2000

MEB

Fig. 13. Data from field observation.

modern atmosphere of religious tolerance (or increased secularism). The walls of these ghettos disappeared along with those of the city. Muslims no longer are opposed to living next to Zoroastrians or Jews, and the limitations imposed upon them have been lifted. Only the Muslim religious leaders (*mulla*s) persist in the ancient antagonism, and their voice in city affairs grows smaller each day.[27] As a result, the ghettos of nineteenth-century Kirman City have virtually disappeared. An examination of the religious composition of the modern Zoroastrian Quarter illustrates the point.

In the 1930's many Zoroastrians of Kirman migrated to Tehran in search of greater economic and social opportunities after Riza Shah recognized them in civil law.[28] Their houses were purchased by Muslims. Now families of both religions live side by side in what was previously a Zoroastrian ghetto (Fig. 13). Though the major social and religious facilities of the Zoroastrian community — the fire-temples, baths, schools, and shrines — are still concentrated in this sector of the city, it is now a religiously mixed residential area.

ALLUVIAL FAN TOWNS AND VILLAGES

The agricultural-weaving villages and towns located on the alluvial fans form part of the hinterland of Kirman City. Though it is reasonable to think of these settlements as belonging to one general class, considerable variety in size, age, function, and location exists among them. The regional subcenters of Mahan and Jupar, for instance, have more than four thousand residents and exhibit many of the characteristics of a Persian city. By contrast, most of the settlements on the northern slopes of the Kuhi Jupar have populations of less than one hundred. Mahan, Jupar, Sehkunj, and Qanaghistan were founded in pre-Islamic times, while Kousar Riz and Muhiabad are only a century old. Some villages are occupied by agriculturalists and herders, others by weavers. Some are located on major trade routes, others in relative isolation.

Despite these variations, the territorial organization, physical setting, and settlement characteristics of all but the smallest villages on the northern slopes of the Kuhi Jupar are similar. All are nuclear, oasis-type settlements separated from neighboring villages and towns by barren slopes. All are watered by qanats tapping the alluvial slopes of the Kuhi Jupar. Structures within these settlements are aligned along the major watercourse, which usually flows northward down the piedmont slope.

Within each line of households a social gradient exists, with the upper class located at the top of the village, the lower classes at the bottom. Specialized economic facilities are rare; their absence is emphasized by the profusion of religious facilities. Except for these, the village is almost completely composed of high-walled household compounds and gardens. Field patterns are similar in arrangement and content; fragmentation is everywhere a problem.

Territorial Organization

In the qanat-watered towns and villages on the slopes of the Kuhi Jupar, the watercourse runs the length of the village, passing by or through each household compound before irrigating the grainfields downslope. The pattern of village structures is linear, and settlements are aligned parallel to the slope of the land along the axes of the alluvial fans (Fig. 14). The village, including its fields, has a triangular shape (Fig. 15). Household compounds form a straight line along the watercourse from the apex of the triangle toward (but not reaching) its base. In the upper section of the triangle, double-cropped gardens extend outward from the compounds, and are located near the houses to prevent theft. The base of the triangle is formed by the communal grainfields, which are cultivated in rotated segments once every three to four years. The various types of land use are spaced according to priority of water use (Fig. 15; see also Appendix A).

Inside the settlement, the location of each household compound determines the quantity and quality of its water supply. Household location with respect to the watercourse, therefore, reflects the social and economic status of its occupants. The prosperous households of landlords, merchants, and religious leaders are in the upper section of the village where water is clean and plentiful, the poorer households of sharecroppers and laborers are downstream where the volume of water is less and it has been polluted by use.[29] In some cases loss in volume from seepage, evaporation, use, and theft is considerable. In Mahan, for example, the Vakilabad qanat has a summer flow of fifty shares (*qasab*s) when entering the village and only thirty shares when emerging from the village for use in the fields. Since shares are measured by time rather than volume, a farmer in lower Mahan sustains a 40% water loss because of the location of his household.[30] Though there is a difference in the price of a share of water depending on where it is used in the village, the price differential is not commensurate with the total water loss. The powerful, therefore, live

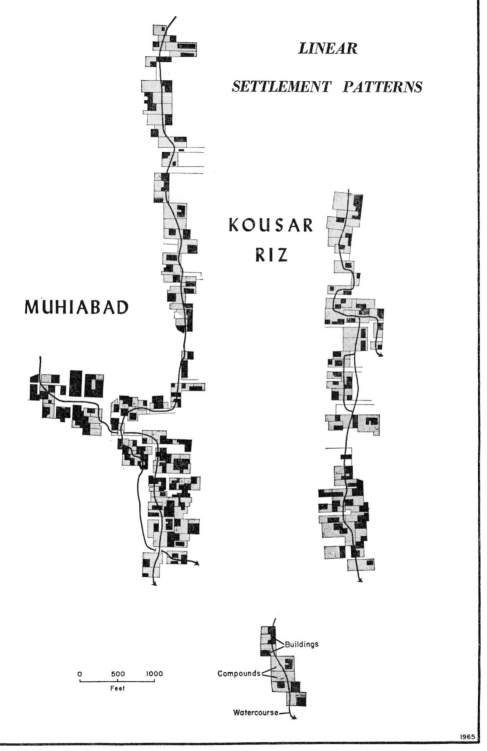

LINEAR

SETTLEMENT PATTERNS

KOUSAR
RIZ

MUHIABAD

0   500   1000
Feet

Buildings

Compounds

Watercourse

1965

Fig. 14. Data from field observation, plane-tabled in field.

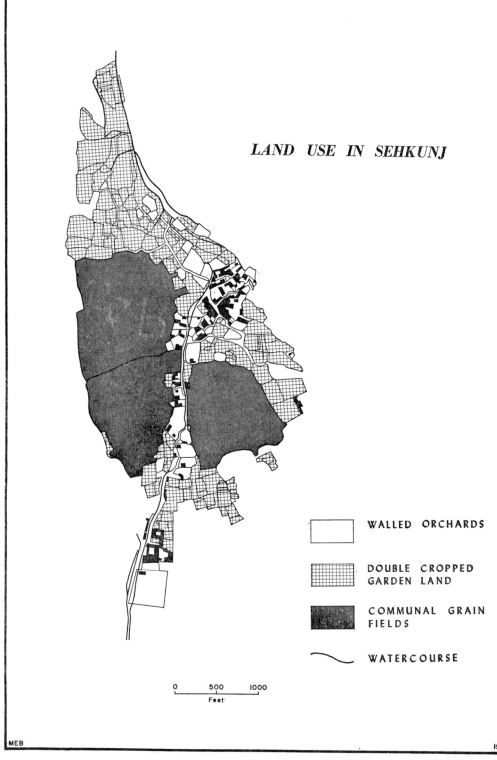

LAND USE IN SEHKUNJ

WALLED ORCHARDS

DOUBLE CROPPED
GARDEN LAND

COMMUNAL GRAIN
FIELDS

WATERCOURSE

0   500   1000
Feet

Fig. 15. Data from field observation, plane-tabled in field.

in the upper section, and often the qanat enters the village at the house or garden of the most influential local landlord.[31]

These social gradients are often obscured by historical development. In Sehkunj, for example, there have been three distinct periods of growth and development (Fig. 16). In the eighteenth century the town of Sehkunj was clustered on a small alluvial terrace where water emerged from the mountains. The village mosque, public baths, and prosperous households were located in this cluster of buildings. Poorer sharecroppers, shepherds, and fuel collectors lived downslope in the lower sector of the town. Late in the nineteenth century a local saint was buried in the cemetery below the town, and a tomb, now called the Shaykh 'Ali Baba Shrine, was constructed over his grave. This shrine rapidly became the focal point of the town, and a tomb, now called the Shaykh 'Ali Baba Shrine, was concenter and established new households near the shrine. Recently, the construction of a new qanat (the Hujatabad qanat) has encouraged the establishment of an entirely new quarter below the Shaykh 'Ali Baba Shrine. Significantly, the qanat was built to enter Sehkunj at the shrine rather than at the old center.

The population of Sehkunj is adjusting to this shift in water supply and another downstream migration of wealthy households, this time from above the shrine to the Hujatabad quarter, is in progress; within twenty years, a readjustment of social status to water supply will probably be completed. Meanwhile, the town of Sehkunj is divided into three sections: the walled center of old Sehkunj, now in partial ruins; the mixed residential quarter above the shrine; and the new Hujatabad quarter, which promises to be the new core of the town.

Because of this social gradient in alluvial fan towns and villages, spatial patterns and morphology change regularly as one passes from the upper section of a town to its lower margins. In the upper section, large compounds attached to walled orchards predominate (Plate 2A). House plans imitate the peristyle plans found in Kirman City and the occupants of these houses are often the most urbanized members of local society. Above these gardens and compounds where the qanat surfaces, the town ends, often at a sharp break in slope at the foot of the mountains.[32]

As one passes downstream along the watercourse, the compounds and houses become smaller and less prepossessing; compound walls are lower, and walled orchards are less common. In this central section the town widens as the qanat stream divides into several channels to distribute water to vegetable gardens located on either side of the lines of household compounds.[33] In large settlements with important religious facilities, a central square may dominate. In smaller places, shops are located amid the houses along the main channel of the qanat. When the village is aligned on the axis of the alluvial fan, dry valleys incised in the fan are the major thoroughfares, and distribution channels follow them. These are often the only passable streets in the settlement, all others being twisting lanes and alleys similar to those of the old residential sections of Kirman City.

In the lower section of the alluvial fan town, walled orchards disappear, though one still finds household gardens of herbs, spices, and vegetables and double-cropped grainfields. The laborers, sharecroppers, unemployed, and beggars live in this section of town; the delay in capital return involved in orchard cultivation puts this beyond their means. The poverty of this section of town is indicated by the cultivation of quick-ripening summer barley instead of commercial crops such as sugar beets, melons, or tomatoes. These households must sacrifice any possibility of purchasing amenities through sale of cash crops in favor of growing basic grains to satisfy immediate needs. Other indices of poverty are the unrepaired walls of the household compounds and the low walls around the fields. The linear pattern of households becomes confused in this part of the settlement, because the main watercourses have split into numerous smaller channels to irrigate the wide area of cultivated land below the settlement. At the base of the village a jumble of small, one- and two-room hovels are occupied by the poorest class.

A strip of double-cropped land separates the occupied area of the village from the grainfields downslope. These fields are in cultivation year round and are rarely fallow. Wheat or sweet barley is planted here in the fall and harvested in the spring. Summer crops such as potatoes, peas, lentils, melons, and sugar beets are planted in the spring and harvested in the fall (see Appendix A). Finally, the water is distributed to the communal wheat and barley fields, which are quite extensive because each plot of land is cultivated only once every three or four years. They are usually cultivated in rotation, but the rotation can be altered if good reason exists. Thus, if one section is flooded by a spring rain, it will be recultivated immediately to take advantage of soil renewal by flood deposition and the restoration of soil moisture. The irrigation channels in the grainfields are more regular than those of the double-cropped area and form a rectangular pattern.

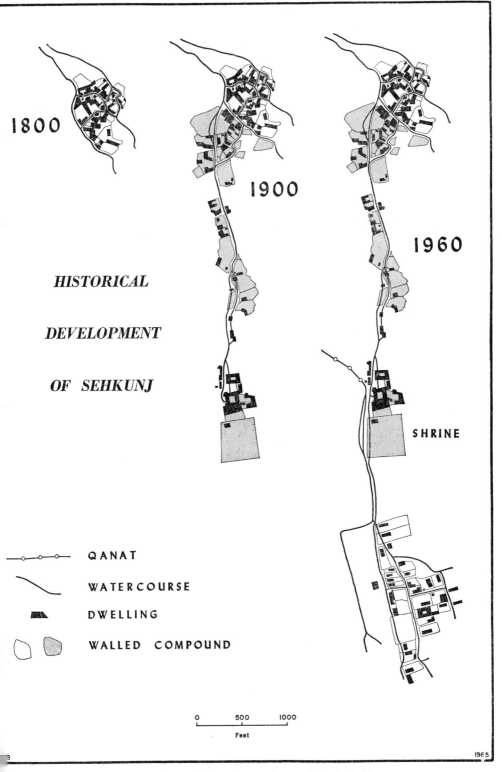

1800

1900

1960

HISTORICAL

DEVELOPMENT

OF SEHKUNJ

SHRINE

○——○——○— QANAT

WATERCOURSE

DWELLING

WALLED COMPOUND

0   500   1000
Feet

1965

. 16. Reconstructed from ruins and interviews, plane-tabled in field.

Village Composition

There are few specialized economic facilities in the alluvial fan towns and villages; most of these settlements are simply collections of household compounds strung out along their watercourses. With the exception of a few shops and gristmills, all nondomestic structures are either religious buildings such as mosques, shrines, and baths or outposts of urban administration. Because the feudal overlord system drains economic surpluses from these settlements through a system of contracts in agriculture, weaving, and herding, any power of internal growth is stifled. One does not find specialized facilities for grain storage, animal protection, or crop processing. Indeed, at present land is so fragmented, animals are owned in such small numbers by so many people, and crop surpluses are so small that these facilities are not needed. Local grain, dairy products, vegetables, and fruits are eaten by the producer or are bartered in the shops of Kirman for salt, sugar, tea, and cloth; all large concentrations of land, crops, herds, and carpets are owned by urban residents.

In contrast with this paucity of economic facilities, the settlements on the slopes of the Kuhi Jupar have been the scene of great religious activity. Religious structures are numerous, probably more so than in other parts of rural Iran, though the strength of religion as a focal point in Iranian peasant life is undisputed.[34] The Shah Ni'matullah Vali Shrine in the town of Mahan, founded in the fifteenth century, is one of the major centers of mysticism in Iran (Plate 2B).[35] The Sufi hospice associated with this shrine was a meeting place for *darvish* mendicants from Iraq, India, and other parts of South and Southwest Asia in the eighteenth and nineteenth centuries. The Mir 'Alamdar Shrine in Jupar is a place of miracles, similar to more important shrines at Qumm and Mashhad. In 1962 the medically documented cure of a woman suffering from gangrene brought several thousand pilgrims to Jupar from as far away as Tehran and Tabriz. Langar, a village of two thousand residents located between Mahan and Jupar, is a center of the Shaykhi sect, the brutal nineteenth-century persecutors of the Bab, Sayyid 'Ali Muhammad of Shiraz, and his religion.[36] This town is still owned by the descendants of Sarkar Aqa, leader of the Shaykhi sect. The ruined village of 'Abdullahabad near Muhiabad is a *qatlagah*, a place where the passion play mourning the martyrdom of Husayn, the grandson of Muhammad, is acted out each year. The little mountain hamlet of Bibigrami is a spa for sufferers of skin diseases. Its pools are green in color from local copper deposits;

this being the sacred color of Islam, the pools are believed by the unlettered to be the "footprints of 'Ali."

As with Christian churches in Europe, these shrines and mosques and their environs are often focal points of social and economic power in their respective settlements. All important meetings are held in them, even when, as in the case of Sehkunj, they lie some distance from the original center of the town. In Mahan the offices of the district governor (*bakhshdar*), the village headman (*kadkhuda*),[37] and other important local officials are in the courtyard of the Shah Ni'matullah Vali Shrine. The shrine of Mir 'Alamdar dominates the central square of Jupar and all township (*dihistan*) offices are located there. No important official enters or leaves either of these towns without first visiting the shrine.

In or near each important shrine or mosque is a cemetery. The larger towns have a special building (*ghasalkhaneh*) near the cemetery where the dead are bathed. The cemeteries of especially sacred shrines such as Shah Ni'matullah Vali, Mir 'Alamdar, and Shaykh 'Ali Baba (Sehkunj) are important facilities for the town and surrounding villages as well, because people believe that the dead gain intercession from the saint of the shrine by burial nearby. In the villages, therefore, only innocent children who do not need special intercession are buried locally; adults are carried to Mahan or Jupar.[38]

Communal baths are also situated near the mosques and shrines. All of the larger settlements in this area have baths, to which peasants from surrounding villages travel regularly to perform religious ablutions and cleanse themselves.[39] A full-scale public bath is owned or rented by a bathkeeper and is used on alternate days by men and women. The bathkeeper employs several workers who wash and massage the patrons, cut hair and nails, and in the past performed circumcisions as well. These workers have a very low social position in Muslim society.[40] The bath itself is usually completely underground; only the roof appears on the surface, a lobed stucco structure resembling a hornet's nest. The interior is a dark, humid lounging room with a tiled pool of warm water at the center. The bath's location in a village is marked by piles of wood and brush to heat the bath water and lines of red-striped toweling drying nearby.

Except for the few structures mentioned above, all buildings in the alluvial fan towns and villages are walled household compounds. The houses are similar to those of Kirman City; one-room dwellings are common, peristyle plans are restricted to the upper class. Even the humblest house is walled, however, for a combination of pragmatic, religious, and cultural reasons. Walls protect the household from the sun, dust storms associated with the "120-day winds of Sistan," and shifting sands. They also provide for easy defense, in a province where nomadic attacks have been a problem historically. But walls also reflect the Islamic desire to shield the household (and particularly its women) from view.[41] Strong wooden and iron doors and L-shaped entryways prevent the passerby from looking into the compound. Walls also satisfy Persian superstitions about the evil eye, which warn everyone to avoid all circumstances that might lead to wonder, awe, or admiration on the part of an observer.

One final structure, the walled orchard or garden, must be noted. Description of Persian gardens in the poetry of Hafiz and Sa'adi and in the reports of Western travelers in Iran have made them one of the best-known elements of the Persian scene.[42] The garden best expresses the spiritual relationship of the Persian to his environment. His appreciation of shade, greenery, and flowing water is enhanced by the desert landscape outside. Two famous gardens in Mahan merit description: Bagh Shahzadeh and the courtyard gardens of the Shah Ni'matullah Vali Shrine. Bagh Shahzadeh was built in 1888–91 by 'Abdul Hamid Mirza, then governor-general of the province of Kirman.[43] The garden is modeled on the Versailles pattern, but the construction is Persian. Situated on a sloping alluvial fan south of Mahan, it is completely enclosed by a twelve-foot adobe wall. A pavilion was built at the foot of the garden, and from this pavilion terraces rise to the tiled summerhouse above. The center of each terrace holds a pool with fountains and shaded walks. Banks of pomegranate, poplar, and Asiatic plane trees occupy the sides of the terraces extending to the walls. The courtyard gardens of the Shah Ni'matullah Vali Shrine are older and more traditionally Persian than those of Bagh Shahzadeh. The garden at the entryway to the shrine (Sahni Atabak) is dominated by a long, rectangular pool surrounded by Judas and cypress trees. The middle courtyard is centered on a cruciform pool, deeply shaded by tall black cypress and pine trees. Four canals separate mixed banks of iris, tulips, and anemones. The plan is formal; the design is based on crossed channels defining four quadrants. This regularity of rows and angles elicits admiration from the Persians. It is reproduced in the famed "garden carpets" of Kirman.

The importance of gardens in village morphology, however, rests on the fact that all Persians appreciate gardens; they have become an integral part of Persian domestic architecture. Most compounds in the village enclose an area which is used as a garden, patio, or simply a yard. This space is filled with trees, vines, flowers, vegetables, herbs, and pools — the content varying with the size of the courtyard and the wealth of the household. The traditional garden emerges most completely in the wealthier homes of Mahan and Jupar. The courtyard is dominated by a central pool, and flower-lined canals divide the garden into sections. A religious element, the concept of sacred water (*kur*), underlies the central position of the pool in many courtyards,[44] but the love of all desert dwellers for flowing water is equally important. In the wealthy homes vegetables such as melons, squash, onions, and garlic recede into the background. Often they are interplanted in vineyards. Beds of alfalfa, the primary winter feed for the sheep, goats, and cattle in the villages, are found in most households. The most common shade trees are cypress, pine, Asiatic plane, ash, willow, poplar, and elm. Among the fruit trees, apple, pear, quince, apricot, peach, cherry, pomegranate, walnut, almond, and mulberry are most usual. In poorer homes flowers and shade trees are replaced by alfalfa beds, fruit-bearing trees, and vines. In these gardens, herbs and spices occupy a more important place, the most common being pennyroyal, wild mustard, and sesame.

Field Patterns

Field patterns are strikingly homogeneous in the various alluvial fan settlements of the Kuhi Jupar. Whether the village is owned by a single absentee owner or by a number of peasant proprietors, village fields are divided into communal wheat fields, double-cropped vegetable land, and walled orchards (see Appendix E). In each village these three types of cultivated land have the same relative position. Peasants favor a combination of fields and crops that will minimize the risk of crop failure and fulfill a variety of family needs. They will work a one-crop field if paid a cash wage, but even then they are reluctant, because this forces them to deal extensively in the city marketplace and convert coins into the family food supply. The landlord is equally reluctant to replace sharecropping agreements with cash wages, fearing peasant idleness and theft.[45] Both of these attitudes reinforce traditional cropping practices and retard consolidation of fields in larger, more economic units.

At Muhiabad, for instance, the landlord attempted to introduce sugar beets as a cash summer replacement crop when opium was outlawed in Iran.[46] Sugar beets were foreign to the household economy; the peasants had to decrease their cultivation of food crops on a market venture and become involved in transactions with the newly constructed sugar beet mill at Bardsir (or Mashiz) some forty miles southwest of Kirman City. The sharecroppers of Muhiabad, therefore, refused to work the sugar beet fields on a sharecropping basis and would work only for cash. The landlord did not wish to assume the entire financial risk of crop failure; thus sugar beets were not cultivated on the large scale originally planned.

Because the peasants and landlords of most alluvial fan villages in the Kirman Basin are integrated into this traditional pattern of economic thought and action, land use patterns vary little from village to village within the region. The only noticeable difference between field patterns in landlord villages compared with villages owned by peasants is the tendency toward greater fragmentation in the latter. The landlord will not hire more sharecroppers than necessary to till his fields, and thus a fixed number of agricultural households and divisions of the cultivated land is achieved. In peasant-owned villages excess population tends to remain in the village; this leads to greater population pressure on the cultivated land and hence greater fragmentation.

MOUNTAIN VILLAGES AND HAMLETS

The Kuhi Jupar Mountains rise steeply from the Kirman plain to heights of more than 11,000 feet. They are dissected by a network of dry valleys formed as flood channels for spring rains and occasional summer thunderstorms. The valleys have steep gradients and are deeply eroded. Their floors are covered with coarse gravel and boulders. Two problems are presented to permanent settlers in these valleys: water supply and lack of level land. Qanats are used to supply domestic and irrigation water. They are less dependable than those of the alluvial fans, being short (less than a kilometer in length) and shallow. Villages are located on small flood terraces on the inside curves of the winding channels and at valley intersections. Fields are planted wherever level land can be found and on slopes as well. As a result, the structure and organization of mountain villages and hamlets vary greatly with local site conditions.

The mountains are clearly a marginal area for permanent settlement. This is reflected in the small number of people living there, the small size of the settlements, the nature of their economy, and the recency of their settlement. Of the nearly 17,000 people living on the northern slopes of the Kuhi Jupar, fewer than seven hundred live in the mountain valleys. Of the thirty-one settlements in these mountain valleys, only one has a population of more than one hundred; only four have over fifty residents (Fig. 10, p. 36). Most mountain settlements rely on a combination of subsistence agriculture, herding, charcoal burning, and fuel collecting for survival. Agriculture is best developed near the mouths of the valleys, in places such as Kahnuj and Mah Char. Herding and charcoal burning are more important near the heads of the valleys, in Daristan, Khankistan, and Chashmeh Kush.

The major economic functions of the mountain settlements in the regional economy of the Kirman Basin are herding and fuel production. Flocks of sheep and goats owned by residents of Kirman City, Mahan, and Jupar are grazed in the mountains. Here isolation and lack of motor-able roads have better preserved the vegetation cover, whereas on the plain it has been stripped away. Currently, increased pressure on available grazing and fuel reserves in the mountains is destroying these resources. When the process is completed, many settlements will have to be abandoned and their residents will return to the plains.

Mountain villages and hamlets differ in appearance from settlements on the alluvial fans (Plate 4A). Most settlements are composed of only three or four structures, and in settlements such as Chashmeh Kush, Baharistan, and Ni'matabad Toujigun, the total population belongs to one family. Household compounds may be walled or unwalled; isolation provides both defense and privacy. The houses cling to valley walls to save level land for cultivation and to avoid flooding. Thus the roof of one house may be a doorstep for the next above. Field stones gathered from the cultivated land provide the basic building material; the cluttered, flat, beehive appearance of the alluvial fan village is not reproduced in this environment.

Nor do the houses conform to a standard pattern. One to four rooms randomly connected form the living unit. Peristyle houses are rare in mountain settlements. There is one at Dareh Gaz and another at Hanak Bala; both are summer residences for the landlord of the village and do not represent local living conditions. Mountain dwellings have thick, field stone walls cemented with mud; only the domed or vaulted roofs are made of adobe. These buildings are well adapted to climate. The thick walls absorb daytime heat and radiate it slowly during the cold nights. Such adjustments are particularly critical for cultivators and shepherds in the mountains, because fuel is one of their major marketable commodities.

Some hamlets located at high elevations in the Kuhi Jupar do not have houses in the usual sense. In Chashmeh Kush, Karimabad Haji 'Ali, and Daristan, the villagers live with their animals in underground shelters in winter and in temporary brush huts in summer (Plate 4B). These caves are dug into the sides of talus slopes a distance of ten or fifteen feet. The roof is low and there is no opening except the doorway, which is about three feet high and two feet wide. These shelters were originally built for animals; their use by people reflects the intense pressure on land in mountain areas.

Animal shelters also vary with elevation (see Appendix C). At lower elevations near the valley mouths, animals are kept in adobe rooms or in pits dug in the corner of the household compound. At middle elevations, underground shelters (*birkand*) are dug in the valley walls opposite the village. In some villages many of these birkands have been built to accommodate the flocks owned by traveling herders and landlords. In such cases, the shelter and village graze are rented each year in return for a small grazing fee and the fertilizer which collects during the winter period. At higher elevations, people and animals alike live in underground shelters.

The organization of territory in the villages and hamlets of the mountains, then, is different from that of settlements on the alluvial fans. Because of their small size, there are no linearity of household compounds and no specialized facilities other than animal shelters. Walled orchards and double-cropped garden land are closer to the settlement than are the wheat fields, but there is no clear hierarchy of water distribution in terms of land use. The fields are scattered up and down the valley both above and below the village, wherever slope and soil conditions are favorable for cultivation. Nor is there a formal rotation system; fields are cultivated or left fallow depending on the available water supply. The source of water in most villages is a shallow qanat, and water supply varies with annual rainfall. Water is stored in a pool located above the settlement and distributed to the fields at night when there will be less evaporation.

In Toujigun, a typical mountain hamlet, the pool is a hundred yards above the alluvial terrace on which the village is built (Fig. 17). The qanat begins one kilometer above the pool and taps a small alluvial fan formed at the intersection of three wadis. Two channels carry water from the pool to the fields. The first of these enters the hamlet of Toujigun and distributes water in the orchard and double-cropped garden lands. The other channel flows at a lesser gradient than the bed of the wadi and

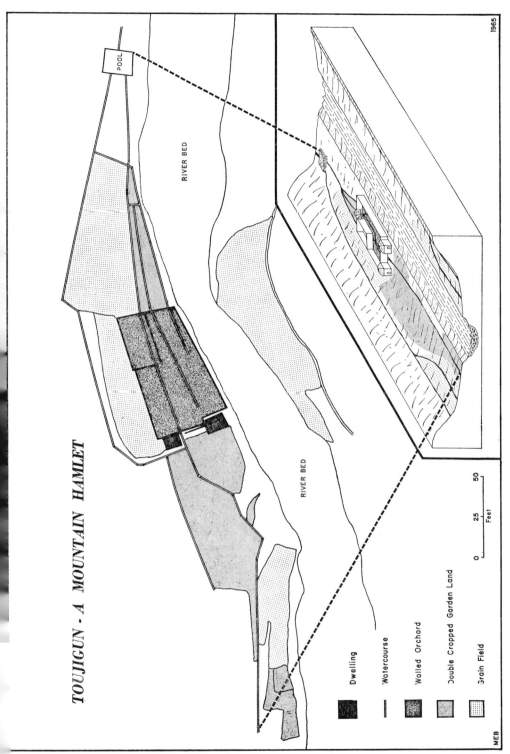

TOUJIGUN - A MOUNTAIN HAMLET

POOL

RIVER BED

RIVER BED

1965

Dwelling

Watercourse

Walled Orchard

Double Cropped Garden Land

Grain Field

0   25   50
        Feet

MEB

Fig. 17. Data from field observation, plane-tabled in field.

carries water to patches of rough hillside land which are cultivated in the wet years and left fallow in the dry.[47] The fields of Toujigun are divided into two types, different in crops, cultivation, and yields. The permanently cultivated land near the settlement is planted in wheat during the winter and in vegetables in the summer. Within the walled garden, alfalfa is grown. These fields are heavily fertilized since manure is available. The rocky hillside land is cultivated irregularly in wheat, barley, peas, and lentils. This land is not plowed deeply (since it is so rocky) but is simply furrowed at planting time to loosen the soil. It is difficult to identify these fields when they are fallow; they differ little from uncultivated land.

The location of mountain valley settlements on small flood terraces and at valley intersections makes flooding a major hazard. Heavy rains or sudden spring thaws wash away entire villages. The town of 'Abdullaha-bad, a settlement once comparable in size with Langar and Qanaghistan, was destroyed by such a flood some years ago, and all settlements in the wadi above it were washed away. To some degree, village morphology in the mountain valleys is designed to avoid these dangers. Compound walls are three to six feet thick at the base and are built along the margins of the stream bed (e.g. at Toujigun). These walls follow the contours of the stream to divert sudden flowage into the channel and away from the village. Reservoir pools are protected from flooding by levees of stone and mud built to a height of six feet on all sides. In winter and early spring, the most likely seasons for floods, village crops are planted as high on the valley walls as possible. But despite these precautions the mountain valleys are dotted with abandoned settlements, many of which are currently being resettled. Among these flooded settlements are Dareh Hasani, Dum Dahaneh Zahrud, Chashmeh Shaghin (now reoccupied), and Ni'matabad. In some cases all structures in the village were destroyed, in others only the qanat. The latter villages are being reoccupied as new settlers from the plain repair the qanats and bring fields back into cultivation.

Chapter 4

Territorial Socioeconomic Structure

People in the Kirman Basin live in four types of settlements, which differ in size, complexity, economic structure, and function: the city, regional subcenters, agricultural-weaving villages, and small villages and hamlets. The economic and social bonds among these various settlements are strong. Topography and the density of settlement in the region have assured easy and continuous communication among them, except in the mountains. Economic interdependence therefore is a dominant characteristic of the regional economy; it is found in agriculture, weaving, and herding. Self-sufficient, independent, internally organized rural settlements, seldom visited and little changed since the time of Christ — a settlement type many writers on the Middle East are fond of — do not exist in the Kirman Basin.

Kirman City is the major administrative and political center of the Kirman Basin and southeastern Iran. Political leaders in rural settlements such as district governors (*bakhshdar*), mayors (*shahrdar*), and village headmen (*kadkhuda*) are appointed to and can be removed from office by the governor-general of the province, who resides in Kirman City. These local leaders settle minor disputes and officiate at local ceremonies; all serious legal disputes are referred directly to Kirman City. Government gendarmerie posts in Mahan and Jupar maintain continuous control over the area. The few professional people in smaller settlements are also government representatives. In Mahan these include six teachers, a doctor, a male nurse, a forestry department official (despite the lack of forests), and several tax collectors.

Kirman City is also the major social and religious center of the basin. Peasants look to it for entertainment and religious leadership. Many attend movies in the city; still more visit its mosques and shrines. On religious holidays and on Fridays (the Muslim sabbath) the bazaar swells with people from Mahan, Jupar, and places much farther away. Tribesmen from Baluchistan with white turbans and flowing robes, weavers from Ravar to the north, villagers from all parts of the province, and traveling mendicants are common sights in the city. Some bring fruit, grain, brush, or charcoal to barter or sell in the bazaar during the early morning hours. Many refuse to sell their goods quickly, for the pleasure of haggling and hearing the week's gossip is not to be missed. The remainder of the day is spent visiting relatives, wandering about the city, and attending religious services. Ancient taxis and buses ply the routes in the basin and beyond to cater to this demand. On every religious holiday, at least one of these vehicles travels from Kirman to Mahan, passes through Langar, Qanaghistan, and Muhiabad to Jupar, and then returns to the city by the same route, a round trip of some seventy miles. Still others go up and down the Yazd–Kirman–Bam highway to collect villagers from surrounding areas. Before cars and buses, peasants walked or rode donkeys to Kirman, and many still do. Wheeled vehicles intensified and expanded an existing pattern; they did not create a new one.[1] The city, then, has always been an important part of peasant life.

Perhaps this interdependence between city and village is most striking in the economic sphere. Kirman City is the financial and administrative center, the economic nucleus, for every major activity in the region. The power elite of the city control the key institutions and basic resources of the province. Landed aristocrats of Kirman finance agriculture. New villages are built and old ones repaired on their command. Every qanat in the Kirman Basin (for which records exist) was built by a member of the urban elite, whether merchant or landlord. Nor has this group relinquished control of the basic elements of production; they own much of the cultivated land and the water which irrigates it. Peasant proprietors are found in the basin, but they do not initiate new economic development except in marginal areas.

By retaining control of the elements of production and then leasing them to villagers, the power elite retain decision-making power. Urbanites decide if fertilizer is to be used, whether tractors are a wise investment, and in many cases which crops are grown. This is not to imply absolute power; landlords are bound by tradition quite as much as peasants. But the fundamental decisions of maintenance and change are theirs, for it is they who finance agriculture. Though social contacts between landlord and peasant may be few (this has been grossly overstated in the literature), the economic bond is firm; their interdependence and respective privileges and duties are at the heart of the agricultural system.

Similar control is maintained in the carpet-weaving industry and in herding. Weavers in villages and towns work for the power elite under a contract system. The carpet merchant supplies the materials, the weaver his labor. The largest herds of sheep and goats in the province are owned by carpet factories in the city and by entrepreneurs who specialize in the wool trade. In essence, the entire economy of the basin is keyed on Kirman City. There is no major segment of the population independent of its influence.[2]

Kirman on its part requires economic support from a wide area of production. The peasantry contribute time and energy, produce and labor, toward the maintenance of the city. Recently these relationships have intensified because Kirman has sought wider and wider relationships with its hinterland to fill the lag in investment opportunities which followed its decline as a military and international trading center. The city is supplied with grain, fruit, and vegetables grown in the gardens and fields of Mahan, Jupar, Langar, Qanaghistan, and many smaller settlements. The hinterland also contributes tax revenues to the city. Tax offices on every major road in Kirman until very recently collected duties on goods flowing in and out of its marketplace.[3] Finally, the raw materials of the carpet-weaving industry are supplied locally. Without these goods and services, the city would certainly decline.

But this very general level of interdependence masks hundreds of minor daily interactions between urbanites and their rural counterparts. The city is the major marketplace for everything the villagers produce. On a given morning, peasants travel to the city to sell a small rug, a mat, a woven cap, stockings, a goat, or any other item in order to buy fundamental necessities such as salt, sugar, tea, or cloth. If his daughter is to be wed or his social position demands that a celebration be held, the peasant asks his landlord or weaving contractor for an advance, and failing that will have recourse to the moneylenders of the bazaar. And debt is a binding tie; many debtors live in villages, most creditors in the city. If a villager has broken the law or the army threatens to induct him, his last appeal will always be to the most powerful urbanite he or his family knows. If he wishes to buy a cup, a plate, a religious photograph or icon, a samovar, or a rug, he will travel to Kirman, where the choice is great and he can hope to find a bargain. The majority of specialized artisans, craftsmen, service workers, and professional people live in Kirman.

Finally there are the small agricultural, weaving, herding, charcoal-burning villages and hamlets on the alluvial fans and in the mountains. Even these show some variety, since any of the above occupations may be the dominant economic activity depending on the location, local resources, and origin of the particular settlement. They are united in being primary producers, and the vast majority of their populations are either farmers, weavers, or herders. Many villages and hamlets are simply offshoots from a parent settlement, particularly those in the mountains. In the past these offspring were called *mazra'eh*, which translates as "hamlet" but indicates that the smaller place is to be treated as an integral part of the larger settlement for tax purposes. Usually settlements located on the water supply lines of a larger settlement have this type of relationship. Thus, the villages and hamlets in the valley south of Langar (Ahmadabad Dogu, Rahimabad, and Zarkuh) are populated by people from Langer who still consider themselves Langari and receive a fixed percentage of Langar's water supply (Fig. 10, p. 36). This same relationship obtains in Kazimabad, Toujigun, and Qudratabad in the Tigiran valley and in the settlements near Mah Char. Peddlers from the parent settlement and sometimes barbers as well travel into the mountains once or twice a month.

This should not suggest that villagers spend the bulk of their time on the road to Kirman or that all villagers live in similar settlements. The cultivator is tied to his field, the shepherd to his flock, and the weaver to his loom. Thus, regional subcenters are necessary to distribute vital goods and services to the rural population. On the northern slopes of the Kuhi Jupar these functions are performed by the towns of Mahan and Jupar. Villagers travel to these centers far oftener than to Kirman City for medicines, for vital elements of the diet (e.g. sugar, tea), on religious holidays, to exchange goods, and in the end for burial. Mahan performs these services for an area including Qanaghistan, Langar, and the mountain settlements of the Kuhi Jupar. The town of Jupar supplies alluvial fan villages as far eastward as Amirabad, including villages such as Isma'ilabad, Shahabad, Kousar Riz, and Muhiabad. In these two towns artisans such as carpenters, well diggers, blacksmiths, coppersmiths, tanners, and brickmakers, and service people such as shopkeepers, barbers, bathkeepers, bakers, druggists, and midwives are found. Local administrators also live here and decide minor disputes concerning ownership, water rights, and other village problems. To a certain extent these occupations are represented in the large villages of Qanaghistan, Langar, and Muhiabad, but their number and importance decline as the settlement grows smaller.

One would expect an organized chain of command in this settlement hierarchy from the decision-making elite of Kirman City through middlemen in the regional subcenter to primary producers in the villages and hamlets, but such is not the case. Arrangements, contracts, and decisions in agriculture, weaving, and herding generally flow directly from the city to the producer. Some landlords deal through intermediaries (*mubashirs*) who represent their interests in local affairs, others do not. In most cases the terms of sharecropping contracts are fixed by tradition. The landlord visits the village in August to reaffirm the contract and again at harvest time to collect his share of the produce. There are no intermediary grain dealers, storers, or processors in Mahan and Jupar. Wheat and barley are harvested from the fields and delivered directly to the city; only the peasant's share (20 to 30%) remains in the hinterland. In weaving, the contract between factory and weaver is also direct. Supplies are sent from the city to the weaver's loom, intermediaries perform regular inspection tours as the carpet progresses, and final payment is made upon delivery in Kirman. There are no carpet shops in the regional subcenters, though there are managers and entrepreneurs who control upward of a hundred looms. Similar arrangements apply to the large herds of sheep and goats.

To be sure, some secondary economic activity is created in the regional subcenters. Local landlords and peasant proprietors sell grain to the weavers of neighboring villages. Independent weavers produce mats or rugs ordered by local residents. Shepherds care for flocks owned by weavers and farmers in the alluvial fan settlements. But these are variations on the major theme in economic activity: urban dominance. The origin and mechanisms of urban control are detailed in Chapter 5.

ECONOMIC STRUCTURE OF KIRMAN CITY

The occupational structure of Kirman City reflects its diverse functions as an administrative, political, commercial, social, and religious center. Its streets are clogged with a variety of specialists: landlords, merchants, booksellers, beggars, hawkers, artisans, civil servants, chauffeurs, weavers, *mulla*s, entertainers, millers, bakers, poets, clerks, bankers, goldsmiths, and a host of other men who serve the city and its hinterland. The professional class composed of teachers (classical and modern), religious

TABLE 4
Generalized Occupational Structure of Kirman City

Occupation	Number	% of total
Professional and administrative	1,943	9.9
Service	2,791	14.1
Commercial	2,089	10.6
Artisans and craftsmen	6,885	34.9
Agriculture	2,586	13.0
Unemployed	1,571	8.0
Not reported	1,891	9.5
TOTAL	19,756	100.0

Source: Government of Iran, *Census District Statistics of the First National Census of Iran, Aban 1335 (November 1956)*, Vol. 17, Part 1 (Tehran: Department of Public Statistics, Ministry of Interior, Government of Iran, 1960), pp. 26, 34–36. These figures represent the total number of males aged 10 years or older, excepting students. The population of Kirman City was too large and diversified to assure complete reliability, although efforts were made to check data in the field. See Appendix F.

leaders, lawyers, doctors, bureaucrats, and clerks makes up a tenth of the male population over ten years old; most of these men (77%) are employed by the government.[4] Service workers form 14% of the labor force, among them barbers, bathkeepers, domestic servants, policemen, and others. The traders of the city (another tenth of the labor force) are divided into two groups, the export-import merchants (wholesalers) and the retail shopkeepers. Many of the former migrated to Tehran when trade declined; but the latter are more numerous than ever, particularly the retailers of cloth, food, and household goods.[5]

Artisans and craftsmen form the largest occupational group in Kirman City, representing nearly 35% of the labor force. Carpet weaving is the major craft (24% of all artisans and craftsmen); it employs designers, dyers, cleaners, carders, and clippers as well as weavers. Unskilled construction workers (including brickmakers) are the largest artisan group (35% of all artisans and craftsmen). Recently, both of these activities have increased in Kirman. Carpet factories have enticed village weavers to the city with offers of better facilities and higher rates of pay. The construction group increased when landless peasants and ambitious sharecroppers migrated to the city in search of work. Having no other skill or training, they carry bricks, clay, dust, and straw for the professional builders. Other large craft groups in Kirman include tailors, blacksmiths, bakers, and carpenters.

Although one does not usually think of farming as a major urban occupation, agriculturalists are numerous in provincial Persian cities. In Kirman they form 13% of the labor force. Among their number are landed aristocrats who own land and water in settlements as distant as the coast of the Persian Gulf, gardeners and sharecroppers who work in the newly constructed orchards and fields (irrigated by deep wells) on the outskirts of the city, and professional gardeners who tend the formal household gardens of the urban elite.[6] In the past, agriculturalists were more numerous; they fed the city when it was under attack and grew fruit and vegetables for the marketplace. The smaller percentage of them in modern Kirman reflects its growing dependence on produce from its hinterland.

The low percentage of unemployed people in Kirman City (8% of the labor force) is deceptive.[7] Many seasonal laborers work in agriculture at harvest time and in construction during spring and early summer. Others work sporadically when there is need for their services — among them donkeymen, domestic servants, and street cleaners. Most of these men probably reported themselves as employed in one or another occupational group. The unemployment rate in Kirman City, therefore, is higher than the figures show.

Most of the people in Kirman City are occupied in secondary and tertiary activities. This in itself does not distinguish Kirman City from other settlements in the region which perform similar functions and have similar occupational structures but operate on a smaller scale in a more restricted area. The principal characteristics which do distinguish Kirman City from smaller places such as Rafsinjan, Bam, Mahan, and Jupar are its full range of social strata and high degree of occupational differentiation.

In Kirman City the social stratification characteristic of many pre-industrial cities is well developed.[8] At the top of the social structure is an urban elite, a small (probably a twentieth of society) group of powerful families who control the elements of production in the city and its hinterland. Beneath this elite group there is a small but growing middle class of intellectuals, second-rank civil servants and bureaucrats, progressive merchants, and professionals, making possibly a tenth of society.[9] Next is the large commoner class composed of petty bazaar merchants, service workers, artisans and craftsmen, and agriculturalists — the bulk of the urban population. At the base of the social order are people isolated by occupation or background from those higher in the socioeconomic scale. In the past, members of the Jewish and Zoroastrian communities of

Kirman were included in this class, but today the main ethnic group still viewed with distaste by society is the Gypsies.[10]

The Urban Elite

Kirman City's upper class is a small, heterogeneous group of leaders drawn from all segments of society but unified in wealth, power, and influence in local affairs. Membership is restricted to individuals with wealth and/or power; entrance cannot be accomplished by family name or contacts alone. To be sure, established families command greater respect than *nouveaux riches*, and a family with a record of past achievement has higher prestige than an equivalent family with an undistinguished past. But these are social shadings. The key to inclusion is ownership — of land, water, animals, or carpets. Accumulation of wealth is usually derived from positions in the governmental, military, or religious hierarchy.

Two traditional groups in the urban elite of Kirman City are the regional political and religious leaders. The political leaders of Kirman, the governor-general and his assistants, are appointed by the central government in Tehran to run both city and province. They have no fixed term of tenure and are frequently removed from office. In the past, political appointments to such provincial governorships were sure roads to fortune (if not fame), and these men acquired large personal fortunes from gifts, bribes, and through manipulation and connivance with members of the local elite. Landlords and merchants favored by one ruler or another would amass riches rapidly; others less fortunate would lose land, water, and carpets. But corruption has declined in recent times. Political appointees are rarely in Kirman long enough to develop intimate contact with one member of the local elite or distaste for another. Hence their impact on the composition of the urban aristocracy, local governmental decisions, and the economy of Kirman is less.

The influence of religious leaders has declined, because secular institutions now perform many of their previous functions. The courts, once the province of *imams* and *mullas*, are now filled with civil judges and lawyers. Religious elementary schools (*maktabs*), supported by private contributions and religious foundations, formerly trained the children of the upper class and shaped their thoughts along traditional lines.[11] Now, government teachers in secular schools train the young, and religion is a minor part of the curriculum. Clerical control of law, education, and mass media has been broken, and thus the wellsprings of religious power are severely limited. That mullas are still treated with great respect by landlords and merchants is probably a tribute to the pervasiveness of their past influence. Young "modern" members of the aristocracy often mock tradition, yet they flatter, subsidize, and defer to religious leaders.

Since the real basis of social and economic power in Kirman is ownership, few religious or resident political leaders in the city fail to root their power firmly in land or carpets. Many landowners of modern Kirman are descendants of powerful government officials, religious leaders, and merchants of the nineteenth century; others belong to the nouveau riche group, men who have accumulated wealth in the bazaar or in civil service and have invested it in land.[12] Nouveaux riches do not view land ownership exclusively as an economic venture, though a substantial amount of their income may derive from it. Land is a tool in their climb to and maintenance of prestige and social power. Any purchase of land is a gain in power, any sale of land symbolizes a (real or imagined) decline in fortunes. Extensive low quality holdings are preferred to fewer high quality properties of equal value, and in some cases landlords retain uneconomic holdings rather than lose prestige by disposing of the land.[13]

The traditional members of the landowning class disdain contact with the masses and surround themselves with managers, clerks, and servants to represent them in dealings with the common people of the city and region. Maids shop for them in the bazaar, clerks handle commercial dealings with retail shopkeepers, and managers negotiate contracts with sharecroppers. Such men conform closely to the stereotype of the Middle Eastern landlord — but they are few in Kirman. Many have migrated to Tehran and others have been replaced by their educated sons, who have a markedly different attitude and approach than their tradition-bound fathers.

The younger members of the landed aristocracy have been educated in Tehran or at Western universities and return to Kirman with progressive technical and (to a lesser extent) social ideas. These men spread knowledge of tractor plowing, fertilization, improved seed, and insecticides throughout their holdings. Most of them are not content simply to be landlords. They are proud of their knowledge and use it as civil servants in government bureaus. They associate informally with middle class contemporaries who share their viewpoint on "modernization"; they do not respect the moralistic attitudes of the commoners toward women, alcoholic beverages, or illegal foods, and they adopt the characteristics of Westernized elements in Tehran society.[14]

In addition to landowners, the elite includes some wholesale import-export merchants (*tajir*) who export carpets, wool, dried fruit, and nuts from Kirman and import sugar, rice, tea, cloth, hardware, and machinery. These men live in large houses in the suburbs of Kirman but work in small, sparsely furnished rooms around the caravanserais. These surroundings are deceptive, for the tajir's money and influence are spread throughout the city at all levels. Most of his capital is in real estate: slum dwellings, orchards, booths in the bazaar, and land and water in surrounding villages. Some is in merchandise, however, and the wealthiest of these merchants are creditors for hundreds of retailers, hawkers, and vendors.

Despite their enormous influence, merchants find entrance into the elite class difficult. Their extensive dealings with lower classes and manipulations for profit have always made them suspect. But a few merchants have achieved upper class status in Kirman, as is to be expected in such a commercial center. And if the merchant who desires inclusion is as socially clever as he is commercially adept, he follows a standard pattern. First, he segregates himself from dealings with the lower classes by hiring the trappings of the landed aristocrat — a host of servants, middlemen, and brokers — and abstains from manual labor of any type. He invests in land, realizing that it is less profitable than trade,[15] to build his image as a member of the upper class. Other less status-conscious merchants are content to manipulate power without position.

The Middle Class

Between the elite and the masses is a growing middle class in Kirman. This group includes representatives of a wide variety of occupations: lesser landlords, lower echelon bureaucrats, young religious leaders, small merchants, shopkeepers of the bazaar, clerks, and professionals, all of whom have less power and wealth than the elite but are above the mass of commoners. The bulk of the middle class is traditional in viewpoint, but a vocal minority is progressive. On the basis of this difference in attitude two groups can be identified: the young and vigorous, Western-trained intelligentsia, who favor modern education, technology, and social progress; and the traditional bazaar retailers, artisans, and craftsmen, who are organized in a complex guild system.

The young intelligentsia are the "modernizers" (or to use Lerner's term, the "transitionals") of Kirman City. Drawn from aristocratic, religious, and commercial backgrounds, they are united in their contempt for traditionalism, emphasizing its worst aspects, and in their desire for change. All are literate and some have a high school education; most have aspirations which they believe can be realized only through revolutionary social change. Thus they form a frustrated, unhappy group, but they have played a positive role in Kirman. Many recent changes in the city such as the paving of major avenues, provision of new bathing facilities (shower baths versus pool baths were a critical issue), the building of an ice factory, and the introduction of numerous paperback bookstores have been initiated and supported by members of the middle class and financed by sympathetic members of the elite.

The bulk of the middle class is composed of retail merchants of the bazaar and master artisans and craftsmen (Plate 6A). In Kirman this class includes cloth sellers, small grocers, carpet sellers and weavers, silversmiths, blacksmiths, carpenters, leather workers, coppersmiths, master tailors, moneylenders, dyers, designers, bathkeepers, shoemakers, potters, booksellers, and other tradesmen. These lower middle class shopkeepers and craftsmen form the heart of the city's economic and social life; they pray regularly at the mosque and attend all religious ceremonies, they converse for hours each day with all classes in their stalls in the bazaar, they belong to a guild and probably a *zurkhana* as well.[16] The artisans and merchants produce luxury goods for the elite and sell lesser products to commoners, villagers, and visiting tribesmen.

Perhaps most important, tradesmen and artisans train the youth of Kirman through a guild system, first as apprentices and later as journeymen. The young men pattern themselves after their guild masters. While performing menial chores as errand boys, they learn that manual labor is the proper function of the lower class, not of the master artisan. They are trained in guild loyalty, regular prayer, and attendance at the mosque.[17] The length of the apprenticeship varies with the ability of the boy, the tenacity of the master, and the difficulty of the craft, but in all cases it is long enough to ensure that the apprentice turned journeyman has absorbed the proper values of the bazaar.

Members of each trade and craft or specialized segment of a trade or craft belong to a guild; membership is a prerequisite for practice of every trade. The guild maintains a monopoly over its given economic activity through informal social pressures rooted in tradition. Some crafts have guild courts which regulate internal disputes and represent members in dealings with other guilds and the government. A guild council formed of elders (*rish safid*) is presided over by the head of the guild.[18] The strongest guilds in Kirman City are the cloth sellers, carpet weavers, shawl makers, rug sellers, and wool sellers. After these come the tailors, potters, blacksmiths, carpenters, coppersmiths and finally noncraft groups such as the bathkeepers, barbers, midwives, storytellers, and darvishes. In some cases, guilds cut across religious boundaries, as with the cloth sellers' guild of Kirman City, which includes Zoroastrians and Jews as well as Muslims.[19] But the members of these religions sell their wares in different parts of the Vakil Bazaar, so that Kirman has three cloth-selling bazaars though only one cloth sellers' guild.

Forces of modernization have nullified many of the economic and social powers of the guilds in Kirman. Guilds are no longer treated as corporate units for taxation purposes, whereas in the past guild members paid government taxes in seven installments to guild leaders. Guild control of the training of middle class youths has been affected by compulsory primary education and military conscription. Guild social and religious activities have been curtailed by government control of assemblies, and identification with the religious class has led to a corresponding loss in prestige. Monopolistic guild control of economic activity has been weakened by the introduction of new techniques and crafts such as automobile repair, mechanized carding and weaving, and truck driving. Finally, government bureaus have assumed regulatory control of economic activity (previously the province of the guild): laws regulating working conditions, minimum health and sanitation standards, and minimum wage laws, though rarely enforced, now place the power of regulation in the hands of bureaucrats rather than of artisans. Continuing changes in industry and commerce seem likely to prevent any return of guilds to their former role in the economic structure of the city.

The Lower Class

The lower class of Kirman City is a large and varied group, comprising well over half its population. The lowest echelons of religious and government service, poor journeymen and unskilled laborers, sharecroppers and gardeners, servants, carriers, lesser shopkeepers, hawkers, and vendors fill the ranks of this commoner group. As a class, it is unified only in the sense that it forms a composite group of similar status in the eyes of the elite. Its three most numerous elements are the vendors, the agriculturalists, and the unskilled laborers.

Hawkers and vendors form one of the most colorful groups in any

Plate 1A. A view of Kirman City from the summit of Qal'ehi Ardashir. The foreground is a new suburb (note bricks drying in sun); the Zoroastrian quarter occupies the background.

Plate 1B. A landlord's house and courtyard garden in Kirman City.

Plate 2A. A view of upper Mahan; trees in background mark the channel of a qanat entering the town. Note the linearity of the household compounds.

Plate 2B. The Shah Ni'matullah Vali Shrine of Mahan, built in the fifteenth century in honor of the famous Sufi saint.

Plate 3A. The small village of 'Aliabad at the foot of the Kuhi Jupar viewed from the Kirman plain.

Plate 3B. A village street scene.

Plate 4A. The mountain village of Husaynabad Mahdi Quli in the Kuhi Jupar.

Plate 4B. Villagers in the mountains live in brush shelters in summer and underground in winter.

Plate 5A. A watercourse in Kirman City. Members of the "traditional" commoner class (left) wash here, as two "modern" bureaucrats pass by.

Plate 5B. In the villages women carry water in goatskin bags.

Plate 6A. The coppersmiths' section of the Vakil Bazaar in Kirman City.

Plate 6B. A religious leader (*mulla*) advising the faithful at the Friday-prayer mosque in Kirman City.

Plate 7A. A water mill near Mahan; note the sprig of wild rue hanging from the ceiling to protect the premises from the "evil eye."

Plate 7B. The carpenter of Langar repairs local tools with native and imported wood.

Plate 8A. Carpet weaving in a village near Kirman. The carpet contractor (right rear) checks the weaver's progress once each month.

Plate 8B. Weaving a Kirman carpet.

Plate 9A. A farmer of Kousar Riz en route to Mahan for marketing and Friday religious services at the Shah Ni'matullah Vali Shrine.

Plate 9B. Two of the "taxis" which carry villagers to Kirman City each morning.

Plate 10A. Threshing wheat (with a *garjin*) in Qanaghistan.

Plate 10B. Winnowing and sifting grain at Qanaghistan.

Plate 11A. Harvesting potatoes at Muhiabad.

Plate 11B. The division of harvest between landlord (right) and peasant (left).

Plate 12A. Flocks of sheep and goats graze on scanty pastures in the Kuhi Jupar.

Plate 12B. Fuel collectors near Daristan return to their village (rear left) with a day's harvest.

Persian city, and Kirman is no exception. They travel about the city calling their wares: water, bread, vegetables, fruit, brooms, cloth, rugs, and hundreds of other things. Each specializes in a particular item, dresses in a particular fashion, and has a unique way of advertising his product. Some work seasonally, such as the sellers of Shahdad oranges, but most travel their routes daily throughout the year. Among the noisiest are the kettle sellers and water sellers, who beat their tins while chanting their wares. The latter are divided into sellers of water from Husaynabad, a spring three miles from the city, and sellers of Kirman City water. The spring water sellers look down on their competitors as handlers of an inferior product. Both drive donkey-powered vehicles with large tanks mounted on the rear axles of World War II jeeps. As these are pulled through the lanes of the city their drivers vie for the attention of the citizens. One of the major reasons for the number and variety of hawkers in Kirman is the restriction of upper class women to the home. It is only when peddlers come to their door that many of these women have the pleasure of examining and purchasing goods.

Most of the agriculturalists in Kirman City are part-time cultivators who combine farming with construction work and other unskilled labor. But even in this group there is some diversity and specialization. A few cultivators have attached themselves to upper class landlords and run errands throughout the city when not working in the fields. These men aspire to positions as watchmen, gatekeepers, or overseers in the household. If successful, they acquire power over several lesser jobs and considerable status among their peers. Another group of agriculturalists specializes in cultivating cash summer crops. Often, by a sharecropping contract, the landlord's household is supplied with fresh vegetables in return for use of an uncultivated plot of land. The remainder of the crop is sold on the outskirts of the bazaar by the cultivator or a member of his family. Several of these gardeners have become famous for the quality of their crops and have developed a faithful clientele among the elite. Such farmers dress in Western clothing and take part in urban social and religious functions; their wives weave carpets or are domestic servants. Finally, there are those cultivators, newly arrived in the city, who have been driven by drought or flood from their villages. These men retain their rural dress, speech, and behavior patterns but assimilate urban characteristics rapidly.

Probably the largest group in the lower class is formed of unskilled laborers. Kirman teems with these: servants, ditchdiggers, haulers, burden bearers, construction workers, donkeymen, and car washers. They are humble in their poverty. Many of these men gather at the western end of the Vakil Bazaar each morning, some with shovels and others without, in hopes that an employer will appear. Carpenters, builders, blacksmiths, and other artisans hire laborers daily from this group. They are paid anywhere from 30 to 40 *rials* ($.40 to $.53) per day after a small gift is given to the employer for providing work, enough money for bread and a bowl of yoghurt.

But there is a group beneath these unskilled laborers, whose status is not only humble but defiling because of occupation or birth. Butchers, barbers, washers in public baths, leather tanners, privy cleaners, night soil collectors, and street scavengers are members of this lowest class. The Gypsies, for instance, are not allowed to touch food or water before use by other members of town society, despite the fact that they are Muslims, nor are they encouraged to settle in Kirman. Intermarriage with Gypsies or others of the defiled class is considered repugnant by elite and commoners alike. In some cases it is expressly forbidden.[20] Forces of change are steadily eliminating people from the group of the unclean, and their numbers are decreasing. Entertainers, for instance, have achieved a type of prominence through their association with the elite. Refrigerated butcher shops and modern barbershops are utilized by upper class Kirmanis, and their proprietors gain respect through this patronage. The craft of leather work is declining and its members are migrating to Tehran in search of other jobs with higher status.

The most striking feature of society in Kirman, then, is the distance between the elite and the lower classes. The social gradient is steep, and differentiation is clear. The prevailing immobility in Kirmani society is ameliorated (at least in the eyes of the residents) by striking cases of vertical mobility. One of the very prominent families in modern Kirman, for example, is of peasant background and achieved wealth and power through speculation in the carpet trade. This case is widely quoted by middle and lower class Kirmanis to establish the possibility of miraculous rise to riches and power through cleverness, luck, and the aid of Allah. The social system in Kirman generally discourages mobility of this type, however, and clear crystallization into distinct classes is the rule. It is the existence of this full range of social strata within Kirman City that distinguishes it from all other settlements in the basin. In the towns and villages there is no comparable elite group and few men of very low status, the social gradient is gentler, and variations in wealth and power are fewer.

THE REGIONAL SUBCENTERS: MAHAN AND JUPAR

Mahan and Jupar, as we have mentioned, are secondary administrative, economic, and religious centers for the people living on the northern slopes of the Kuhi Jupar. These functions date from the Middle Ages, when Mahan and Jupar grew into towns because of favorable location on major trade routes. After the construction of the Shah Ni'matullah

TABLE 5
Generalized Occupational Structures of Mahan and Jupar

Occupation	No. of heads of households	% of total
Mahan		
Professional	76	4.4
Service	101	6.8
Weaving industry	452	30.3
Artisans and craftsmen	184	12.3
Agriculturalists and herders	509	34.1
Unemployed	182	12.1
TOTAL	1,504	100.0
Jupar		
Professional	29	3.3
Service	49	5.6
Weaving industry	353	40.5
Artisans and craftsmen	108	12.4
Agriculturalists and herders	236	27.1
Unemployed	96	11.1
TOTAL	871	100.0

Data based on original village questionnaires and IBM cards from the 1956 Census of Iran. The cards were checked thoroughly in the field. A more detailed occupational breakdown is included in Appendix F. See Note to Table 4.

Vali Shrine in the fifteenth century, Mahan outstripped its rival and became the county (*bakhsh*) administrative center governing the two townships (*dihistan*s) of Mahan and Jupar.

The occupational structure of Mahan and Jupar exhibits many urban characteristics. Full-time agriculturalists and herders compose only one-third or fewer of the heads of households; the bulk of the population are artisans, craftsmen, weavers, shopkeepers, traders, and service workers. In Mahan particularly the occupational diversification of the market town is found. This characteristic differentiates Mahan and Jupar from

Langar, Qanaghistan, Muhiabad, and other smaller settlements on the slopes of the Kuhi Jupar.

The Upper and Middle Classes

The upper and middle classes of Mahan and Jupar are not as distinctively different as in Kirman City. Their members are neither as powerful nor as exclusive as the urban elite. The leaders of the resident upper and middle classes are the county governor, mayor, and village headman (all appointed by the governor-general of Kirman), members of the town council, wealthy shopkeepers, local landlords, doctors, bank managers, some teachers, a priest, and several carpet factory managers. These men exercise power over the town and surrounding villages but are careful not to interfere with direct commands from the urban elite. Thus, a local carpet factory manager may hire or fire a weaver or punish individuals through local officials for theft or poor weaving, but has no voice in the pattern, design, size, or number of carpets woven. Locally, he is a highly respected member of the community, but in Kirman he is simply a hired representative. The village headman selects military conscripts to fill the local quota, but if a landlord needs a particular sharecropper, the headman will not interfere. The county governor settles land and water disputes when local residents are involved, but if the assets of a land-owner are at stake, he will withdraw completely from the dispute. Even the few professionals — the doctors, teachers, and mullas — are completely subservient to the powers that be in Kirman. They all do everything in their power to maintain smooth, frictionless relations with that powerful group.

Membership in the resident elite is based on a variety of factors which span occupational boundaries. One of the government teachers, for example, is the grandson of a famous religious leader and has inherited shares in the Mahan water supply. Shopkeepers in this group own land in town and have servants who run their retail shops. Because the degree of wealth and power attainable in Mahan and Jupar is limited by the size of the population and resource base, great variations in wealth are not found; secondary factors such as level of education, piety, and family background play a greater role in determining an individual's position than they do in Kirman City.

Many members of the resident upper and middle classes mimic the trappings, manners, and attitudes of the urban elite of Kirman City. They use urban furnishings (notably chairs and tables) in their homes, disdain working with their hands, practice the exaggerated politeness of the urban upper class, and emphasize their privileged position in town society through displays of conspicuous consumption and studied leisure. In some cases this imitation is carried to an extreme. A banker in Mahan, for instance, believed it inconsistent with his position to drive an automobile, and hired a chauffeur. As he owned a Volkswagen, this caused great discomfort to his family and friends by overcrowding the rear seat. Despite this cultivated urban orientation, the resident elite have far greater contact with the commoner class in the towns than do the elite of Kirman City. It is impossible for them to be completely divorced from manual labor.

The Commoner Class: Agriculturalists and Craftsmen

Most of the people in Mahan and Jupar are either agriculturalists (peasant proprietors, sharecroppers, tenant renters, and agricultural laborers) or craftsmen who weave carpets and rugs and make mats, felts, donkeybags, shoes, and clothing. The agriculturalists are the traditional core of the population, the transmitters of rural culture in these urbanized town settings. They wear distinctive peasant garb — blue cotton trousers, long shirts, and felt caps — in contrast with the Western clothing of the artisans and craftsmen. They are conscious of their long residence in the area and refer to the weavers as *khushnishin* or "new settlers." Because the water supply is relatively stable in Mahan and Jupar, these farmers are closely tied to the land. Tenancy and sharecropping rights are handed down from father to son for generations. Variations in speech and manner further emphasize their apartness.

The artisans and craftsmen are members of the largest single occupational group in Mahan and Jupar (Plates 7A, B). Most are carpet weavers, but carpenters, blacksmiths, tinsmiths, mechanics, tailors, shoemakers, bakers, tanners, and qanat builders also live in these towns. Most weavers inherit their craft, but recently second and third sons of peasant owners and sharecroppers have been forced off the land by population growth and have become weaving apprentices. The weavers are more closely linked with urban life than the agriculturalists. Market prices of wool and dyes, current wages for carding, spinning, and dyeing wool, and the international export trade in Kirmani carpets are of far greater concern to them than the advent of the spring rains or the condition of this year's crops.

But peasants and weavers alike balance their time and energy to produce as many of the basic necessities of life as possible. Farmers till part of the communal grainfield, part of the double-cropped garden area, and if possible some walled garden or orchard land. By working three different types of land, they can supply their household needs for food and fodder. In the winter villagers scour the uplands in search of brush and wood for the potter's kiln, the village bath, or for household fuel. Farmers also work as day laborers hauling mud and straw for a builder or turning a windlass to lift dirt from a qanat. Weavers cultivate gardens and keep animals to reduce the number of items they must purchase in the city.[21]

Rural households typically own several chickens, a few goats or sheep, a donkey or a cow. If a weaver or farmer does not own a donkey or cow, he must rent them from donkeymen and cattle owners. Animals therefore are often shared by several households of an extended family to lessen this expense. Donkeys are the major beasts of burden in Mahan and Jupar. They are used for short-distance hauling of carpets, wool, dirt, dung, wood, and produce. Cattle are rarely used for transport; their major task is plowing the fields. Sheep and goats supply meat, milk, wool, hair, and down for domestic use and sale. These animals often represent the accumulated capital of each household and are bought from other villagers or from transient herders in good years and sold in the city in famine years.[22] The small gardens within the household compounds are largely devoted to alfalfa, fruit trees, and herbs.

Women and children also contribute to the family economy. They weave carpets, short-napped coarse rugs (*gilim*), and loosely woven woolen mats (*jajim*). Carpet weavers earn a high wage (by local standards), so a woman skilled in carpet weaving has no difficulty in finding a husband. Less talented women work at lesser crafts, spinning wool into yarn, cleaning hair from the down of Kashmir goats, and making woolen hats, stockings, and felts. In the poorest households women work as day laborers in the fields, sowing grain, weeding, and harvesting the crops, or else they collect wild rue seeds to sell for protection against the evil eye.

The bottom of society in Mahan and Jupar is rounded out by the poorest elements of the commoner class: beggars, scavengers, and the many unemployed. As a group, these people are poverty-stricken, live in ruined dwellings at the base of the town, and have little chance of improving their position. More than a tenth of the population is unemployed most of the year.[23] Only in the harvest season, the bottleneck in the agricultural system, is work available (see Appendix A). Many have migrated from satellite villages to these towns with the same aspirations as their counterparts who emigrated to Kirman. Both groups lead a marginal existence.

In the regional subcenters of Mahan and Jupar, then, there is less occupational diversity than in Kirman City, and the distance between the top and bottom of the social structure is smaller. The social gradient is compressed because the elite class is less clearly separated from the masses and the lowest elements (e.g. defiling occupations) are poorly represented. But Mahan and Jupar do have more complex social and economic structures than smaller settlements on the slopes of the Kuhi Jupar. Through their mixture of urban and rural people important regional functions are served: food production and provision of labor for the city, and transfer of goods and raw materials between Kirman City and the villages and hamlets of the Kuhi Jupar.

LARGE AGRICULTURAL-WEAVING VILLAGES

Qanaghistan, Langar, and Muhiabad are intermediate in size and complexity between the regional subcenters of Mahan and Jupar and the small villages and hamlets of the alluvial fans and mountain valleys. Each of these large villages has more than a thousand residents, and a few professionals, service workers, and artisans who satisfy local needs. These centers have few facilities — a bath, a small shrine, a mill, and several shops — but these are enough to attract villagers from nearby smaller settlements when a plow needs mending, a funeral is to be held, grain must be milled, or a guest arrives and there is no tea in the house. In these settlements, all members of society fall within the bounds of the commoner class. The few shopkeepers, millers, and bathkeepers work part-time in agriculture or weaving. There is some diversification of labor, but less specialization of laborers. Except for minor service activities, the population has a single regional function: it supplies the urban market with carpets and crops.

Most of the wage earners in Qanaghistan, Langar, and Muhiabad are either agriculturalists or weavers. Muhiabad and Qanaghistan are primarily weaving centers, but in Langar agriculturalists and herders are a majority. Langar is located where the Tigiran valley opens onto the alluvial fan, and has pasture and water rights in this valley; thus few of its people (2.8%) are unemployed. In Qanaghistan the landlords have failed to repair the water supply system, and their stern religious beliefs (Shaykhi sect) are not attractive to weavers; hence unemployment is extremely high (15.3%).

In all three of these large villages the occupation division between weavers and cultivators is the most significant social division. There is little cooperation or exchange between the two groups. The agriculturalists cannot supply weavers with foodstuffs, since most are sharecroppers and have no surplus. Weavers do not buy wool directly from herders; both groups work under contracts with carpet factories in Kirman City. Nor

TABLE 6

Generalized Occupational Structures of the Large Agricultural-Weaving Villages

Occupation	No. of heads of households	% of total
Qanaghistan		
Professional	4	0.9
Service	27	6.1
Weaving industry	218	49.2
Artisans and craftsmen	50	11.3
Agriculturalists and herders	76	17.2
Unemployed	68	15.3
TOTAL	443	100.0
Langar		
Professional	6	1.4
Service	16	3.8
Weaving industry	147	34.4
Artisans and craftsmen	23	5.4
Agriculturalists and herders	223	52.2
Unemployed	12	2.8
TOTAL	427	100.0
Muhiabad		
Professional	3	1.2
Service	5	2.0
Weaving industry	133	52.6
Artisans and craftsmen	15	5.9
Agriculturalists and herders	79	31.2
Unemployed	18	7.1
TOTAL	253	100.0

Source: See notes to Tables 4 and 5.

do weavers sell carpets or mats to the peasants. Their best market for non-contract merchandise is in the bazaar in Kirman City. Most transactions therefore pass through Kirman City, Mahan, or Jupar. But there is one minor area of cooperation between weavers and agriculturalists: the payment of dues to the priests, barbers, carpenters, and blacksmiths. A standard sum is collected from each household in the village to support these facilities. The amount of the levy varies from place to place depending on the number of facilities and the total population. Agriculturalists pay directly from the harvest either before or after the division of crop between the landlord and the peasant. Weavers pay in cash throughout the year.

SMALL VILLAGES AND HAMLETS

Only in the small villages and hamlets on the alluvial fans and in the mountain valleys of the Kuhi Jupar can one find a rural peasantry similar to that described in the Middle Eastern literature.[24] These settlements have fewer than four hundred residents[25] and are occupied by peasant proprietors, sharecroppers, herders, and fuel collectors who are closely tied to the land. Differences among individuals are slight; all are equally lacking in power and wealth. Over a period of time most residents become interrelated by blood or marriage, which gives the settlement a cohesiveness that is lacking in town and city.

Agriculture is the major economic activity in small villages and hamlets. Almost three out of every four households (73.9%) derive their principal income from agriculture. Weaving is practiced in less than a tenth of the households, because craftsmen migrate to larger settlements where wages are higher and facilities are better. The few nonagriculturalists in these places are unskilled laborers and charcoal burners, who remain in the villages by preference or because there is no work for them in the towns. The only members of the professional class found in small villages and hamlets are teachers assigned there by the Education Office in Kirman City.

But even here one must speak guardedly about an isolated traditional peasantry unaffected by the economic and social changes occurring in the larger centers of the basin. The settlers are still serviced by traveling peddlers and barbers from alluvial fan towns. Their land and water (ex-

TABLE 7

Generalized Occupational Structures of the Small Villages and Hamlets

Occupation	No. of heads of households	% of total
Professional	3	0.7
Service	6	1.3
Weaving industry	42	9.2
Artisans and craftsmen	54	11.8
Agriculturalists and herders	333	73.9
Unemployed	19	3.1
TOTAL	457	100.0

Source: See notes to Tables 4 and 5. This table includes data for 18 small villages and hamlets in the region which were covered in the 1956 Census.

cept in the Hanak valley) are owned by urban or town residents. Their products, whether charcoal, wheat, or wool, are destined for an urban market. On the other hand, barter is more common in these small villages and hamlets, their inhabitants dress uniformly in rural costumes, and their speech and manners differ from those of urban dwellers.

To a considerable extent, the location of the village or hamlet determines its degree of isolation and ruralness. Mountain hamlets are the most isolated settlements in the basin. From some of these a trip to the alluvial fans may take as long as a day. Life is difficult and primitive in such places, but land hunger, grazing resources, and available fuel supplies are attracting new settlers from the plain each year. The possibility of bringing water to the surface without a large capital investment attracts some. Others simply come to work as sharecroppers or herders because there is no work on the plain. As this process intensifies, the small villages and hamlets will undoubtedly be drawn more completely into the urban-dominated regional economy of the basin.

Chapter 5

Urban Dominance and the Regional Economy

The preceding descriptions of city, town, village, and hamlet reveal one major fact: settlement, economy, and society in Kirman are urban-dominated. Why in a land purportedly filled with self-sufficient villages should such a rational, fully developed, regional pattern of settlement and economic organization exist? Its genesis probably lies in the settlement history and physical environment of Kirman. That settlement was initiated here by the advanced urban society of Sassanian Iran is not surprising. The basin is a marginal environment at best. Its winters are cold, its summers hot; above all, it is so dry that all crops must be irrigated. Development of this land by technologically primitive tribal groups was unlikely, though not impossible. Substantial capital had to be invested in irrigation devices (qanats), without which organized permanent settlement would be difficult. Nor was the motive for establishing settlement in Kirman unusual; defensive outposts are frequently birthplaces of cities in marginal areas. So Kirman City was founded for political reasons; and later, when population increased, settlement expanded onto nearby alluvial fans and into the mountain valleys to utilize their various environmental assets.

But if the genesis of urban dominance in Kirman is not perplexing, its continued existence — some sixteen hundred years later — certainly is. Established mechanisms to maintain urban dominance are surely necessary to explain such continuity. It is the modern forms of these mechanisms and the ways in which they function to concentrate wealth and power in the city that form the heart of this chapter. In the view taken here, the social and economic structure of modern Iran is seen as fundamentally similar to the feudal structures of Parthian and Sassasian Iran. The peasantry is an integral, functioning part of a larger society, not a divorced element.[1] After all, agriculture has always been the fundamental source of governmental income in Iran, and it is unreasonable to suppose that the powerful and shrewd men who led Iran to fame in the past did so with three-quarters of its population existing in isolation beyond the influence of urban centers. Some have suggested (in opposition to modern land distribution laws) that Iran's peasantry survived precisely because it had few relationships with the great cities and societies that periodically rose and fell. Further, according to this reasoning, modern efforts to bring villages within the scope of governmental administration endanger this survival. The evidence from Kirman suggests the reverse: the villager of Iran, whether sharecropper, weaver, or herder, is inextricably involved in an urban-dominated, regional economic organization and probably was so in the past.

MAINTENANCE OF URBAN DOMINANCE

Traditional systems ensure the maintenance of urban dominance in the three major economic realms of Kirman. In agriculture, the mechanism is the land tenure system; in animal husbandry, herding contracts; and in craft activities, weaving contracts. In each sphere, the upper class of Kirman City retains ownership of the production factors. Thus, in agriculture, land and water are principally owned by large landowners (*arbabi*); in animal husbandry the sheep and goats are owned by urban residents; and in weaving the large flocks, dye-houses, and looms are owned by carpet merchants. These elements are rented by members of the elite to lesser individuals — farmers, weavers, and shepherds — who, in return for their labor receive a subsistence wage.[2]

Land Tenure

The majority of the agriculturalists in Kirman are landless sharecroppers,[3] who cultivate the land on the basis of annual written or verbal contracts with landowners. This contract guarantees the sharecroppers a percentage of the harvest in return for their labor and any other element that they contribute, such as fertilizer, draft animals, or seed. Theoretically, the division of crop is based on five factors — land, water, draft animals, seed, and labor — and one-fifth of the harvest is allotted to the supplier of each factor. In practice, sharecropping contracts vary from settlement to settlement. Usually the peasant supplies the labor and the landlord provides water, land, seed, and draft animals. The sharecropper receives 30% of the harvest and the landlord 70%. There is no distinction between winter cereal crops and summer crops,[4] but the division of tree crops depends on the size of the orchard. If few tree crops are grown, the peasant's share is 30%, if orchards are extensive it will be only 20%.

The distribution of sharecropping agreements throughout the basin provides a clue to the criteria most critical in the division of crops. At lower elevations in stable alluvial fan villages the peasant receives 30% of ground crops and 20% of tree crops in return for his labor. In the mountain valleys the peasant's share of ground crops is still 30%, but his share in the tree crops increases from 20% to 30%. In high mountain hamlets sharecroppers receive 50% of the total harvest. In all areas the peasant supplies the same element, labor, and the landlord supplies all other factors in the production of the crop. These differences in the terms of crop-sharing agreements appear to vary according to the needs of the peasant household relative to crop yields. Because yields are lower in the mountain valleys and high mountain hamlets, the peasant's share is correspondingly higher.[5]

The actual division of the crop takes place on the threshing floor. Before the crop is divided into the landlord's share (*minal*) and the peasant's share (*insaba*), deductions are levied for the carpenter, blacksmith, bathkeeper, crop-watcher, water distributor, and village headman. In most cases these dues amount to 10 or 15% of the total harvest. In Mahan, for example, the water distributor theoretically receives no share in the harvest, but a token offer of five *mann* of wheat (15 kg.) is an investment in the future. The village headman receives one kilogram of wheat for every share in the water supply. Further deductions for personal services are paid individually, since a choice of baths, carpenters, and blacksmiths is available.

A number of secondary factors are also considered in crop-sharing agreements in Kirman. Usually the peasant has the right to the same proportion of straw as of grain. In some cases, however, the landlord takes all the wheat straw and the peasant all the barley straw. In the mountains the peasants keep both wheat and barley straw. In large settlements the sharecroppers receive one-third of the grain and straw left in the fields and on the threshing floor after the harvest. In smaller places this debris is not collected; the peasants graze their sheep and goats on the stubble.

Because the landlord provides every essential for cultivation except labor, the sharecropper is little more than a landless laborer and thus has no security of tenure. This lack of security is particularly critical in the Kirman region because unemployment is so high. Sharecroppers can be evicted from the land at any time during the year, though it is rarely done until after the harvest. The peasant plows the land with no guarantee that he will sow it. The landlord has full powers of ownership and use of the land. To some extent this is modified by local custom in the more stable villages on the alluvial fans. Here, peasants transmit sharecropping rights from father to son. This does not mean that the peasant cultivates the same land at all times, for the landlord may redistribute tenure rights at will. But customarily land is left in the hands of the same peasant for many years unless some disagreement occurs. In these stable settlements the peasants own their houses and even some agricultural implements.

Insecurity is a greater problem in the mountain valleys of the Kuhi Jupar. Here, sharecroppers do not work the same village or field from year to year; they work a valley or a region. Within one valley, as the fortunes of each village rise or fall depending on winter rains and the condition of the qanat, peasants migrate from place to place to maintain an equilibrium between population and water supply.[6]

Given these conditions of insecurity of tenure, arbitrary redistribution of land, and unstable water supply, it is clear that the sharecropper's status and standard of living are extremely low. He cultivates cereals in a marginal environment, receives 30% of the harvest, from which dues must be subtracted, and has no cooperative marketing facilities. He must survive periods of want and depend on the landlord or a moneylender in the bazaar to tide him over these bad years.[7] All loans are raised on the security of next year's harvest. Usually the landlord is willing (and expected) to supply the needed grain, because if the sharecropper is indebted to a moneylender, he may steal from the harvest to meet his commitments. Surprisingly, debt is not viewed as a totally negative condition by the sharecropper in Kirman. Some measure of security is derived from the fact that the landlord will lend him grain, and it is clearly understood that the landlord will not take so much of the next harvest that the sharecropper cannot feed his family. But debt keeps the sharecropper at the subsistence level; he works his way from harvest to harvest with little prospect of bettering his condition.

Herding Contracts

The urban elite also retain control of production factors in herding. Most of the sheep and goats grazed in nearby mountain pastures are owned by carpet merchants, wool dealers, and landowners of Kirman City. Through ownership of land and water in alluvial fan settlements, these men have maintained control of pasture resources. But their dominance is less complete in herding than in agriculture or weaving. There are independent sheep owners — residents of Mahan and Jupar and traveling shepherds from Baluchistan, southern Kirman, and Yazd — who own animals and rent graze.[8] There are also shepherds who work for a village, caring for the flocks of its residents, in return for wages. But whether the flock is owned by an urban resident, a traveling sheepherder, or a group of villagers, the shepherds work under a contract system.[9]

Herding contracts have striking similarities to sharecropping contracts. Both are initiated in autumn when the winter grains are sown; both are binding for one year. Some shepherds are paid a fixed annual wage (like tenant renters), others receive a percentage of the milk and lamb or kid crops (like sharecroppers). The criterion for determining shepherds' wages is also similar to that used in the tenure system. Shepherds must be paid a subsistence wage; thus, a man with many children is paid more than one with few.[10] Only where this minimum standard is satisfied is the shepherd paid on the basis of the other factors such as the number of animals herded, the condition of local graze, or available village facilities.

Sheep and goats owned by landlords and carpet merchants in Kirman City are farmed out to shepherds under a variety of contracts. In every case the owner supplies animals, graze, and housing for the shepherd. Shepherds who work for a fixed annual wage (ranging from 3,000 to 4,500 rials [$40 to $60]) are paid in cash or kind in monthly installments; they receive no wool, milk products, or lambs. Other shepherds graze a flock for one year and return the initial number of animals of each age group to the owner, keeping the lambs but delivering all milk products and wool to the owner. Under a third type of contract, the shepherd is paid a small cash sum and receives a percentage of the flock's milk products and all lambs and kids above a minimum number.[11] In all of these contracts wool, the principal commercial product from a carpet merchant's viewpoint, is the property of the owners.

Herding contracts between shepherds and villagers are more variable. At Hujatabad the shepherd is paid 3,500 rials ($46.66) per year plus clothing and shelter in the village. The shepherd of Kupang receives 4,000 rials ($53.33) per year, the other terms being the same. In some hamlets in the Hanak valley the shepherds are paid on a per animal basis. In Hanak Bala and Hanak Pa'yin shepherds receive 3 kg. of wheat and .75 kg. of barley per animal per year; the wheat is eaten by their families, the barley by their dogs.[12] At Daristan, however, the shepherd receives half the milk, half the progeny, but none of the wool or down produced by the flock.[13] In Mahan shepherds are paid 10 rials ($.13) per animal per month, 3 kg. of wheat when each lamb or kid is born, and one-seventh of the flock's milk production.

Weaving Contracts

Capital from Kirman City subsidizes and standardizes weaving. The agents of large Iranian and Western carpet firms live in the city, which is the principal collecting point for wool and dyes produced throughout the province. The primary role of the city in this industry is indicated by the fact that the designs of village-woven carpets are identical to those of Kirman City and that nearly three-quarters of the village weavers are under contract with carpet factories located in Kirman City.[14] The organization of the industry is strikingly similar to the systems in agriculture and herding described above. The elements of production — wool, dyes, designs, and looms — are owned by carpet factories, wool merchants, and entrepreneurs in Kirman City. Each carpet is subsidized through several processes — washing, sorting, dyeing, carding, spinning, weaving, and clipping — by these urbanites.[15] Craftsmen are paid a subsistence wage for their labor; the profits are accumulated by the entrepreneurs and merchants. The production process may be organized in several different ways depending on the size of the carpet firm.

The largest carpet firms in Kirman City keep a stable of designers, draftsmen, and weavers, and own dye-houses and weaving factories, some with as many as forty or fifty looms. These firms hire the best weavers from villages and towns throughout the province and bring them to Kirman. When the demand for carpets is great, there is a lively competition for master weavers. Wages are high, the weavers are given houses rent-free, and a subsidy is granted to the weaver conditional upon his continued work.[16] But master weavers are few and the demand for Kirmani carpets is declining, so that this system of operation is confined to a few large, well-established weaving houses in Kirman, the only firms capable of controlling the entire production process.

More commonly, the large carpet firms in Kirman City (particularly those owned by Europeans) sign contracts for the production of a certain number of carpets of specified design, color, and size, with weaving entrepreneurs, middlemen, and brokers who are active members in the weaving guilds. Such a man controls anywhere from ten to one hundred weavers in Kirman City and surrounding weaving centers through debt and/or influence. The carpet firm supplies all materials to this subcontractor except for the loom; he in turn negotiates contracts with individual weavers, handles the distribution of materials to them, and oversees the production of the carpets (Plates 8A, B). The entrepreneur's success depends on careful administration of contracts and the production of high-quality, well-woven carpets.[17] His value is measured by his ability to detect faulty weaving and synthetic dyes and his vigor in urging the weavers to work quickly and well. Individual contracts are negotiated for each carpet by the carpet firm and the entrepreneur. The price varies with the design, color, and density of the carpet.[18] Complicated designs such as the famous teardrop pattern are expensive.[19] Those with many colors or great density are also expensive.

The entrepreneur negotiates a contract with the weaver for the desired carpet. In a typical contract, the entrepreneur supplies the weaver with dyed wool already spun into yarn and warp threads. If the entrepreneur supplies the loom, the weaver must rent it. The weaver is paid in six or seven installments. The initial payment is given before he begins, when an agreement has been reached. It usually amounts to about 10% of the total contract. Other payments are made as the work progresses, and the final payment when the carpet is completed. This last payment is adjusted to account for any defects in weaving which lessen the value of the carpet. The unit of payment in Kirman is 16,000 knots (*sad nishan*), 100 rows each 160 knots in length. A skillful weaver can produce 16,000 knots a day, for which he is paid from 50 to 60 rials ($.66 to $.80). The monthly income of a trained weaver therefore is less than $20, a small fraction of the carpet's market value.

The alternatives to these contracts for a weaver are few; thus non-contract weavers are a minority in Kirman. Carpets woven by private weavers are usually of inferior (70/35) quality and may contain numerous defects. Private weavers cannot afford to purchase the wool for an entire carpet from one lot; hence variations in color and density lessen its value. Also because the *jufti* knot (tying four warp threads together instead of two) is nearly impossible to detect once the carpet is woven, carpet firms and customers are reluctant to buy carpets of questionable origin.

The major influence of urban dominance on rural settlements in the Kirman Basin is to retard independent town and village economic growth and specialization. Carpet designs are uniform in all settlements and cropping patterns vary little from place to place, because economic activity is standardized by the urban elite. What specialization does exist, such as concentration of herding in mountain hamlets, Langar, and Jupar, is directly related to differences in local environments. In every economic sphere, rural settlements are drained of vitality by contracts which concentrate profits in the city. But local economic organization does exist in the larger towns and villages. For the most part this activity is administrative rather than wealth-producing. It regulates resource use, but does not represent the interests of peasants vis-à-vis urban landlords or merchants. Its minor importance as compared with city-town or city-village economic activity needs to be emphasized, because the importance of internal village organization has been overstated in the Middle Eastern literature.

Village Farming Organization

In large rural settlements, formal village-level decisions regulate the rotation and distribution of water, the dates of sowing and rotation of cropland, the levying of dues and taxes to support local officials and service personnel, and the appointment of village officials such as the water distributor and crop-watcher. In smaller settlements cooperation on these matters is handled informally.

The most critical community decisions involve the water supply. Some of these, such as the rotation of water, are determined by tradition. Others such as the maintenance of qanats are recurring problems which vary with winter rains, summer dust storms, and the local water table. In Mahan, formal meetings of the owners (both resident and nonresident) of each qanat are held to decide maintenance questions when the flow of the qanat is decreasing; each owner has a vote proportionate to his share in the total flow of the qanat.[20]

Water distribution is another constant problem in the larger settlements, where water must be guided through a maze of channels to the right field at the right time. This is the task of that locally appointed official, the water distributor.[21] He is a respected and trusted man, locally called "the bailiff of water" (*mubashiri ab*), who is appointed by vote of water owners. His duties involve not only supervision of water distribution but administration of the reserve fund for qanat repair and regulation of disputes rising out of conflicting water rights.[22] Where variations in crop combinations exist, the water distributor administers all borrowing and trading of water within the rotation system. He knows when each owner needs water, where it can be acquired, and what terms will effect an exchange. His salary is derived from these water arrangements; hence he is often called "the water dealer."

Local regulation is also necessary in decisions relating to land use within each village. The dates of plowing and sowing and cropping patterns must be coordinated with water distribution so that needs and supply are in balance. Winter grains are rotated in large blocks to take advantage of existing irrigation networks.[23] The number of large blocks is determined by local topography, soils, and ownership conditions. Such coordination requires conformity on the part of the individual owner to village-level decisions and contributes to the homogeneity of cropping patterns from place to place. The specific choice of crop is still decided by the owner, but the food needs of most peasant families, soil and water conditions, and other factors make it essential that the principal effort be expended on producing winter grains. There is greater individual choice in the selection of summer crops.

In settlements where cultivated fields are extensive, another local official, the crop-watcher, is found. This office represents a local community solution to the problem of insecurity; thus, the crop-watcher is elected locally by the peasantry with the concurrence of the village owners.[24] He is charged with protecting village crops against damage and theft, and sleeps in a small, round, adobe hut in the middle of the fields. The crop-watcher is paid by deductions from the harvest or a fixed wage in cash or kind, amounting to about 5,000 rials ($67) per year.

The regulatory nature of village-level cooperation is apparent. It is probable that constant demands of maintaining qanats, protecting crops, and regulating water distribution and cropping patterns encouraged such coordination and proved its necessity. Without it, the potential size of settlements would be severely limited. In the one settlement in the region where administration failed, chaos resulted. At Sehkunj shortage of irrigation water led to a duplication of water deeds by the owners, so that water claims exceeded water supply. No decision was reached concerning water regulation, and distribution is now decided by lots cast daily by the farmers. The farmer with the last hour's water is responsible for distribution, and his day is spent attempting to prevent others from taking water; if he fails, he gets no water and so tries to steal it from another man the next day. The situation is so confused that no local official will become involved. As a result, farmers have begun to leave Sehkunj to work as sharecroppers in nearby villages. The importance of village-level organization is emphasized by this example, but such organization should not be confused with creative economic activity.

Other Village-Level Organization

In weaving, guilds regulate some economic activity in the regional subcenters and large alluvial fan villages (see pp. 75–76). As in agriculture, guilds do not represent members in dealings with the carpet firms of Kirman City, except when a guild leader is also a weaving contractor. The guilds do not press weaving factories to pay higher wages or provide better working conditions. They function as cooperative societies, and their powers are limited by the contract system through which weavers deal individually and directly with the carpet factory or one of its agents.

As in Kirman City, rural guilds limit knowledge of the weaving craft to guild members and control entrance into the profession by the apprenticeship system.[25] They also arbitrate disputes among guild members and between guildsmen and outsiders. But guild control is less restrictive in these rural areas than it is in the city. Some farmers work part-time at low rates (on a piecework basis) for professional weavers during the winter. In many households women and children weave carpets and spin yarn while the men work in the fields. Full-time professional weavers will accept a farmer's son or daughter as an apprentice if paid for their trouble. In theory the guild exercises restrictive control, but in practice it is lenient, particularly since the use of spinning machines in Kirman City has caused greater competition for apprentice positions in Mahan and Jupar.

The principal functions of rural weaving guilds are social. If a weaver dies, guild members are present at the grave and efforts are made to find work for his widow and children. If a weaver is ill, other weavers devote hours to his loom so that the family will still receive income. Guild members attend religious ceremonies and social events together and march as a group in religious processions during the month of Muharram. In one settlement, Mahan, there is a specific shrine dedicated to weavers which is rarely used by farmers or herders. Essentially, rural guilds protect the welfare of their members without economic restrictions; they provide some measure of security to a weaver where the larger economic system provides none.

There is no local organization in herding comparable to those in agriculture or weaving. The very nature of this activity, its dependence on migration to and from grazing areas, disperses shepherds and their flocks over wide areas and precludes such a development.

Chapter 6

Stability and Change in Kirman

Numerous forces of modernization are challenging traditional
patterns of Kirmani life, but few changes have been generated
internally in the city or towns of Kirman. Modern concepts and materials
spread from Tehran, take root in the imitative minds of the urban middle
class, and then diffuse to villages owned by progressive members of the
urban elite. The innovators are many: educated sons of landowners and
carpet merchants, officials sent to Kirman and its villages by the central government, representatives of American and Iranian development
agencies, and a host of unconscious innovators — the shopkeepers and
merchants of Kirman who sell radios, stoves, plastic goods, pressure
lanterns, newspapers, bicycles, tractors, and hundreds of other new
elements of material culture. The urban elite and the middle class mimic
the tastes and decisions of their counterparts in Tehran; there is little
creative energy in this provincial city.[1]

That change has occurred in Kirman is particularly important for two
reasons. First, Kirman is located more than six hundred miles away from
the capital city and center of change, Tehran. Second, change in Kirman
tends to be limited by regional migration patterns. Members of the urban
elite and the salaried middle class frequently migrate to Tehran and
other large Persian cities, thereby lessening the strength of the small
cadre of urban "transitionals."[2] Rural immigrants, on the other hand,
tend to reinforce the folk mentality and traditional value systems of the
city. Because of these two forces, one might reasonably expect that
similar processes of change have been in operation in other Persian
provinces to *at least* the same degree as in Kirman.

Underlying the very evident changes in material culture, technology,
and social values are forces dating back forty years to the rise of Riza

Shah in the 1920's. The spread of transportation facilities intensified existing patterns of urban-rural communication. Establishment of effective, continuous control by government forces over tribal areas increased stability and security. Government involvement in local political affairs, water supply problems, conservation of resources, labor conditions, medical facilities, and other social issues added a new dimension to provincial life. Above all, the consistent agreement among political leaders after Riza Shah — that change is needed, is desirable, and can be accomplished — has influenced local leaders to follow their example. There can be no doubt that a technological revolution spurred by Westernization is sweeping Iran; it is changing traditional political concepts, moral standards, and religious values.[3]

It is the social structure of Kirman that has felt the impact of Westernization most deeply.[4] The twin pillars of nineteenth-century Kirmani social life, the patrilocal extended family and the Islamic clergy, have shown little resilience in the face of modern forces of change. Surprisingly, the magic of technology has wrought scant change in the heart of the economy — the contract system. The traditional organization of resources functions in established ways through established channels. This system corresponds to Steward's "culture core," a series of economic arrangements which vary little, precisely because they are deeply involved in the production process.[5]

SOCIAL CHANGE

The structure of society in nineteenth-century Kirman City was based on the clear division separating the upper class from the commoners. But within each of these groups considerable differentiation existed, and indeed the most striking features of Kirmani society were, as has been noted above, the steepness of its social gradient and the distance between top and bottom. Power and wealth were concentrated on the uppermost levels; income variations among the commoner group were minor except at the lowest level, that of the beggars, prostitutes, and unemployed. Vertical mobility was virtually nonexistent. Within each level, social status was based on noneconomic factors such as day-to-day religious behavior, kinship affiliation, occupation, and level of education.

The basic unit of social organization in nineteenth-century Kirman was the large extended family, which included a man and his wife, their unmarried children, married sons, and other relatives, all living together in one household compound. Usually this organization was most clearly realized in the upper levels of Kirmani society; the urban poor were rarely able to support such large households and maintained "limited" extended families, *familles souches*.[6] These family organizations functioned as economic units, and their resources were managed by the oldest (or most capable) male. It was his duty to provide security for family members, to keep family property intact, and if possible to enhance the family's status. Because of the lack of social mobility in nineteenth-century Persian society, family position was a primary factor in economic well-being. Individual interests were subordinate to those of the group; and decisions concerning marriage, migration, occupation, and behavior were often the products of family meetings. Interconnections among families were carefully planned from birth, and cross-cousin marriages were quite common. Though somewhat unwieldy, these extended families presented a solid front to the community; their members were welded into a cooperative unit by the fact that advancement or failure on the part of any member attached to all members.

Religion was the fundamental extrafamilial unifying force in nineteenth-century Kirman.[7] Religious leaders wielded enormous power, economically through religious endowments (the *vaqf* system), spiritually through religious injunctions, and socially through their control of the courts, education, and mass media. A young boy's early training (unless his family was poverty-stricken) took place in a religious elementary school (*maktab*), supported by private contributions and religious foundations.[8] Here, religious values and practice were stressed. The child learned the proper prayer formulae, the special obligations of the Ramazan fast and the Muharram mourning period, and recitations from the Koran; his mind was firmly shaped along traditional lines. Religious norms, thus installed, were highly prescriptive, leading to an unusual degree of social conformity within the various classes. Within the city over a hundred mosques, shrines, and secondary religious facilities attested to the primary role of religion in Kirman's social fabric.

The dominant characteristic of social patterns in nineteenth-century Kirman, then, was stability. Social horizons were limited by family status and the dictates of Islam; social and physical mobility were limited by a society in which the sacred prevailed over the secular and the economy was based on status. There was probably little rural-urban migration either to or from Kirman, and the city's population of 40,000 remained static. To be sure, peasants migrated to Kirman in times of crisis for protection and in times of disaster for political assistance; but given the stable preindustrial economy of the city, they soon returned to their villages. The merchants and traders of Kirman developed extraregional relationships with other Persian cities, and elite families often had connections with the capital; but these relationships had little impact on the daily and annual rhythm of society and economy in Kirman.

New cultural values have upset and weakened the power of the family and the church in modern Kirman. Economic opportunities, the possibility of migration to other cities, shifting residence patterns, and increased social mobility all conspired to undermine the traditional patrilocal extended family.[9] As individualism and a competitive spirit spurred the youth of the city, filial obedience, acceptance of cross-cousin marriage, respect for age, and subservience to family interests weakened. These trends were accelerated by a redefinition of high status in terms of the new values: education and particularly specialized knowledge, accomplishment, and modernism.

The principle of secularization weakened the power and influence of the clergy.[10] The judicial system was overhauled along the lines of the Napoleonic Code, and secular law was given primacy over religious law (*shari'a*). Religious schools have been replaced by secular schools in which government teachers train the children and religion is a minor part of the curriculum. Clerical control of law, education, and mass media has been broken; thus the sources of religious power are severely limited. In Kirman City, secularization led to a decrease in the number of clergy and a restriction of their influence; religious structures have fallen into disrepair and less capital is invested in vaqf properties. Among all but the lowest classes of the city, a desire for social and economic advancement has superseded the intense concern with Islamic faith and practice which characterized the preceding century.

ECONOMIC CHANGE

Economic change has been less pervasive than social change in Kirman. One cannot speak of a shift from subsistence to money economy, because there never was a subsistence economy in the sense of self-reliant, self-sufficient economic activity in rural areas of Kirman. Involvement in the urban marketplace has been stimulated by more efficient and rapid transportation, but the pattern existed long before automobiles and taxis came into use. There is increased economic diversification in Kirman City, and even some cases of technological unemployment, but these are minor variations.

Two economic changes which are most striking in appearance (though in reality of lesser importance) are first the tremendously rapid change in material culture in Kirman and second, economic diversification. In the realm of village and town life, ready-made clothes are replacing home-made products, the superiority of kerosene stoves over charcoal braziers is recognized by all, and inexpensive foreign dishes and utensils are preferred to local products. Foreign manufacture is considered to be a guarantee of quality, so that many elements are adopted in unmodified state, though others may be modified or rejected if they conflict strongly with traditional values. For the most part, this increase in foreign goods has simply meant that a hawker now carries different wares and chants their virtues in different terms; the shopkeeper still retains all the characteristics of his class though he sells merchandise unknown in Kirman before this decade.

But there are new economic activities created by the expansion of technology — among them gas stations, repair shops, electrical plants, ice factories, pharmacies, and photography shops. These are concentrated in Kirman City, though one can now buy gasoline, aspirin tablets, and have electricity for four hours a day in Mahan. Some of these new activities have replaced other traditional crafts. Thus, after a new ice factory was completed, the ancient storehouses for ice fell into disrepair; when horses were replaced by automobiles, the blacksmith's trade shifted to repair of iron shares, axes, chains, and shovels; potters, coppersmiths, and tailors now supply a smaller share of the commoner market. The elements of economic change are obvious, but change itself is superficial. It has not modified the prevailing economic organization of the area.

The settlement pattern and the three major sectors of the economy — agriculture, weaving, and herding — have all experienced minor changes. Settlement has expanded to accommodate an expanding population. In agriculture there have been crop changes, introduction of new tools and techniques, and an increase in agricultural knowledge. Weaving designs, dyes, and techniques have altered. In herding there has been a shift in animal concentration both in space and throughout the population. But the stable pattern described above is intact. Kirman has changed just enough to avert major change and its attendant social implications.

Change in the Pattern of Settlement

Iran's population has increased in the last fifty years. Major forces stimulating population increase are the lowering of infant mortality rates because of more widespread availability of medicines, health campaigns, improved sanitation, the banning of opium, and the eradication of malaria.[11] In Kirman, population growth has been slower than in other parts of Iran, because the region is still recovering from the devastations of the eighteenth century, because the shift in capital from Isfahan to Qazvin and Tehran left Kirman remote from the centers of power, and because trade with India has declined sharply. In the middle of the nineteenth century Kirman City had approximately 40,000 residents.[12] Fifty years later the city's population was 45,000 or 50,000 though travelers still considered Kirman one of the poorest cities in Persia.[13] In 1956 Kirman City's population exceeded 60,000, in spite of a major emigration of landlords, artisans, and landless peasants to Tehran after World War II.[14]

The populations of Mahan, Jupar, and other rural settlements increased more markedly. Mahan, a village of 2,000 inhabitants in 1904–1905, now has a population of more than 6,000.[15] The people of Jupar, Sehkunj, Muhiabad, Langar, and Qanaghistan claim that their settlements have grown considerably. Though no statistics are available to prove this point, there is general agreement among the older inhabitants that resident populations have doubled in the last twenty years.

To meet increased local food demands, the cultivated area has been expanded and grain is imported. Several new qanats were and are being built on the alluvial fans at Deh Hunari, Javadieh, and Hujatabad, and many older channels have been repaired. At Shahabad, for example, the owners expanded the settlement by lengthening and deepening the tunnel of the qanat. Part of the village water supply was rented to subsidize repair costs, and the water supply has increased 40% in the last eight years.[16] Other settlements such as Jupar, Langar, Kousar Riz, Hanak Bala, and Daristan have also invested in qanat repairs (Fig. 9, p. 34).[17]

But the major settlement expansion has not developed within the framework of the traditional qanat system; deep wells powered by diesel pumps and European windmills are providing water for expanding orchards and fields on the central plain.[18] Deep wells are used on the plain where the water table lies at a depth of less than one hundred feet. They are concentrated near Kirman City to avoid conflict with qanat owners, who object to drilling near their property. On the alluvial fans the water table is several hundred feet beneath the surface, so qanats are preferred.

Deep wells have a number of significant advantages over qanats on the Kirman plain.[19] They are not limited by slope and soil conditions and can be placed at locations convenient in terms of transportation, market, or other conditions. Also, deep wells draw water from the permanent aquifer, eliminating seasonal variations; and water is not wasted when demand falls short of supply. Their major disadvantages are high construction costs and continuing maintenance and fuel costs. In addition, deep wells cannot be constructed from local materials by local laborers as can qanats. But they can supply water to Kirman City more economically than the long qanats which cross the plain, and this has been recognized by the landlords of Kirman. There are now sixty to eighty deep wells located around Kirman City.

Several factors have retarded settlement expansion based on deep wells in Kirman. The laws of "borders" (harim) have limited their use to the immediate suburbs of Kirman City. Deep well owners try to avoid subterranean aquifers tapped by qanat channels, but there is still considerable local suspicion on this score. Decreased flow in any qanat leads to immediate accusations that the nearest deep well has drained the water table. Because many Kirmani families own shares in qanats, this antagonism is widespread enough to affect the social position of deep well owners. Difficulties are further compounded by limited knowledge of local subterranean aquifers and ignorance of the distribution of qanat tunnels beneath the plain. It is not unusual for an entire village whose qanat has dried to descend on the governor-general's office demanding immediate redress. If efforts at compromise fail and the villagers' crops wilt in the fields, the personal safety of the accused deep well owner can become precarious. New land distribution laws have attempted to balance these factors and indirectly encourage deep well development by exempting land watered by deep wells from distribution to sharecropping peasants.[20] By adopting deep wells, then, the Kirmani landlords ensure their continued ownership of the land.

Another settlement expansion is occurring in the mountain valleys of the Kuhi Jupar.[21] Here the process is simply a repetition of past settlement sequences; initial settlement by charcoal burners and fuel collectors is followed by semipermanent agricultural-herding settlements established along the water supply lines of parent villages on the plains.[22] Landless peasants leave the plains to cultivate small patches of land in the mountain valleys. Hamlets such as Kazimabad, Toujigun, Mazra'eh Shur, and Chashmeh Kush have been established within the living memory of local inhabitants (Fig. 10, p. 36).

The intensity of population pressure in these mountain valleys is extreme. In the Hanak valley, for example, people migrate from one hamlet to another depending on which has the greatest water supply in a given year. All qanats are shallow and fluctuate with annual rainfall; population fluctuates in direct proportion. In 1956 the village of Mah Char had a population of 57 people, in 1960 only 31 residents, in 1962 more than 60.[23] These changes were caused by families moving from Mah Char to Narmakan in a bad year and back again in a good one. Because the population is composed of peasant owners, they always remain near their holdings in hopes that the next year's rains will bring better fortune.

Thus settlement is expanding everywhere in the basin. In rural areas, the expansion is manifested in intensified use of existing qanats and re-settlement of abandoned places. On the plain, deep wells allow expansion into former desert areas and the establishment of new villages and gardens. Whether this expansion is temporary or permanent is uncertain. It is certain, however, that the criteria for locating future settlements have changed from those which were decisive in the development of the traditional pattern.

Change in Agriculture

When in 1955 the central government banned the cultivation and use of opium, the change affected every cultivator in the basin. Opium had been the principal cash summer crop of the region. It needed little water yet produced an easily marketable crop of high value and low weight. Kirman's environment was excellent for poppy cultivation, and connoisseurs still speak of the wonderful opium from the fields of Mahan. Poppy seeds were planted in seedbeds in November and December and transplanted into the fields in January and February. Only two or three irrigations, at fifteen-day intervals in April and May, were needed. The crop harvested in June and July averaged yields of 1.5 to 2 pounds of crude opium per acre.[24]

The impact of the Opium Law of 1955 on Kirmani agriculture was great.[25] Replacement crops such as potatoes, sugar beets, alfalfa, and to a lesser extent cummin seed and saffron, were cultivated. Sugar beets were limited to large landlord holdings on major roads where direct communication with the sugar beet mill at Bardsir was possible. Cummin seed and saffron were difficult to market (though their growing habits are similar to the poppy), and potatoes and alfalfa are low value crops. All agriculturalists therefore lost income. Large landlords were aided by the construction of the sugar beet mill but peasant proprietors' holdings were too fragmented to convert to sugar beets. Sharecroppers lost income because the opium crop was divided 50–50, whereas potatoes, sugar beets, and alfalfa are divided on the standard 70–30 basis. Thus the sharecropper was forced both to cultivate crops of lower value and to receive a lower percentage of the harvest.

Other changes in agriculture are less widespread. Because change is initiated by urban landlords, the spatial distribution of new techniques and tools follows no pattern. Adjoining villages use implements from different eras, neighboring fields are cultivated in quite different ways; practices in villages near the city may be traditional while those in others farther away are modern. The critical factors in agricultural change have been the temperament, education, and financial status of the landowner. The large landowners have introduced changes most readily; they are the only agriculturalists financially capable of doing so. Tractor farming, for example, is restricted to their fields, because other holdings are too fragmented and owners of smaller holdings are too poor. But chemical fertilizers are used by many owners; large landlords use them on summer and winter crops, smaller owners only on summer crops.

The integration of tractor farming into traditional Iranian agriculture provides a concrete example of economic change. Land tenure contracts begin at sowing time and end at the harvest; they do not include a commitment for preliminary preparation of the land. In the past, landlords paid daily wages to sharecroppers who tilled the land with nail plows. After the introduction of tractor plowing, these sharecroppers were paid a smaller total wage (because fewer days labor were involved) for rebuilding the irrigation channels and were compensated by the increase in wheat and barley yields. The net impact of tractor farming in the village has been quite limited; the sharecropper receives approximately the same subsistence wage as in the past. Only the landlords gain by the higher yields — the principal reason they support this innovation. The multiple ramifications usually associated with the introduction of tractors have not occurred in Kirman.

But not all the tools of modern agriculture can be integrated into traditional Iranian agriculture successfully: the moldboard plow is an example of an innovation that failed; it has nowhere replaced the oft-maligned nail plow, which has distinct advantages over its more modern counterpart. The light, wooden nail plow can maneuver in small irregular plots bounded by irrigation ditches. It leaves no open furrow at one side of the field, which would create irrigation problems by collecting too much precious water. The nail plow is inexpensive to construct, can be built entirely from local materials, and requires little maintenance. It can be pulled by small native draft animals which are too weak to pull a moldboard plow through the hard, stony soils of Kirman.[26] In short, the nail plow is adjusted to local agricultural conditions.

In sum, then, the introduction of technological advances such as the tractor, deep well irrigation, chemical fertilizer, and pesticides has had surprisingly little impact on the traditional system of agriculture in Kirman; these innovations have been assimilated without great disturbance. To be sure, yields have increased, as development people are quick to point out, but the profits return to the city; the village and its farmers are little changed.

Change in Herding and Associated Activities

The period of recent change has had a major impact on the herding sector of the Kirman economy. Over the years, generations of sheep and goats have overgrazed natural pastures, and numberless fuel collectors and charcoal burners have stripped woody plants from the land (Plates 12A, B). Now, it appears, a critical point has been reached. Increased population and expanding settlement, the demands of carpet merchants and wool sellers for more raw materials, and fuel collectors using trucks and jeeps have initiated a rapid and thorough deterioration of the remaining natural vegetation (see Chapter 1 and Appendix C). By 1962 this intensified resource use had already led to several important changes in animal husbandry, herding, and village life.

First, deterioration of natural graze led to increased reliance on cultivated fodder and a concentration of animal ownership among agriculturalists in rural areas. According to local informants, villagers on the flanks of the Kuhi Jupar grazed cattle and donkeys, sheep and goats within sight of the village thirty years ago.[27] Many householders owned animals because all had grazing rights. But increased population pressure (animal as well as human) destroyed natural pastures near settlements. Cattle and donkeys no longer graze; they are fed entirely on cultivated crops (except for weeds in fallow fields). The most common plant in the household garden therefore is alfalfa, a crop unknown in Kirman thirty years ago. Only agriculturalists who grow fodder can afford to feed many animals. Thus, most locally owned cattle and donkeys are owned by full- or part-time farmers. Villagers are now beginning to rely on fodder grasses for sheep as well as cattle, and as this trend intensifies, sheep ownership will be concentrated among agriculturalists and goats will be confined to the mountains.

Second, destruction of grazing resources and fuel sources on the plains spurred settlement expansion and a concentration of large flocks of sheep and goats in the mountain valleys of the Kuhi Jupar. After World War II, motorized fuel collectors efficiently stripped the plains of trees and shrubs. Even before this, shepherds were ranging long distances for graze. Both groups soon looked elsewhere for needed resources. Hamlets were established in the mountains as outliers of parent settlements to serve as supply centers for charcoal burners, transient fuel collectors, and shepherds. Many were merely a collection of underground shelters where one could take cover in severe weather. Initially, shepherds used the mountains only for summer graze, but soon they settled permanently in these hamlets. This movement into the mountains changed the composition of the flocks, because goats are better mountain animals than sheep. Shepherds in the Tigiran and Hanak valleys claim that fifteen years ago these areas supported flocks of sheep; sheep now graze here only during the spring flush. It is difficult to ascertain whether or not this has led to an increase in the total number of goats as compared with sheep in the basin. If so, it presents a very real threat to the carpet-weaving industry of Kirman City.

Finally, destruction of the last remaining local forests on the plains has created a major fuel problem for all villagers. In particular, the scarcity of charcoal has influenced cropping patterns in the orchards of Mahan, Jupar, and smaller settlements. Fruit and shade trees, traditionally grown along watercourses and in Persian gardens, are disappearing. The high price of charcoal has led to sharecropping agreements between villagers and charcoal burners or the outright sale of woodlots. In most smaller settlements almond, apricot, mulberry, and poplar trees have been cut and burned for charcoal. In other villages, trees are cut and soaked in kerosene, an inefficient but inexpensive substitute for kerosene or charcoal. As a result, walled orchards are a rare sight. In mountain villages where fuel is most desperately needed, orchards are rare, abandoned gardens are common. Five years ago a commission studied this problem. It advised the villagers to take goats and sheep off the land and to use kerosene for fuel. The villagers still tell jokes about this commission.

Change in Carpet Weaving

After World War II, demand for Kirmani carpets on the world market declined. Fashions had changed and the postwar generation preferred simple, neutral carpeting to the bright, ornate Persian products. Kirman designers responded to this pressure by producing simple medallion carpets with pastel backgrounds instead of French floral designs. But in this market Kirman carpets had other competitors: hand-woven products from Puerto Rico and Ireland and modern, high-quality, machine-woven rugs.

At the same time, the quality of Kirman carpets declined because of deterioration in the standard of design, the use of imported dyes, and the weaving of imperfect knots. The variety and excellence of design disappeared when designers adapted their products to the vagaries of taste and style. New styles invariably tended toward uniformity, and designers were employed in reproducing large numbers of similar carpets. Imported dyes were not used in Kirmani carpets, but their use in other Persian weaving centers threatened the reputation of all Persian carpets. The weaving of imperfect knots, however, was widespread in Kirman.[28] Once defective knots were tied, they could not be detected.

The carpet-weaving industry of Kirman responded to these pressures by attempting to centralize the industry. This concentrated weavers, spinners, dyers, and other craftsmen of the region in Kirman City and nearby centers. Large carpet factories imported weavers and dyers to exercise direct control over the production process. Dyes were cooked in the factory, women washed and spun wool in the yard, and the weavers were constantly watched. Smaller companies which could not compete on this level used subcontractors and brokers to supervise the various stages of production. As the smallest firms were forced out of major weaving centers, a minor backflow took place in the tide of craftsman urbanization. These firms encouraged weaving in remote mountain districts among newly settled tribal people where inferior dyes and the jufti knot were unknown. In all areas, private weavers were placed under contract with urban firms.

A second change in the carpet-weaving industry of Kirman was the mechanization of several preliminary phases of production. Initially, machines were used to card dyed wool. This proved economical and produced more uniform colors, a fact of importance in carpets with large, solid, pastel backgrounds. Recently, a spinning plant has been built in Kirman City, an innovation deeply resented by the 8,000 city and village women who supplemented family income by spinning wool into yarn. Also, the traditional master weavers who chanted complex carpet designs to apprentices have been replaced by simple, standardized scale drawings.

But these changes have not altered the condition of the weaver in Kirman, whose plight was so compelling in the 1920's and 1930's that it was discussed in the League of Nations, the Persian press, and the Iranian Senate. The master weaver of Kirman still feeds his family on an income of roughly $20 a month. His looms are in dimly lit, damp, odorous rooms. Much of the weaving is done by children from five to fifteen years old who work from dawn to sunset in summer and from dawn until three hours after sunset (with candles) in winter. These children are weak, pale, tubercular, and in some cases deformed by long hours of sitting in one position.[29] In the villages, such conditions are less prevalent, but nowhere has the carpet-weaving industry brought prosperity to its laborers. Nor have these changes altered the industry's dependence on the fluctuations of international style in a rapidly changing world. From a national and international viewpoint its stability is questionable.

Chapter 7

Conclusions

From a geographical viewpoint, the nature of urban dominance, its growth in earlier feudal periods, and continued existence in the modern era have several ramifications. If the patterns of the Kirman Basin are representative — and there is good reason to believe they are — the functions of Middle Eastern cities and villages, the social and economic organization of the Middle Eastern peasantry, and the nature of the modernization process in this region bear further discussion.

Cities in the Middle East are almost habitually described as international commercial clearinghouses. Their location at the "crossroads" of the Old World and importance as connecting points in the flow of goods and ideas between East and West have been stressed to the point of exaggeration. From a European vantage point, the raison d'être of cities such as Mashhad, Tehran, Tabriz, Isfahan, and Kirman has historically been international trade; the very mention of them suggests caravanserais, the silk trade, and Eastern spices. That few people in such cities are engaged in international commerce, that each of these cities forms the center of a rich agricultural area,[1] and that most of these cities manufacture specialized products (e.g. carpets) by processing raw materials from their hinterlands are rarely mentioned. The critical regional functions of the Middle Eastern city have been ignored.

The case in point, Kirman City, is the administrative, economic, and social capital of southeastern Iran. Most Kirmanis are engaged in collecting and processing raw materials from the hinterland and in distributing goods, materials, and services to this wider area. Even in the nineteenth century, when Kirman was an important commercial center on the Indian highway, its wealth was based on local production of nuts, dried fruit, spices, shawls, and carpets — not on the transshipment trade. The

111

city is in no sense an isolate; it is the focal point of a regionally organized settlement pattern. The pattern is less obvious than in more humid regions because of the critical role of water supply and the overriding influence of qanats in settlement location. But the clear hierarchy of settlements, their ranking in age, size, water hinterlands, and pasture rights, is evidence of a rational pattern of settlement developed and maintained by continuous communication among all sectors. The existence of Kirman, then, rests on coordination and exploitation of resources in surrounding areas, not on fortuitous location on a trade route.

The traditional description of Middle Eastern "villages" as physically isolated, homogeneous, subsistence settlements occupied primarily by agriculturalists is even more distorted. Rural settlements in the Middle East are deceptive. From a distance they look isolated, because they are separated from neighboring settlements by miles of barren land, and the line between desert and sown is sharp. Internally, this initial impression is hardened by the unimposing morphology of the settlement, the elementary character of its economic facilities, and its poverty. But in Kirman isolated self-subsistent settlements do not exist, and if the history of the area has been correctly interpreted, they probably never did. All settlements maintain communication with Kirman City in varying degrees. The pronounced separation of settlements on the landscape is produced by the distribution of aquifers needed for water supply, the availability of level areas for cultivation, and a variety of other factors. The internal underdevelopment of these places — even large settlements such as Mahan and Jupar — has been produced by the prevailing economy, not by physical isolation.

Furthermore, rural settlements in the Kirman Basin are not homogeneous in structure or occupations. They differ in size and complexity from regional subcenters to simple hamlets. Their morphologies vary with site conditions, historical development, and regional functions. Some have specialized economies: those with dependable water supplies are agricultural, others with extensive pastures concentrate on herding, and some have been designed to exploit a single environmental asset such as fuel or graze. This diversity of settlement morphology is reflected in complex occupational structures. All of the larger rural settlements house weavers, herders, agriculturalists, service workers, professionals, and artisans; agriculturalists are often a minority. In fact the occupational structures of Mahan, Jupar, Langar, and Qanaghistan are quite similar to that of Kirman City — and perhaps even more significantly to Alberts' village of Davarabad[2] in northern Iran and Gulick's village of Al-Munṣif[3] in Lebanon.

These settlement characteristics immediately cast doubt on the relevance of the usual characterizations of Middle Eastern rural life. Terms such as "traditional agrarian folk community"[4] and "peasant society"[5] imply basic assumptions which are not supported by the evidence from Kirman. Settlements there are not uniformly small, homogeneous, self-sufficient entities. They do not exhibit the organic and functional unity elaborated in Redfield. Nor are they occupied by men in effective control of a piece of land and attached to it by ties of tradition and sentiment.[6] Kroeber's definition is more appropriate: the people of the Kirman Basin live in close relation to urban centers and form a segment of a larger whole; they constitute "part-societies."[7] Consideration of a single settlement, then, divorced from its geographical setting is unrealistic.

Because the peasant village is urban-oriented, study of larger and more complete systems — regions — is indicated. It is here that the data from Kirman are most suggestive. The territorial economic patterns in the basin document the persistence of a feudal structure in agriculture (the land tenure system has long been recognized) and in other economic activities. Contracts between landlord and peasant, carpet manager and weaver, and wool merchant and herder are strikingly similar. These relationships partly explain the similarities in urban and rural economic structures and the "urbanized" characteristics of most Kirmani villagers.[8] There may be a gradient, what Miner called a "folk-urban continuum," with few people representing either of the polar concepts.[9]

Finally the evidence from Kirman suggests that the impact of modernization in the Middle East has altered social patterns more deeply than economic organization. The weakening of traditional family patterns has given rise to greater anonymity and social disorganization, particularly among the urban middle class. Because this middle class is the most vital "force for change" in the region, these trends will undoubtedly intensify.[10] The decline of the Islamic clergy, which through inept and rigid leadership has managed to become a symbol of regression for reformers in most Middle Eastern countries, poses an even more serious problem, for as the leaders of tomorrow hastily discard tradition, they increasingly find themselves adrift in a moral void.

Compounding this problem is the persistence of the economic basis of Iran's feudal society. In this country economic change has merely altered the trappings of the elite; they have made concessions to the modern era without losing control of the economy.[11] The urban upper class has succeeded in controlling the dissemination of critical elements of the new technology and manipulates these to ensure continued rural subordination to urban demands. The elements of change remain interlaced in an ancient fabric. Thus while Kirman, Iran, and probably the Middle East as well are poised on the brink of revolutionary social change, feudal economic patterns remain intact: the system still concentrates wealth in the hands of a small elite, still weakens forces of growth in smaller places, and thereby perpetuates a society with a nonproductive, wealthy elite resting uneasily atop a poverty-stricken mass.

Reference Matter

Appendix A

AGRICULTURE IN KIRMAN: CROPS, TOOLS,
AND TECHNIQUES

Crops

Cultivated land in the Kirman Basin is almost completely irrigated.[1] Seasonal and annual fluctuations in water supply govern the combination of crops grown in each settlement. In spring qanats are swollen by winter rains, while in late summer and autumn their channels are nearly dry.[2] Agriculturalists select that combination of summer crops which yields the most food or cash without exceeding the available water supply. In dry years peas and barley are planted because these crops use little water; in wetter years cash crops which use greater amounts of water, such as sugar beets, melons, and tomatoes, are grown. Walled orchards, which must be irrigated the year round, occupy only a small percentage of the cultivated area.

The typical cropping pattern of Kirmani villages is dominated by winter cereals, but includes a variety of secondary cash and subsistence crops. This pattern is repeated over wide areas of the Central Plateau of Iran, except where forces of modernization are creating enclaves of agricultural specialization. In Rafsinjan, for example, the local economy is based on one cash crop, pistachios, and groves of pistachio trees are replacing cereal crops at a rate of a thousand hectares a year.[3] Modern textile mills in Isfahan have encouraged cotton cultivation in nearby areas; while in the Bardsir area southwest of Kirman City the sugar beet mill has encouraged the growing of sugar beets as a summer cash crop, replacing the earlier opium.[4] But these areas of crop specialization are exceptions. Table 8 illustrates the usual cropping pattern for four settlements of various sizes located in different physical environments in the Kirman Basin. There is little variation in cropping patterns despite differences in village ownership and site conditions. Over three-fifths of the cultivated area is planted in wheat, less than one-fifth in barley and one-fifth in double-cropped vegetable land and walled orchards. These figures represent land in crops, excluding fallow land — which would amount to two, three, or four times the area in cereal crops, depending on local crop rotations.

117

TABLE 8
Land in Crops in Selected Villages of the Kirman Basin

Settlement	% Winter wheat	% Winter barley	% Summer crops	% Walled orchards
Kousar Riz	70	14	14	2
Qadirabad	55	23	14	8
Kazimabad	70	23	5	2
Baharistan	63	15	22	0
ROUGH AVERAGE	65	19	13	3

Data collected in the field in 1962. In the case of the three smaller settlements (Qadirabad, Kazimabad, and Baharistan), the percentages were achieved by conversion of local equivalents. In the case of Kousar Riz a plane-tabled map was planimetered to estimate the percentage cultivated in each crop.

Winter wheat and barley occupy nearly 85% of the land in crops in the settlements of the Kirman Basin. Leavened wheat bread is the staple food of the peasantry; barley bread is used as a substitute during famine periods. A number of varieties of wheat are grown locally; all are sown in early autumn and harvested in spring.[5] Three varieties of barley are grown: (1) sweet barley, which is eaten as bread by the poorer classes; (2) an all-purpose medium grade barley used for food and fodder; and (3) sour barley used specifically as an animal fodder. The two better grade barleys are sown and harvested with the wheat crop. Sour barley is cultivated as a late summer crop, sown in August and harvested in October.

Wheat yields vary from village to village and from field to field within each village. The highest yields are reaped in villages owned by interested members of the landed aristocracy, and/or peasant proprietors. The lowest wheat yields are found in mountain hamlets, where freezing temperatures, scarcity of level land, stony soils, and a more conservative, less educated, and less settled population contribute to keeping agriculture marginal. In large settlements on the alluvial fans, wheat yields average 53 bu./acre (3 *mann/qasab*) when the land is plowed by tractor or spade and chemical fertilizer is used.[6] In mountain hamlets where more primitive techniques are used, they range from 2.5 to 4.5 bu./acre. Under average conditions of cultivation, wheat fields produce approximately 18–22 bu./acre.[7] Yields are measured by so many times the amount of seed sown rather than by wheat production per unit of area, as is true in many other parts of the world. Usually wheat is sown at a rate of 2–3.5 bu./acre; wheat yields then vary from ratios of 2:1 in the poorest areas to 45:1 in the best areas, with an average return of approximately 15:1 or 20:1. Despite these great variations, wheat yields in Kirman are some of the highest found anywhere on the Central Plateau of Iran.[8]

Barley, when cultivated as a winter crop, is sown at the same time as wheat and harvested earlier. The land is immediately replanted, so that the area in winter barley is roughly equal to the area planted in summer vegetables in each settlement. Barley is also grown as a spring or late summer crop when there is a shortage of water, because it uses less water than other crops and matures earlier. In the poorest settlements barley is grown continuously as a summer crop. Barley yields do not vary as much as wheat yields, because there is greater uniformity in techniques of cultivation. The highest yields range from 25 to 30 bu./acre; the average is approximately 4–5 bu./acre (¼ mann/qasab).[9] Barley is sown at a rate of 2.5 bu./acre and produces seed ratios of about 2:1 or 3:1, though they may rise as high as 18:1 or 20:1.

The bulk of the remaining land in crops is devoted to summer crops. There is great variation in these crop combinations from village to village. The choice of summer crops depends on the location of the village (mountains or plains), size of holdings, and type of ownership. This land is rarely fallow; it is composed of small irregularly shaped parcels found in the middle and upper sections of the village and beneath the trees in walled orchards. Among the summer crops grown in Kirman are melons, potatoes, tomatoes, cucumbers, sugar beets, lentils, field peas, green beans, and eggplant; these are planted in late February and early March on the plains and about twenty days later in the mountains. They are irrigated every six days during the hot season and are harvested in late summer.

Potatoes and peas are the most important subsistence summer crops grown in summer. Potatoes can be harvested early if the water supply system fails or if there is a food shortage. The risk of total crop failure therefore is minimal. Potato yields vary from 89 to 213 bu./acre, with an average yield of about 142 bu./acre.[10] Peas are grown in the mountain hamlets and in alluvial fan settlements which have little water, such as Qadirabad, Kuhan Chinar, and Sehkunj. In mountain hamlets peas are grown on plowed land and on stony, unplowed hillsides, so that yields vary widely. In 1962 locusts invaded the region and destroyed most of the pea fields, but under normal conditions yields of 35 bu./acre are expected on fertilized, plowed land and yields of 4.5 bu./acre on unplowed hillside land.

The most important cash summer crops in Kirman are melons, sugar beets, tomatoes, cucumbers, and eggplant. Tomatoes and sugar beets were introduced into the basin ten years ago as replacement crops for government-outlawed opium. Occasionally these crops are found in household gardens, but usually they are cultivated as cash crops on land owned by a landed proprietor. Several types of melons are grown locally; cantaloupes (*kharbuzeh*), watermelons (*hindavaneh*), and honeydew melons (*garmak*) are most important. Yields for summer cash crops are difficult to ascertain; they are scientifically cultivated in one village and suffer from lack of irrigation water in the next. Sugar beets are cultivated in large fields owned by absentee landlords. The produce is sold under contract to the sugar beet mill at Bardsir At harvest time a truck from this factory tours the villages buying the crop at a rate of 1,000 rials ($13.33) per metric ton.[11] This method of collection limits sugar beet cultivation to settlements located on major roads such as Mahan, Kousar Riz, and Jupar. Average yields are relatively low in the Kirman Basin, usually about 282 bu./acre.

In addition to these cash and subsistence summer crops, a variety of vegetables, fruit, and herbs of lesser importance are grown in household gardens. The most important of these low-acreage crops is alfalfa, the only forage crop grown in the region except for some small patches of root beets in mountain hamlets. Alfalfa is grown in small plots in the household compounds of the peasantry and beneath the shade and fruit trees in the walled orchards of the wealthy. Its roots are left in the ground for a period of seven years. Each year three to seven crops are produced, depending on the age of the plants, the length of the growing season (mountains versus plains), competition for irrigation water, and fertilization practices. In Kirman alfalfa is grown exclusively as a fodder crop, though in Rafsinjan it is used as a green manure in the pistachio groves. Alfalfa is fed green to plow oxen, donkeys, and weaning lambs and kids in summer; but most of the crop is dried in small windrows. Alfalfa yields are lower in the mountains because of the shorter growing season. At Baharistan, for example, four crops of alfalfa produce less than one half ton (0.43) of hay per acre per year. In alluvial fan settlements seven crops of alfalfa produce 4–11 tons of hay per acre per year. Other minor garden vegetables, herbs, and spices include carrots, lettuce, squash, cabbage, linseed, sesame, saffron, henna, and castor beans. The only garden vegetables grown in every settlement are onions and garlic.

The final category of cultivated land, the walled orchard, is found primarily in the larger settlements of the region — in Kirman City, Mahan, and Jupar, where nonagriculturalists have gardens and the wealthier classes live. In no settlement do walled orchards exceed a tenth of the cultivated area, mainly because they must be irrigated the year round. A variety of trees in these gardens produce fruit for the Kirman marketplace, an important source of cash to the villagers. The most common fruit trees are pomegranate, apple, quince, pear, apricot, plum, peach, fig, and mulberry. Among the important nut and shade trees are walnut, almond, and hazelnut. The small size of holdings limits the use of insecticides; thus fruit is generally of poor quality though having an excellent flavor. Orchards are irrigated once a month from September to May and every ten days from May to September.

Tools

Agricultural implements in Kirman are built of local materials and repaired by local artisans — except for iron plowshares and spades, which are imported into the region. The wooden nail plow is used in every village.[12] It has a single handle and an iron-sheathed share; only the front edge of the share is made of iron. The share is attached to the beam of the plow by means of wooden pegs and leather thongs. The plow is pulled by a pair of oxen or a mixed team of oxen, mules, and donkeys. Two wooden hoops extend downward from the yoke to encircle the necks of the animals. The team, yoke, and plow together are called a *band gav*; the plow or plowshare alone is called a *gav ahan*. Such a plow pierces the soil to a depth of four to seven inches. It does not invert a furrow slice.

The clods of hard earth left behind after plowing with the nail plow must be broken apart before seed is sown. Two implements are used for this purpose, a primitive harrow (*rindeh*) or a flat, heavy oaken plank with a smooth underside (*takhteh*).[13] A team pulls the harrow or plank across the furrows with two men standing on it to add pressure. The harrow has bits if iron imbedded in its underside to pulverize the surface. In villages which have neither of these implements (usually mountain hamlets), clods are laboriously broken with spades, mattocks, and clubs by young boys and women.

Very few ancillary implements are used in agriculture. In mountain hamlets, wooden mattocks with iron tips and sledge hammers are employed to break stony soils. Where potatoes and melons are cultivated, an implement called the *panjeh* piles the soil in ridges separated by deep furrows. The panjeh is a curved metal or wooden plate with seven or eight widely spaced teeth attached to a long handle. As a farmer presses it into the ground his assistant pulls on the rope tied to its base to pile the soil into ridges.[14] The older panjeh have five wooden teeth, hence the name, which means "hand"; newer ones are made of curved iron. In addition, a variety of hand tools are used in the villages of Kirman. Among these are wooden rakes, weeding implements, sickles, winnowing forks, and wooden or iron spades. Hoes were not seen during the field period. A primitive wooden thresher (*garjin*) with four or five rollers is also used (Plate 10A).

Cultivation Techniques

Wheat and barley are cultivated in two different ways depending on local conditions. In alluvial fan villages the land is plowed with a nail plow to a depth of four to seven inches, depending on the hardness of the soil. It is then leveled with a harrow or plank, flooded, and left to dry. When the topsoil turns white, the field is "ready for work" (*bekar amadeh*). In mountain hamlets the land is first cleared of boulders and stones washed into the valley by winter floods. The stones are broken with a sledge and collected in piles. In some cases the field is then plowed and smoothed with a plank before sowing, but usually plowing and sowing are simultaneous: a small boy follows the nail plow and sows the seed broadcast. The amount of seed used varies with the capability of the soil. On rocky hillside land, wheat is sown at a rate of 2 bu./acre; in alluvial fan fields the rate is 3.5 bu./acre.

Variations on these patterns can be found. In Amirabad, west of Mahan, for instance, after a winter flood softened the topsoil the crop was planted without initial plowing. Where there is sufficient water to soften the land by flooding, the initial plowing can be omitted. The more traditional farmers in the region sow broadcast on unplowed surfaces and cover the seed by plowing and leveling. In the peasant proprietor villages of the Hanak valley, the land is dug to a depth of nearly two feet with a spade; yields here are higher than on land plowed with a nail plow or a tractor, all other conditions being equal.[15] The spade is used only on double-cropped vegetable land; the communal wheat fields are too large for it and rocky hillside land is too hard. Sharecroppers will spade the land only if the landlord pays extra wages.

Crop rotation practices vary from village to village with the amount of level land and water available. In mountain hamlets wheat fields are cultivated on alternate years (*do ayish*).[16] An exception to this rule is Mah Char, which is located at the intersection of several valleys and has an abundance of level land. Here the wheat fields lie fallow for three years and are cultivated every fourth year (*chahar ayish*). In alluvial fan villages a four-year rotation is common. At Sehkunj a three-year rotation (wheat–barley–fallow) is used. In villages where flooding occurs periodically, rotation is irregular, and fields are left fallow only when yields begin to decline. Fallow fields are never weeded, irrigated, or plowed; they receive nutrients only when sheep and goats graze on harvest stubble and weeds.

On double-cropped vegetable land, rotation systems are more complicated. In Qanaghistan a wheat–potato–wheat–potato or wheat–potato–fallow–potato rotation is used. The former serves on fields located near town which receive more fertilizer, the latter on poorer soils farther from the settlement. In Mahan wheat–sugar beet–wheat–melon and wheat–sugar beet–fallow–melon rotations are used in the same way. In general, the use of fallow and rotation systems is keyed more to water supply than to soil conditions. Though agriculturalists are aware that one piece of land is "strong" and another "weak" and act on this knowledge, there is no systematic use of leguminous crops to build soil fertility.[17]

The preparation of garden land for summer crops is intensive. More labor and capital per acre are invested in summer cash crops than in winter grains. The soil is tilled with spades or in larger settlements (Mahan, Jupar, and Qanaghistan) with tractors. The land is flooded, fertilized, and reflooded to decompose the manure before planting. Potatoes, melons, cucumbers, squash, and tomatoes are planted in hills constructed with a panjeh. The seeds are sown by women and children, by hand or with a digging stick. Millet, peas, and sugar beets are planted on flat land, sown broadcast, and spread evenly by crisscrossing the area with a harrow or a rake. Small grains are planted either in rows behind a nail plow, irregularly with a digging stick, or broadcast.

Manure and other fertilizers are widely used on cash summer crops. Their value is universally recognized. If fertilizer is not used, it is because of the poverty of the owner. According to local belief, animal manure strengthens the soil for seven years; but it is in short supply because camel, cow, and donkey dung are burned as cooking fuel. Only sheep and goat manure and night soil are available for the fields. Mountain villagers sell manure to agriculturalists on the plains in the spring, after the underground shelters in which the goats and sheep are housed during the winter have been cleaned. Privy cleaners sell night soil the year round. Chemical fertilizers are used mainly on the estates of landed proprietors.[18]

The fields in large settlements are better fertilized than those in smaller places, since farmers can scour the streets for household sewage and animal droppings. The double-cropped vegetable land of Mahan, Jupar, Langar, and Qanaghistan is continuously fertilized and continuously cultivated. Any available fertilizer is laid in the troughs between rows of melons, tomatoes, and cucumbers. This decomposes with each successive six-day irrigation. Night soil is used on onions and tomatoes; animal fertilizer is preferred for root beets, turnips, and potatoes; chemical fertilizer is used on sugar beets, potatoes, and alfalfa. If the potato or sugar beet crop is not maturing properly, chemical fertilizer is applied when the plants are six to eight inches high. When it is used on alfalfa, a crop can be cut every fifteen to twenty-five days during the summer instead of every forty days. On potatoes, a common weed called *khur* (English ?) is used in the valleys as a green manure; and in the mountains, where khur does not grow, the wild rue plant (*dashti*) serves the same purpose. The usefulness of these weeds has been discovered by the pistachio growers of Rafsinjan, and truckloads of dried weeds are now carried from Mahan and Jupar for use in the pistachio groves. In 1962 nearly 500 tons of khur and dashti were carried from the Mahan region to Rafsinjan. This stripping of weeds from harvested fields will undoubtedly speed soil erosion considerably.

Irrigation is accomplished by periodic inundation of the fields. Water rotations vary from village to village depending on the number of share-holders in the qanat, village tradition, and local soil and cropping conditions. Water is carried from the qanat to the fields in unlined diversion channels with numerous dikes and dams. Each bend or cutoff in the water channel, each diversion of the water, is a vestige of some past business transaction, marriage agreement, or inheritance settlement. In large settlements a local official (*mirab*) supervises the distribution of water through this maze of channels. In smaller villages the peasants distribute the water themselves. In all settlements the irrigation channels coincide with ownership boundaries, and the areas enclosed by these ditches vary from 50 to 375 square meters, but are rarely larger. The irrigation channels require constant maintenance, which is the responsibility of the sharecropper. In Kirman they are con-structed and maintained with spades and panjehs, though in other parts of Iran animal-drawn border-dikers are used.[19] This system of irrigation retards the spread of tractors because considerable labor is involved in reconstruct-ing the channels after the land has been plowed.

Harvesting, winnowing, and threshing form a bottleneck in the agricultural cycle. The labor shortage at this season is eased by the northward migration of three to four hundred families of dark-skinned, colorfully dressed people from Narmashir, a district of Baluchistan. These people — men, women, and children — harvest wheat and barley with a crude, short-handled knife with an eight- to ten-inch toothed blade. The grain is cut close to the ground, leaving a low stubble for the grazing sheep and goats.

The threshing floor is a level plot of sun-dried earth. The grain, piled in a large ring, is threshed by a garjin drawn in decreasing circles around the pile. If the village has no thresher, donkeys and cows trample the pile until the grain is separated from the straw. The grain is then thrown into the wind with a wooden fork and passed through two sieves of progressively finer mesh to separate out the chaff (Plate 10B). Both grain and straw are transported from the threshing floor to the village on donkeys after the crop has been divided between the landlord, peasant, and various local officials and service workers who have liens on the crop (Plate 11B). The sharecropper's portion is usually milled in the home by hand, while the landlord's share is ground in a water mill (Plate 7A) or in one of the new electric mills at Sehkunj, Mahan, or Kirman.

Appendix B

WEAVING A KIRMAN CARPET

The production of a Kirman carpet begins with the purchase, washing, and soaking of local wools. Kirman sheep produce fine carpet wools — so fine in fact that the woolen mills of Isfahan and Yazd import Kirmani wool, thereby forcing the weaving factories of Kirman to import lesser grade wools from Mashhad and Kirmanshah. Local sheep produce two clips of wool each year, a long-staple spring clip and a softer, shorter autumn clip; they are mixed together in the carpets. In 1962 high quality Kirmani wool sold locally for 42 to 38 *tuman*s ($5.60–$6.40) per *batmann* (6 lbs. 14 oz.).

Once purchased, the wool is washed by the women of Kirman for a daily wage of 25 to 30 rials ($.33–$.40), then sorted by color. White wools are used for the light pastel blue and pink backgrounds of the modern Kirman medallion carpets, yellow for more vivid colors, and brown and black for very dark colors. The wool is soaked in alum over a slow fire to clean away the fat. Then it is given to one of the dyers of Kirman, who are famous for the wide variety of colors they can produce. Each color has a different price; the bright reds are most expensive, the browns least so. At present Kirman is the only major weaving center in Persia where natural dyestuffs (excepting indigo) have not been replaced with imported dyes, a fact that adds to the value and beauty of Kirman carpets.

Most of the large dye-houses are located in Kirman City, though some firms have established dye-houses in secondary weaving centers such as Mahan and Jupar. In the city, dyes are boiled in large earthenware vats three to five feet in height. They are heated by kerosene under pressure and and are capable of handling as much as 50 to 60 kg. of wool in one batch. Dyeing in the smaller weaving centers is done in smaller earthenware vats in which 20 to 30 kg. of wool can be dyed, and brush is the major fuel.

The principal dyestuffs used in Kirman are synthetic indigo,[1] cochineal, madder, weld, walnut husks, pomegranate rind, vine leaves, henna, and straw. Synthetic indigo is used to produce the rich blues in modern Kirmani carpets. The indigo plant still grows wild in the area, but it is used only in carpets woven by some Baluchi tribes. Because natural and synthetic indigo

125

have the same chemical composition, the color of Kirmani carpets is not affected. Cochineal is used for brilliant reds. It is imported from India (and more recently from Mexico), where it is produced from dried bodies of female scale insects. Madder (*Rubia tinctorum*) is also used as a red dye in Kirman, though cochineal is preferred. The plant grows wild in the foothills and is cultivated in some household gardens in weaving centers.[2] Synthetic madder (alizarin) is not used in Kirman.

The weld plant (*Reseda luteola*) also grows wild in the Kirman area, and its leaves and flowers produce a yellow dye used in the finest Kirman carpets. The plant is locally called *isparak* or dyer's weed. When combined with indigo, weld produces a variety of shades of green. Vine leaves and pomegranate rind are used in less expensive Kirman carpets. Vine leaves yield a bright, harsh yellow and pomegranate rind dyes a brownish-yellow color; both are inferior to weld. Walnut husks produce fine tan and brown colors. They are inexpensive and plentiful. Walnut husks are often combined with madder, weld, and other dyestuffs to produce different shades. Henna is used for a bright orange-yellow color. The leaves of the plant are pounded into a powder which is mixed with water, pomegranate rind, or walnut husks to achieve various shadings. Alum is used as a mordant for every dye except cochineal.

After the wool is dyed, it is carded to mix various shadings and achieve a uniform color. This is necessary because the wool closest to the animal's skin has accumulated more fat and thus absorbs less dye. Most of the wool in Kirman is carded in one of the four power-driven carding plants in the city. Occasionally one sees a hand-carder (*hallaj*) on the streets of Kirman, who still earns a living with the ancient bow, but most of these men have been driven into other occupations by the machines.

Dyed wool is spun into yarn by women in Kirman City or in nearby villages and towns, for a wage of about 60 rials per mann ($.80/6 lbs. 10 oz.).[3] The wool is hand-spun on small local wooden spinning wheels, made by Gypsies who travel through Kirman during the harvest season. Until 1961 hand-spinning was a major industry in the Kirman Basin and an important source of income for village women. In 1948, 8,000 women were engaged in spinning, being paid at that time 35 rials per batmann (6 lbs. 14 oz.).[4] Two years ago, when a machine spinning plant was built in Kirman, fewer women were needed and many turned to making coarse, short-napped rugs (*gilim*) and loosely woven woolen mats (*jajim*) for supplementary income.

The dyed yarn and warp thread are finally given to the weaver by a subcontractor working for one of the major Kirmani carpet firms. The weaver's first task is to lay the warp threads and prepare the loom for weaving. Usually the warp strands are stretched between two stakes driven into the ground and transferred to the loom. Cotton thread with ten or eleven well-twisted strands is used for both the warp (*tun*) and the weft (*putun*) of the carpets, except for the third (central) weft, which is very thin. The looms of Kirman are made of poplar, because it is a straight tree which grows rapidly along the banks of watercourses. Two types of looms are used, the large roller-beam type, which is common in Kirman City, and the village type. Both are stationary upright looms; horizontal looms are used only by the tribal people. Roller-beam looms are used to weave large carpets. Their major advantage is that by turning the beam to raise and lower the carpet instead of loosening the warp strands, a greater and more even tension can be maintained and a straighter carpet is produced. Village looms are simpler and cruder. The warp strands are attached in bunches to the upper and lower beams by ropes which are loosened as the carpet is raised and lowered. Tension is maintained by driving wedges into the sides of the loom. In both types, the weaver sits on a plank which is raised as the weaving progresses to a height of four or five feet. At that point the carpet is turned on the roller-beam type, and the wedges are removed on the village type to lower the carpet.

After the warp is laid, the weaving begins (Plates 8A, B). A colored piece of yarn is knotted around each pair of warp strings. Only the Farsi or Persian knot (sometimes called the Senneh knot) is woven in Kirman. Spools of various colored yarns hang above the weaver's head and these yarns are woven into the carpet according to a prescribed pattern. In the past the design was chanted by one of the master weavers, but now charts are used. When a row of knots is completed, three wefts are passed in and out of the warp strands and are beaten into place with a comb beater. Kirman is one of the few places in Persia where three wefts instead of the usual one or two are used. The extra weft does not strengthen the carpet in any way and is apparently woven by tradition rather than for any practical purpose. The weaver continues this process for months, working from dawn till sunset until the carpet is completed.

The woven carpet is bound at both ends with a strip of cloth formed by weaving the warp and weft strands together. The ends are knotted to complete the fringe. At this point the weaver's task is finished, and the carpet is transported to a carpet factory in Kirman City, where the yarn is clipped to a specified length. This is done in a single operation by trained clippers using sharp, curved knives about a foot in length.[5] The carpet is then ready to be marketed locally or exported to the merchant houses of Tehran. From Tehran, it is usually exported to the United States through the southern port of Khurramshahr.

Appendix C

ANIMAL HUSBANDRY IN KIRMAN

Cattle and Donkeys

In the settlements of Kirman, cattle are used as draft animals; their principal function is to plow the soil.[1] Milk, meat, and hides are important by-products, but cattle are rarely raised for these purposes, except in Kirman City, where some of the wealthier families keep one or two cows for milk. Both cows and bulls pull plows, in pairs or in emergencies with a donkey. Kirmani cattle are a mixed breed purchased over the years from traveling cattlemen of Khurasan, Baluchistan, Yazd, and Kirman who buy, sell, and trade animals from all regions. Most cattle are undernourished and overworked — small, weak, and thin. Planned breeding is virtually unknown in the region.

Cattle are put to work in their third year, and their ages are reckoned from that date. In the second year they are trained to harness on the threshing floor. If a bull adapts to such work, it will pull a plow the following year; if not, it is either sold or castrated to make it more compliant.[2] Cattle usually work for nine to eleven years and are butchered only when old or sick. Beef, needless to say, is not a favored meat. The cost of a young, healthy draft animal ranges from 400 to 500 tumans ($53.33–$66.66) — nearly a year's income for the average agriculturalist. A farmer with no draft animal must rent one at a rate of 50 rials per day.

And few cultivators can afford to own one. Roughly four-fifths of the families in Mahan Bakhsh own no cattle, despite the fact that more than a third of the population is in agriculture. Cattle renters are found in the larger centers (particularly Mahan, Jupar, Langar, Qanaghistan, and Muhiabad), who rent out animals at lower rates than an ordinary farmer would. These men own cattle of various ages and strengths and constantly buy, sell, and exchange animals for profit. In recent years their trading has been hurt by the introduction of tractor farming.

Milk is an important by-product for cattle owners, though it is not a major article of commerce. Cow milk is considered to be inferior to either sheep or

128

TABLE 9
Location and Ownership of Cattle, Mahan Bakhsh, 1956

Settlement type	Number of heads of households	Percent of heads of households with			
		no cattle	1 head of cattle	2 cattle	over 2 cattle
Regional subcenters					
Mahan	1,525	82	14	3	1
Jupar	873	80	10	9	1
Large alluvial fan villages					
Qanaghistan	447	85	11	3	1
Langar	307	84	6	6	4
Muhiabad	252	76	18	5	1
Small alluvial fan villages	268	58	30	10	2
Mountain hamlets	166	63	30	6	1
TOTAL AND AVERAGES	3,838	79	14	6	1

Source: Tables 9–16 are based on unpublished materials collected during the Census of November 1956 and have not been checked in the field. The figures do not indicate definite ownership but the number of animals housed overnight in each household compound. On the plains this is identical with ownership, but in the mountains it is not. The reliability of the figures is uncertain.

goat milk because it produces less yoghurt, clarified butter, and cheese per liter. Milk is always boiled before using, because most cows have tuberculosis. An average cow in Kirman produces about 3 kg. of milk per day and is milked twice a day, in the morning and at sunset, for about nine months. The cow produces about 450 lbs. of milk per year, most of it during the first five or six months of the lactation period.[3] If a cow fails to produce this amount of milk, it is fattened and slaughtered or sold to one of the cattle entrepreneurs.

Donkeys are the universal pack animals in the Kirman Basin. Farmers, weavers, and laborers use them for short-distance hauling and transportation.[4] Larger transport animals (camels, horses, and mules) have to a great extent been replaced by trucks.[5] Donkeys carry fertilizer, tools, and seed to the fields in the sowing season and haul grain and straw back to the village at harvest time. Donkeys are particularly important to mountain dwellers, because no roads exist in that region; they haul brush, charcoal, wool, and produce to the plains and carry tea, sugar, cloth and other essentials back. It is not surprising, therefore, that almost three-quarters of the mountain families own at least one donkey. In the towns of Mahan and Jupar the figure is nearer one-quarter, for there are donkeymen, professional haulers, in all larger settlements, who earn their living carrying materials and renting

TABLE 10
Location and Size of Cattle Holdings, Mahan Bakhsh, 1956

Settlement type	Number of cattle	Percent of cattle owned		
		singly	in pairs	in lots of 3 or more
Regional subcenters				
Mahan	349	62	30	8
Jupar	292	30	53	17
Large alluvial fan villages				
Qanaghistan	83	58	29	13
Langar	95	18	42	40
Muhiabad	83	53	34	13
Small alluvial fan villages	161	50	33	17
Mountain hamlets	71	72	28	2
TOTAL AND AVERAGES	1,134	48	37	15

Source: See note to Table 9.

TABLE 11
Location and Ownership of Donkeys, Mahan Bakhsh, 1956

Settlement type	Number of heads of households	Percent of heads of households with			
		no donkeys	1 donkey	2 donkeys	over 2 donkeys
Regional subcenters					
Mahan	1,525	74	22	3	1
Jupar	873	68	19	11	2
Large alluvial fan villages					
Qanaghistan	447	71	23	4	2
Langar	307	57	33	8	2
Muhiabad	252	68	25	6	1
Small alluvial fan villages	268	30	43	21	6
Mountain hamlets	166	28	35	28	9
TOTAL AND AVERAGES	3,838	66	24	8	2

Source: See note to Table 9.

TABLE 12
Location and Size of Donkey Holdings, Mahan Bakhsh, 1956

Settlement type	Number of donkeys	Percent of donkeys owned		
		singly	in pairs	in lots of 3 or more
Regional subcenters				
Mahan	468	72	20	8
Jupar	411	40	46	14
Large alluvial fan villages				
Qanaghistan	171	60	21	19
Langar	173	59	28	13
Muhiabad	104	59	33	8
Small alluvial fan villages	290	39	39	22
Mountain hamlets	214	27	44	29
TOTAL AND AVERAGES	1,831	51	33	16

Source: See note to Table 9.

donkeys. Thus almost half the donkeys in the Mahan region are owned by only a tenth of the population.

Cattle and donkeys are stabled in small adobe rooms or pens inside the household compounds. They are kept indoors to escape the summer sun, the winter cold, and the ever-present possibility of theft. In spring and fall they graze on stubble and weeds in the harvested and fallow fields;[6] but grazing provides little fodder for them because sheep and goats have stripped the land bare near settlements. Cattle and donkey owners increasingly must depend on cultivated fodder. Sour barley, straw, and alfalfa are the mainstays of the animal diet, and root beets, potato, cucumber, and sugar beet leaves are used when available.

Sheep and Goats

The sheep and goats of Kirman are hardy native animals adapted to the marginal graze and severe winters of the Central Plateau (Plate 12A).[7] Locally, these sheep are called "Kirmani," but actually they belong to the Baluchi breed found throughout eastern Iran. Baluchi sheep are small, compact animals with white bodies and black markings on the nose, legs, and feet. Their wool is shipped to every major weaving center in Iran for use in high quality carpets. These sheep are excellent foragers. The goats in Kirman belong to the Ra'in breed, a local variant of the Kashmir goats found on high plateaus throughout Asia. They are small animals, weighing anywhere from 40 to 80 lbs., with black, brown, reddish, grey, or white coats. Their thick undercoat of down, an adaptation to cold winters, is their most valuable product.

TABLE 13
Location and Ownership of Sheep, Mahan Bakhsh, 1956

| Settlement type | Number of heads of households | Percent of heads of households with | | | |
		no sheep	1–10 sheep	11–25 sheep	over 25 sheep
Regional subcenters					
Mahan	1,525	69	30	1	0
Jupar	873	58	39	2	1
Large alluvial fan villages					
Qanaghistan	447	69	29	1	1
Langar	307	66	26	5	3
Muhiabad	252	56	42	1	1
Small alluvial fan villages	268	37	54	5	4
Mountain hamlets	166	38	42	10	10
TOTAL AND AVERAGES	3,838	62	35	2	1

Source: See note to Table 9.

Herding is a major commercial enterprise in mountain settlements, and professional shepherds form about a quarter of the population. They work for landlords, wool dealers, carpet merchants, and peasant proprietors, herding large flocks ranging in size from 200 to 500 animals. Goats and sheep are housed in the mountain hamlets, because of superior grazing resources, though most are owned by urban residents. Local people own few sheep, because goats are better adapted to the rigors of mountain life. In alluvial fan villages herding is a secondary activity. Flocks are smaller, usually from 50 to 150 animals. They are jointly owned by sharecroppers, peasant proprietors, weavers, and artisans. Sheep constitute about half the flock. The shepherds are not professionals; they are young boys and old men recruited from the ranks of the unemployed. These shepherds collect animals from each household in the morning, take them to pasture near the settlement during the day, and return them to their owners in the evening. Each animal is daubed with brightly colored carpet dyes to mark its ownership and to protect it from the evil eye.

The spring months are the busiest season for shepherds because lambing occurs in February and March. Lambs and kids are allowed to nurse at will for a few days, after which each ewe and she-goat is fitted with a leather bag covering the udder.[8] In the mountains lambs and kids move with the flock because it is often absent from the village for days. On the plains, however, they are kept in household compounds; pasturage is apt to be a long distance away and these young animals are too weak to make the trip. In the mountains ewes and she-goats are milked at noon by the shepherd in fieldstone enclosures which dot the mountain valleys. Shepherds drive the milkers into

TABLE 14
Location and Size of Sheep Holdings, Mahan Bakhsh, 1956

Settlement type	Number of sheep	Percent of sheep owned in flocks of		
		1–10	11–25	over 25
Regional subcenters				
Mahan	1,539	71	13	16
Jupar	1,685	55	12	33
Large alluvial fan villages				
Qanaghistan	562	57	16	27
Langar	1,397	27	17	56
Muhiabad	462	49	6	45
Small alluvial fan villages	1,084	38	20	42
Mountain hamlets	1,763	18	17	65
TOTAL AND AVERAGES	8,492	43	15	42

Source: See note to Table 9.

these rough pens and milk them as they pass through the narrow entryway. On the plains the women of the village milk each animal every morning and evening, before it is entrusted to the shepherd and after it returns home from grazing. A ewe or she-goat gives .5 to 1.5 liters of milk each day in addition to feeding its young. This milk can be sold in the form of yoghurt or cheese for 5–8 rials per kg., producing an average income of 150–200 rials ($2.00–$2.66) per animal per year.

Sheep and goats are shorn in late spring and early summer. The techniques of shearing are inefficient and only ten sheep or fifteen goats can be clipped each day. Fleece weights average 1.5 kg. for Baluchi sheep and .5–.75 kg. for Ra'in goats. Shearing completed, the shepherd has little work until late summer when graze becomes scarce and the flocks must be driven deeper and deeper into the mountains. In winter, mountain flocks are kept in underground shelters and are fed various fodders provided by their owner. The flocks on the plains continue to graze until the coldest days of December.

Peasants keep sheep and goats for curds, clarified butter, yoghurt, and cheese, and for wool, down, hair, and fertilizer. The wool products of peasant-owned animals are often used in the home. The milk products, particularly yoghurt, are eaten whenever available and form the major source of protein in the peasant diet. But despite the varied benefits of owning sheep and goats, most of the households in the Mahan region do not own either. The number of animals in each settlement varies with the condition and extent of its pastures. In Langar and Jupar, which have large grazing areas extending into the mountain valleys, the number of animals per family is greater than in Mahan, Qanaghistan, or Muhiabad.

TABLE 15
Location and Ownership of Goats, Mahan Bakhsh, 1956

Settlement type	Number of heads of households	Percent of heads of households with			
		no goats	1–10 goats	11–25 goats	over 25 goats
Regional subcenters					
Mahan	1,525	82	16	1	1
Jupar	873	60	38	1	1
Large alluvial fan villages					
Qanaghistan	447	85	14	1	..
Langar	307	76	19	3	2
Muhiabad	252	65	34	..	1
Small alluvial fan villages	268	25	61	6	8
Mountain hamlets	166	50	7	16	27
TOTAL AND AVERAGES	3,838	70	25	2	3

Source: See note to Table 9.

TABLE 16
Location and Size of Goat Holdings, Mahan Bakhsh, 1956

Settlement type	Number of goats	Percent of goats owned in flocks of		
		1–10	11–25	over 25
Regional subcenters				
Mahan	1,442	31	18	51
Jupar	2,009	36	23	41
Large alluvial fan villages				
Qanaghistan	365	36	9	55
Langar	793	19	27	54
Muhiabad	426	31	11	58
Small alluvial fan villages	2,478	15	20	65
Mountain hamlets	6,017	1	7	92
TOTAL AND AVERAGES	13,530	15	14	71

Source: See note to Table 9.

Appendix D

QANATS IN KIRMAN

Nature and Distribution of Qanats

Qanats, as we have said, are gently sloping tunnels dug in loose, alluvial sediments (Fig. 6). In excavating them the diggers must have fresh air and tunnel spoil must be removed, so the tunnels are connected to the surface with a series of vertical shafts through which fresh air enters and excavated dirt leaves. After the tunnel and shafts are constructed, ground water percolates into the tunnel and flows along its path to emerge at the surface. Unlike other traditional irrigation devices such as the counterpoised sweep (*shaduf*), the waterwheel (*dulab*), and the noria (*na'ura*), when the qanat is completed, no power source other than gravity is needed to maintain flow.

The size of a qanat may vary considerably. In the mountains short tunnels less than a kilometer in length are common, but the qanats which supply water to Kirman City extend southward a distance up to thirty miles underground to tap ground water from the alluvial foothills of the Kuhi Jupar range (Fig. 7). The sources of these qanat tunnels lie at a depth of two to three hundred feet. The deepest known qanat in Iran is located at Birjand; its tunnel begins at a depth of nine hundred feet.[1] Usually qanats are constructed individually, but occasionally they are built in pairs, with twin tunnels constructed side by side connected by passages. This type of construction facilitates maintenance of the channels. Water can be diverted back and forth between the two channels as the workmen clean first one and then the other tunnel. Twin qanats are not found in the Kirman Basin.

The ideal topography for qanat construction is a piedmont alluvial plain, where gently sloping tunnels can intersect a sloping water table. This setting exists in many arid regions of the Old World; in most, qanats are or have been used to bring irrigation water to the surface. In Iran, where alluvial plains are common, qanats are widely used. Tabriz, Hamadan, Qazvin, Saveh, Tehran, Kashan, Yazd, Kirman, and Shiraz rely on qanats for domestic and irrigation water. It is estimated that nearly fifteen million acres of cultivated land, one-third to one-half of the irrigated area of Iran, is

watered by 37,500 qanats, of which an estimated 21,000 are in fully operating
order and 16,500 are used but need repair.[2] Their aggregate length has been
placed at more than 100,000 miles, their total discharge at 20,000 cubic
meters per second.[3] Though these data are suspect, having never been
verified by field work, there is no doubt that qanats are the major source of
irrigation water in Iran.

East of Iran, qanats are used in Afghanistan, Central Asia, and Chinese
Turkestan (Sinkiang). Here they are called by the Persian term (*kariz*)
rather than the Arabic (qanat).[4] In Afghanistan they are the major source
of irrigation water in the south and southeast, especially around the city of
Qandahar.[5] In Pakistani Baluchistan, approximately two-thirds of the water
used in the city of Quetta is supplied by qanats.[6] In China qanats were used
in the second century B.C. and are still found in the Turfan Basin.[7]

To the west, qanats can be found in Mesopotamia, the Levant, and Saudi
Arabia. From there they were spread by the Arabs across North Africa and
into Cyprus and Spain. In Iraq qanats are found in the mountain foothills of
the north and east. They are still used to supply water at Kirkuk and Arbil.[8]
Farther east, in the foothills of the Zagros, the city of Sulaymaniyah receives
its entire water supply from qanats.[9] In the Levant qanats are found only
in the drier parts of Syria and Jordan, where they are incorrectly believed to
be of Roman origin. Qanats were introduced into Cyprus by the Arabs but
are no longer used.[10] In Arabia they are used in Oman, on the Hadhramaut
coast, and in Yemen. Qanats also supply water to the Al Kharj oasis southeast of Riyadh and to Al Qatif near Dhahran.[11]

Qanats (*foggaras*) are found in North Africa on the northern and southern
slopes of the Atlas Mountains and are particularly concentrated near the
city of Marrakech.[12] In Algeria they have been constructed on the borders
of the Tademait Plateau, in the Tidikelt district, and in neighboring areas.[13]
They are used in Egypt only at the Kharga oasis, where the fifth-century B.C.
Persian monarch, Darius, had infiltration channels dug in the soft sandstone to supplement surface water supplies.[14] The Arabs introduced the
concept of qanat technology into Spain, and from there it was carried to
South America. In the Atacama region of Chile qanats are used to supply
water to the cities of Iquique and Pica.[15] They are also found in parts of
Mexico.

Qanat Construction

In earlier times the slaves and captives of the Achaemenian and Sassanian
kings were trained to construct and maintain qanat tunnels. In recent times
this task has been handled by a hereditary class of professional qanat diggers
called *muqanni*s. These men migrate from place to place in central Iran when
a flood destroys qanats in one area or a lowered water table demands that
qanat tunnels be lengthened in another. In Kirman muqannis from Na'in,
Rafsinjan, Bam, Birjand, and Yazd are found as well as native Kirmanis.
These men form a special artisan class. Digging qanats is a tiring and haz-
ardous profession, and floods and cave-ins in the tunnels are frequent. As a

result, muqannis command high wages and are highly regarded in the community. There is universal respect for their superstitions (e.g. a muqanni will not work if he sneezed that morning). The fact that a prayer is said over the muqanni as he descends into the qanat deeply impresses the villagers.

Selection of site is the first step in the construction of a qanat. Conditions governing this selection include local slope conditions, ground water supplies, and the proposed location of the new settlement. These factors are weighed by an expert, usually one of the older, more famous muqannis, who decides where a trial well should be dug. Favorable sites usually lie near the mouth of a wadi, though where the water table is deep and the qanat long the general topographic setting is more indicative of the likely location of subterranean water supplies.

When the expert has decided on the site, a team of workers led by a muqanni digs a vertical shaft deep enough to penetrate the permanent ground water table. The muqanni must be certain that this well has penetrated either the permanent water table or a constant flow of ground water on an impermeable stratum. If there is doubt as to the permanence of the water supply, more test holes are dug to determine the extent of the aquifer and the depth of the water table. When a trial well proves to have sufficient water, it will become the starting point for the construction of a qanat tunnel. This shaft will be called the "mother well" (*madari chah*) of the qanat, though the term is misleading because water is not removed from the ground at this point. The length of the qanat is measured from the mother well to the point where water surfaces. The depth of the mother well may vary from ten to several hundred feet.

Next, the muqanni must establish the alignment and grade of the qanat; this is the most difficult engineering task in the entire operation. The qanat must be aligned so that a gently sloping tunnel from the water-filled base of the mother well will surface *above* the irrigated fields of the settlement. If the tunnel emerges some distance away from the settlement, water must flow on the surface in an open channel to the houses and fields. In such cases, evaporation and seepage become major problems. If the gradient of the tunnel is too steep, water rushing down the tunnel will erode the walls and soon destroy it. The maximum gradient in a short qanat is approximately $1/1,000$ or $1/1,500$; in a long qanat the tunnel is nearly horizontal. Using only a string or a level, a skilled muqanni can establish such a grade even when the tunnel passes beneath several miles of rough terrain.[16]

The long qanats from the alluvial fans at the foot of the Kuhi Jupar (Fig. 7) are completely submerged until they reach Kirman City, for an open stream running across the central plain would surely disappear in the sands. To decrease the slope of these qanats, several tunnels bend westward toward Jupar and then turn north toward Kirman City. If these qanats ran due north, their tunnel gradients would be too steep. The qanats of Mahan and Jupar cannot be completely submerged. Their mother wells are located in the Kuhi Jupar, two to three thousand feet higher than the settlements. It is impossible for the qanats to remain underground, because the difference in elevation is too great; the water is carried in open surface streams. The Mah Char qanat of Mahan, for instance, flows on the surface for fifteen miles from the villages of Abgarm, Mah Char, and Roughanu to Mahan (Figs. 9, 10). The channel of this open stream crosses rough terrain, and approximately a quarter of the water is lost in seepage and evaporation. There is some attempt to decrease this loss, however. The landowners of Mahan hire a summer laborer who shovels fine clay dust into the stream at its origin. The clay dust cements the bed of the stream and decreases seepage. If this were not done, very little water would arrive at Mahan. Generally, seepage and evaporation in qanats which surface far from settlements amounts to a loss of 20 to 35% of the total water supply. At Turbati Haydari in Khurasan, for instance, only 25% of the water produced by qanats reaches the fields.[17]

The qanats of Kousar Riz and Muhiabad also run long distances as surface streams (Fig. 9). These qanats surface in the mountains south of Jupar and flow in tree-lined channels for eight miles to the fields of Kousar Riz and Muhiabad. Their courses are unusual, because their channels run eastward along the alluvial fans rather than emerging from the mountains directly above the settlements. As a result, their channels have silted, and the peasants have built levees around them which rise six to eight feet above the surface of the fan. A final example of this type of qanat is the Ab Kush qanat which supplies water to Langar. Its mother well lies deep in the Kuhi Jupar mountains, and water flows in an open channel down a steep mountain valley. Tubes of hollow wood have been built into the valley walls to carry the water to Langar. All of these qanats — Mah Char of Mahan, Kousar Riz, Muhiabad, and Ab Kush of Langar — emphasize the desirability of having the qanat surface as near as possible to the settlement. Where this is not possible, the cost of water is high and the amount which finally reaches the cultivated fields is low.

After the alignment and grade of the qanat have been established, the muqanni begins the actual construction of the tunnel. Work starts in the dry section of the qanat at the downslope end. The tunnel is dug back toward the mother well, with vertical shafts connecting the tunnel to the surface at intervals of 150–300 feet. In some cases the vertical shafts are dug first; then the tunnel is constructed to connect the bottoms of these shafts.

A team of men collaborates in the construction of a qanat. The leader is a muqanni, a skilled well digger. With a small pick and shovel he excavates a tunnel two or three feet wide and three to four feet high. An apprentice packs the dirt into a rubber bucket, and two laborers at the surface haul the dirt up the shaft by turning a windlass. If the qanat tunnel lies at a depth of more than three hundred feet, a second windlass will be set up in a niche half way down the vertical shaft and the dirt will be transferred from one bucket to another at this point. In 1962 a team of men constructing a qanat received 500 rials ($6.66) per day, a very high wage for Kirman.[18]

The major problems in constructing a qanat occur when the tunnel enters the water-bearing section. Here the muqanni works with water flowing around him, ventilation is poor, and the chances of cave-ins are great. Because of these hazards many qanat diggers are drowned or suffocated each year in the tunnels. In some cases the shafts fill with water before having reached the proper depth; the muqanni must dig upward beneath this pool and avoid the rush of water when a breakthrough is made.[19] If the tunnel passes through an area of soft sand, clay hoops (*nays*) are inserted in the tunnel to support the channel and prevent collapse (Fig. 6). Where ventilation is poor, extra vertical shafts are dug to prevent suffocation. Every muqanni carries a castor oil lamp; when the air has too little oxygen to keep its flame lit, he leaves the tunnel and another shaft is built. In Yazd, where the qanats are very deep, vertical shafts are built on either side of the tunnel. A lamp placed at the bottom of one shaft draws air down the other to improve ventilation.[20]

The time required to build a qanat varies with the capital of the owner, underground soil and water conditions, the amount of water desired, and the skill of the muqanni. In 1961–62 two new qanats were initiated at Deh Hunari and Javadieh near Jupar and one was completed at Hujatabad near Sehkunj (Fig. 10). The Hujatabad qanat is only one kilometer in length, with a mother well 130 feet deep, but it has been twenty-seven years in construction because of three changes in ownership. All three of these qanats have been planned to provide water for settlements high on the alluvial fans. No new qanats have been built near Kirman City during the present generation. Qanats are still the least expensive means of bringing water to the surface on the alluvial fans, but deep wells are more economical on the plain.

The cost of qanat construction in the Kirman Basin can be estimated from data for the Javadieh qanat (Table 17). Construction began in 1941 and one team of qanat diggers worked regularly for seventeen years to bring

TABLE 17
Construction Costs of the Javadieh Qanat

	Rials	Dollars
1 team of diggers for 17 years at 103 rials per day	525,300	7,004
1 team of diggers for 4 years at 500 rials per day	600,000	8,000
1 team of diggers for 4 years at 500 rials per night	600,000	8,000
30,000 clay hoops at 25 rials	750,000	10,000
TOTAL COST	2,475,300	33,004

Note: These figures are approximations. It is assumed that the teams did not work on Fridays or religious and civil holidays and thus worked a 300-day year. Beckett's 1950 figure of 22 rials per day for a laborer's wage is used as an average for the first 17 years; one team of workers would receive 103 rials per day (three laborers at 22 rials per day, one muqanni at 37). Wages from 1958 to 1962 are assumed to be the same as they were during the field period (1961–62). The figure of 25 rials for each clay hoop is an average. Whole clay hoops cost 40 rials apiece, broken hoops cost 15 rials. In the tunnels a broken hoop is placed between two whole hoops, hence the average of 25 rials apiece. Beckett (1953), pp. 54–55.

water to the surface. In 1958 small amounts of water began to flow down the channel, and the owner hired a second team of diggers to work at night. Now, the Javadieh qanat is three kilometers long, extending from Jupar into the hills west of Shahabad. The tunnel divides into two branches with two mother wells at 150 and 165 feet respectively. The entire tunnel is lined with clay hoops because of loose sand. The qanat now provides sufficient water to irrigate less than one-half acre of land every twenty-four hours.

On this basis, qanats appear to cost approximately $10,000 per kilometer to build. The Javadieh qanat cost more, $11,000 per kilometer, because the entire tunnel was lined with hoops. The high costs of this relatively short qanat indicate the monumental expense of constructing one of the long qanats to Kirman City. A deep qanat to Kirman City, 18 miles in length with a mother well 270 feet deep cost approximately $213,000 when completed in 1950. If one recalculated this figure to account for inflation and increased wages, the capital cost of this qanat today would be $387,000. Hence qanats are no longer the most economical method of supplying water to Kirman City.

Appendix E

LAND OWNERSHIP IN KIRMAN[1]

Most agriculturalists in Iran are sharecropping tenants. In 1962 an estimated 60% of Iranian farmers owned no land and another 23% owned less than one hectare of cultivated land.[2] These proportions are representative of ownership conditions in Kirman. Large absentee landowners (*arbabi*), including traditional landed aristocrats and nouveaux riches merchants and bureaucrats, owned about half the cultivated land. Lesser resident and absentee landlords (*khurdeh malik*) — the weavers, shopkeepers, artisans, craftsmen, petty religious and civil officials of Kirman, Mahan, and Jupar — owned about one-tenth.[3] Endowed land (*vaqf*) dedicated to religious or charitable purposes amounted to one-quarter; peasant proprietors owned and cultivated the remainder.[4]

Large Absentee Landlordship

The large landed proprietors can be divided into two subclasses, traditional landed aristocrats and nouveaux riches landlords. The traditional landed aristocrat does not view land ownership solely as an economic venture, for the prestige and social power of any family in the elite class are based on land ownership. The longer a family has owned land the greater its patriarchal sense of responsibility for the well-being of its peasantry is likely to be. Sharecroppers in villages owned by members of the aristocracy are more secure than those in villages owned by the nouveaux riches. In bad years the traditional landlord tides the peasant over the winter with loans of grain, sugar, tea, and cloth. These loans are repaid at harvest time or, if the harvest is bad, are forgotten. Such arrangements are often handled by an overseer (*mubashir*) who lives in the village and represents the landlord's interests in the organization and administration of village affairs. The mubashir bridges the social and physical gap between the landed aristocrat of Kirman City or Tehran and the sharecropper.

The nouveaux riches invest in land for social rather than economic reasons. The new villages built by members of this class (Deh Hunari and Javadieh) are showplaces and summer residences, not investments. These landlords

141

TABLE 18
Ownership of Land and Water, Mahan Bakhsh

Settlement	Population	Percent of total land in control of		
		absentee owners	peasant proprietors	religious endowments
Regional subcenters				
Mahan	6,239	50	33	17
Jupar	4,187	54	42	4
Large villages				
Qanaghistan	1,846	56	33	11
Langar	1,506	59	23	18
Muhiabad	1,004	100	. .	. .
Alluvial fan villages and hamlets				
Shahabad	271	94	2	4
Isma'ilabad	239	95	1	4
Sehkunj	236	. .	99	1
Kousar Riz	171	50	. .	50
'Arababad	147	100	. .	. .
Karimabad (Jupar)	79	100	. .	. .
Zinilabad	72	100	. .	. .
Amirabad	57	100	. .	. .
'Aliabad	28	100	. .	. .
Karimabad Sardar	22	100	. .	. .
'Abdullahabad	20	67	. .	33
Husaynabad Akhlaqi	18	100	. .	. .
Qadirabad	11	67	33	. .
Hakimabad	7	100	. .	. .
Mountain villages and hamlets				
Kahnuj	175	. .	100	. .
Daristan	73	50	50	. .
Husaynabad Mahdi Quli	63	100	. .	. .
Mah Char	57	100	. .	. .
Hanak Bala and Pa'yin	45	100	. .	. .
Roughanu	45	50	50	. .
Narmakan	34	67	. .	33
Karimabad Haji 'Ali	33	100	. .	. .
Kazimabad	27	100	. .	. .
Hasanabad	26	33	67	. .
Zahrud	18	50	50	. .
Dareh Gaz	15	. .	. .	100
Toujigun	15	. .	100	. .
Qalatu	13	100	. .	. .
Shurabad	10	100	. .	. .
Baharistan	9	100	. .	. .
Qudratabad	7	. .	100	. .

TABLE 18 (*continued*)

| Settlement | Population | Percent of total land in control of | | |
		absentee owners	peasant proprietors	religious endowments
Mahdiabad	6	100	. .	. .
Chashmeh Kush	5	100	. .	. .
Ni'matabad Toujigun	5	100	. .	. .
Zarkuh	4	100	. .	. .
Khankistan	2	100	. .	. .

Source: These percentages are based on data compiled from the original village questionnaires of the 1956 Iranian Census. They were all checked in the field and some of the changes noted between 1956 and 1962 are presented in Table 19. The percentages were derived by converting local measures.

are less hampered by traditional landlord-peasant relationships and are less patriarchal. Such landlords try to replace sharecropping agreements with cash wages to avoid problems in village administration and to prevent distribution of their holdings under the new land reform laws. Other new landlords have invested in land as speculators. Technically, these men are not owners; they simply rent land from absentee landed aristocrats. This is the most destructive type of tenure found in the Kirman Basin, because the renter has no permanent interest in either the land or the sharecroppers. Rental agreements are rarely longer than five years; profits must be forthcoming immediately.

Small Nonfarming Ownership

The second category of land ownership in the Kirman Basin, the holdings of lesser nonfarmer owners (khurdeh malik), is found principally in the larger towns. This land is owned by local weavers, shopkeepers, artisans, and so on, who have invested in land for security and to acquire pasture rights; by descendants of former landed aristocrats whose holdings have become fragmented through inheritance and/or sale; and by peasant proprietors who have migrated to the city but have not sold their land in the village.

For a man with limited capital, investment in land is more secure than ventures in the bazaar. The most adventurous small owners combine their holdings and hire a sharecropper to work the land in return for 30% of the harvest. The owner supplies seed and fertilizer and assumes most of the risk of crop failure. Less adventurous (and more numerous) small owners rent their land for a fixed sum each year, so that all risk devolves on the renter. Rental agreements are so common among small holders in Mahan that fixed rental rates for shares in each qanat have developed.[5]

In terms of land use, certain generalizations about small nonfarmer holdings can be made. First, these holdings tend to fragment rather than consolidate, because the limited capital of the small holder makes him vulnerable to natural disasters such as floods, dust storms, or shifting sand and to any economic setback. For the same reason, agricultural methods on these holdings are traditional. Small owners lack capital for tractor plowing, chemical fertilizer, or other modern agricultural techniques. Also, since much of the land is rented on a short-term basis, the stimuli for permanent improvement are weak. Finally, these small holdings are highly mobile properties. A group of speculators in Mahan buy and sell these holdings and have made enormous profits in recent years because increased pressure on the cultivated area has steadily inflated land values. For these reasons — though no data are available to test the reasoning — it seems likely that soil conditions and crop yields are poorer on small owner holdings than on landed estates or peasant proprietors' land.

Religious Endowments

The fundamental characteristic of endowed holdings [6] is that the property, whether land, water, a house, mill or bath, is held in perpetuity, and revenues from this property must be devoted to a religious or charitable purpose. Landholdings in this category, therefore, cannot decrease in size by inheritance or sale.

Property may be dedicated to a variety of communal or private purposes.[7] Communal charitable endowments are the most important type of vaqf holdings in Kirman; they can be classified by the purpose for which the revenue is used. Some are dedicated to supplying food, clothing, and shelter to the poor; others to educating the illiterate. But the most common religious endowments in Kirman subsidize the passion plays held annually in Muharram to mourn the martyrdom of Husayn. These celebrations were outlawed by Riza Shah, and the administration of such properties was placed under the control of the Ministry of Education. After Riza Shah's exile, however, passion plays were revived, and revenues from vaqf land are again used to support them.

Religious endowments are administered by an official (*mutavalli*) appointed by the founder of the endowment. This man is not a trustee (for the property belongs to God), but acts as manager of the property and determines the sharecropping or renting agreements under which it is cultivated. Revenues from vaqf properties are collected by the Education offices in Mahan and Kirman City. They are divided by law into specific proportions. From the total revenue, 25% is utilized for repairs and maintenance of the land, water, and buildings; 10% is paid to the manager, 5% to the man who watches the manager,[8] and 5% is kept in a reserve fund for emergencies. The Education Office receives 9% for administrative costs. The remaining 46% is used for the declared purpose of the trust.[9]

In Mahan most religious endowments are rented on a short-term basis for a fixed sum. Often the manager rents the property to himself, to a relative, or to a business partner. Rental rates therefore are extremely low and little money is actually gathered for religious purposes. The tenant (even if he

TABLE 19
Some Changes of Ownership in Mahan Bakhsh, 1956–62

Location	absentee owners	peasant proprietors	religious endowments	Reason for change
Alluvial fan villages				
'Aliabad	96	4	. .	Death of owner led to sale of his wife's dowry to a peasant proprietor.
Karimabad				
Sardar	83	17	. .	Death of owner led to division among sons and sale of one *dang* (one-sixth).
Qadirabad	23	77	. .	Qanat destroyed by flood. Owner sold part of village for capital to make repairs.
Hujatabad	100	. .	. .	New qanat and new village completed in 1958.
Mountain hamlets				
Daristan	17	83	. .	Sale of land by owner to peasants and local shepherd.
Hanak Bala				
and Pa'yin	25	75	. .	Death of father who lived in Kirman. Inheritance by resident sons, hence increase in peasant proprietorship.
Roughanu	. .	50	50	Death of owner, willed land in vaqf with son as mutavalli.
Karimabad				
Haji 'Ali	67	. .	33	One-third of village willed to vaqf on death of childless owner.
Zahrud	29	71	. .	Return to village land by son upon death of nonresident father.
Toujigun	67	33	. .	Peasant proprietors migrated to Langar after children learned weaving. Increase in absentee ownership.
Qudratabad	100	. .	. .	Death of peasant proprietor. Sale by son to carpet merchant of Langar.
Qalatu	92	8	. .	Half dang of village bought by potter after joint owners could not agree on use of kiln.

Source: See note to Table 18.

is the mutavalli) has no permanent interest in the condition of the property. Most properties are neglected, and this neglect is becoming worse because the central government is threatening to appropriate endowed holdings and distribute them to sharecropping peasants. This danger has stimulated further collusion among all concerned to embezzle funds intended for repairs and for the reserve fund.

Peasant Proprietorship

The fourth category of landholding in Kirman is peasant proprietorship. Peasant proprietors are concentrated in the regional subcenters (Mahan and Jupar), where larger holdings have fragmented, and in the Hanak valley, the most isolated settled area in the region. Peasant proprietor holdings tend to be small, since capital is limited and the acreage is farmed as a family concern. The peasant proprietor supplies all essentials for cultivation. He is usually a better farmer than the sharecropper, working harder and more thoroughly. Productivity, however, varies with location. In the Hanak valley yields are low because the land is poor and the proprietor must cope with frequent floods and frosts. In the towns such natural catastrophes are less frequent and yields are somewhat higher.

Some Ownership Changes: 1956–62 [10]

A variety of factors influence land ownership in Kirman; some stabilize and enlarge holdings while others induce fragmentation. The former include the prestige value of land and the use of handholdings as secure investments. The latter are the inheritance system, which operates at all social and economic levels; the high maintenance and repair costs of qanat irrigation; and the use of land and water as dowries by small owners.

The stabilizing forces in land ownership in Kirman appear to be dominant at the present time. Few changes between 1956 (Table 18) and 1962 (Table 19) were found in the field.[11] Land hunger spurred by population expansion has encouraged owners to keep their properties. Changes that did occur during this period, with the exception of two properties which were dedicated as religious endowments, caused a decrease in the size of holding. All were among small owners or peasant proprietors. Most of the changes occurred when, upon the death of the owner, the property was split among the heirs (Karimabad Sardar, Hanak Bala and Pa'yin, Qudratabad).[12] In one case (Qadirabad) floods destroyed the qanat and the owner sold part of his land to meet repair costs. At Toujigun peasant proprietors sold their holdings and migrated to Langar. The changes are too few and fragmented to provide a reliable pattern.

Appendix F

DETAILED OCCUPATIONAL STRUCTURE
OF SETTLEMENTS IN KIRMAN

Data for Kirman City are from Government of Iran, *Census District Statistics of the First National Census of Iran, Aban 1335 (November 1956)*, Vol. 17, Part 1 (1960), pp. 34–36. Figures given for number of men include all males over 10 years of age except students.

The data for regional subcenters, large villages, and small villages and hamlets are from original village questionnaires of the 1956 Iranian Census and tabulated IBM cards for each head of household. All data were checked in the field. Number of men shown under these classifications includes only heads of households.

Occupation	*No. of Men*	*% Total*
KIRMAN CITY		
Professional		
Biological and agricultural work	6	
Medical and health sciences	77	
Teaching and tutoring	234	
Legal occupations	47	
Religious and social welfare work	104	
Art, writing, entertaining	11	
Other professions	163	
	642	3
Administrative		
Managerial and administrative work	159	
Clerical occupations	1,142	
	1,301	7

147

Occupation	No. of Men	% Total
Service		
Protective service	523	
Domestic and personal service	840	
Miscellaneous service	137	
Manual labor	426	
Motor vehicle driving	789	
Animal-drawn vehicle driving	76	
	2,791	14
Commercial		
Retail selling (in establishments)	1,970	
Wholesale selling	119	
	2,089	11
Artisans and Craftsmen		
Textiles (not carpetmaking)	150	
Carpet weaving	1,643	
Garments and leather products	756	
Basketry and brush making	2	
Woodworking and carpentry	283	
Metalworking	607	
Electrical work	41	
Construction	2,284	
Construction machinery	26	
Printing and bookbinding	31	
Ceramic and pottery	13	
Chemicals	81	
Pelt and hide treating	29	
Food processing	552	
Mineral treating	151	
Well drilling	184	
Labor in well drilling	6	
Miscellaneous craft occupations	13	
Labor in craft occupations	33	
	6,885	35
Agriculture and Other Primary Activities		
Farming	2,431	
Hunting	2	
Fishing	2	
Forestry	5	
Labor in farming	146	
	2,586	13

Occupation	No. of Men	% Total
Unemployed	1,571	8
Not reported	1,891	9
TOTAL KIRMAN CITY	19,756	100

REGIONAL SUBCENTERS

MAHAN

Professional

Administrators	2	
Police	13	
Secretaries	25	
Teachers	11	
Priests	12	
Doctors and nurses	3	
Clerics	10	
	76	5

Service

Shopkeepers	54	
Wholesalers	2	
Transportation	13	
Domestic and personal service, barbers, bathkeepers	24	
Armed service and communication	5	
Protective service	3	
	101	7

Weaving Industry

Factory managers	12	
Private weavers	30	
Contract weavers	342	
Noncarpet weavers	68	
	452	30

Artisans and Craftsmen

Carpenters	17	
Blacksmiths and tinsmiths	11	
Mechanics	2	
Tailors and shoemakers	26	
Bakers and confectioners	32	
Construction workers	82	
Qanat builders	2	
Lime and charcoal burners	12	
	184	12

Occupation	No. of Men	% Total
Agriculture and Herding		
Landlords	13	
Peasant proprietors and sharecroppers	313	
Shepherds and laborers	175	
Water officials and crop-watchers	8	
	509	34
Unemployed	182	12
TOTAL MAHAN	1,504	100

JUPAR

Occupation	No. of Men	% Total
Professional		
Administrators	1	
Police	4	
Secretaries	4	
Teachers	5	
Priests	5	
Doctors and nurses	4	
Clerics	6	
	29	3
Service		
Shopkeepers	36	
Transportation	5	
Domestic and personal service, barbers, bathkeepers	7	
Protective service	1	
	49	6
Weaving Industry		
Factory managers	2	
Private weavers	225	
Contract weavers	116	
Noncarpet weavers	10	
	353	41
Artisans and Craftsmen		
Carpenters	5	
Blacksmiths and tinsmiths	7	
Mechanics	1	
Tailors and shoemakers	16	
Bakers and confectioners	14	
Construction workers	24	
Qanat builders	28	

Occupation	No. of Men	% Total
Lime and charcoal burners	5	
Leather tanners	8	
	108	12

Agriculture and Herding

Landlords	11	
Peasant proprietors and sharecroppers	169	
Shepherds and laborers	55	
Water officials and crop-watchers	1	
	236	27
Unemployed	96	11
TOTAL JUPAR	871	100

LARGE VILLAGES

LANGAR

Professional

Administrators	3	
Priests	3	
	6	1

Service

Shopkeepers	12	
Domestic and personal service, barbers, bathkeepers	4	
	16	4

Weaving Industry

Contract weavers	147	34

Artisans and Craftsmen

Blacksmiths and tinsmiths	3	
Tailors and shoemakers	1	
Construction workers	15	
Qanat builders	4	
	23	6

Agriculture and Herding

Landlords	5	
Peasant proprietors and sharecroppers	200	
Shepherds and laborers	18	
	223	52
Unemployed	12	3
TOTAL LANGAR	427	100

Occupation	No. of Men	% Total
QANAGHISTAN		
Professional		
Administrators	1	
Priests	1	
Clerics	2	
	4	1
Service		
Shopkeepers	23	
Transportation	2	
Domestic and personal service, barbers, bathkeepers	2	
	27	6
Weaving Industry		
Factory managers	9	
Private weavers	7	
Contract weavers	194	
Noncarpet weavers	8	
	218	49
Artisans and Craftsmen		
Carpenters	1	
Blacksmiths and tinsmiths	2	
Tailors and shoemakers	5	
Bakers and confectioners	10	
Construction workers	30	
Qanat builders	2	
	50	12
Agriculture and Herding		
Peasant proprietors and sharecroppers	69	
Shepherds and laborers	7	
	76	17
Unemployed	68	15
TOTAL QANAGHISTAN	443	100
MUHIABAD		
Professional		
Administrators	1	
Priests	2	
	3	1

Occupation	No. of Men	% Total
Service		
Shopkeepers	1	
Domestic and personal service, barbers, bathkeepers	4	
	5	2
Weaving Industry		
Private weavers	46	
Contract weavers	85	
Noncarpet weavers	2	
	133	53
Artisans and Craftsmen		
Blacksmiths and tinsmiths	2	
Tailors and shoemakers	3	
Construction workers	9	
Qanat builders	1	
	15	6
Agriculture and Herding		
Peasant proprietors and sharecroppers	66	
Shepherds and laborers	13	
	79	32
Unemployed	18	7
TOTAL MUHIABAD	253	100

SMALL VILLAGES AND HAMLETS

	No. of Men	% Total
Professional		
Teachers	3	..
Service		
Shopkeepers	2	
Transportation	2	
Domestic and personal service, barbers, bathkeepers	2	
	6	2
Weaving Industry		
Private weavers	5	
Contract weavers	22	
Noncarpet weavers	15	
	42	9

Occupation	No. of Men	% Total
Artisans and Craftsmen		
Carpenters	1	
Blacksmiths and tinsmiths	1	
Construction workers	28	
Qanat builders	9	
Lime and charcoal burners	15	
	54	12
Agriculture and Herding		
Landlords	5	
Peasant proprietors and sharecroppers	234	
Shepherds and laborers	91	
Water officials and crop-watchers	3	
	333	74
Unemployed	19	3
TOTAL SMALL VILLAGES AND HAMLETS	457	100

Notes

1 The First National Census of Iran (November 1956) has been published in 129 volumes in English and Persian by the Department of Public Statistics, Ministry of Interior in Tehran. The specific volume devoted to Kirman City is Government of Iran, *Census District Statistics of the First National Census of Iran, Aban 1335 (November 1956)*, Vol. 17, *Zarand and Kerman Census Districts*, Part 1, *Kerman* (1960).

2 *Kerman*: Army Map Service, 1:253,400, 1942, Sheet No. H–40J; *Bahramabad*: Army Map Service, 1:253,440, 1942, Sheet No. H–40I. These are being revised by Army Map Service mapping teams.

3 The Sahab Geographical and Drafting Institute (P.O. Box 236, Tehran) sells maps of most Iranian cities.

Introduction

1 This tripartite division of Middle Eastern society has been used by many authors. See Elizabeth E. Bacon, "A Preliminary Attempt to Determine the Culture Areas of Asia," *Southwestern Journal of Anthropology*, 2 (1946): 117–32; Jacques Weulersse, *Paysans de Syrie et du Proche-Orient* (1946), pp. 60–66; Raphael Patai, "Nomadism: Middle Eastern and Central Asian," *Southwestern Journal of Anthropology*, 7 (1951): 401–14; idem, "The Middle East as a Culture Area," *Middle East Journal*, 6 (1952): 1–21; Carleton S. Coon, *Caravan: The Story of the Middle East* (1958), pp. 171–259; Louis Sweet, *Tell Ṭoqaan: A Syrian Village* (1960), pp. 1–6, 228–30; Gabriel Baer, *Population and Society in the Arab East* (1964), pp. 119–203.

2 Robert C. Alberts agrees with this viewpoint. He notes "a multitude of gaps in our present knowledge of the Middle East where impressions, intuition and stereotypes often substitute for facts. In part this situation has come about from disproportionate emphasis in investigation of socio-cultural patterning and change among the three fundamental types of ecological entities in the Middle Eastern scene." Alberts, *Social Struc-*

ture and Culture Change in an Iranian Village (1963), p. 2. Also see discussion in Laura Nader, "Communication between Village and City in the Modern Middle East," *Human Organization*, 24 (1965): 18–24.

3   Studies using the city as a unit include Jacques Weulersse, "Antioche, essai de géographie urbaine," *Bulletin d'études orientales*, 4 (1934): 27–79; Roger Le Tourneau, *Fès avant le protectorat* (1949); Horace Miner, *The Primitive City of Timbuctoo* (1953); K. Scharlau, "Moderne Umgestaltungen in Grundriss iranischer Stadte," *Erdkunde*, 15 (1961): 180–91; John I. Clarke, *The Iranian City of Shiraz* (1963); Xavier de Planhol, "Abadan: morphologie et fonction du tissu urbain," *Revue géographique de l'Est*, 4 (1964): 338–85; idem, *Recherches sur la géographie humaine de l'Iran septentrional* (1964), pp. 59–76. Two refreshingly different comparative studies are Planhol, *The World of Islam* (1959), and Gideon Sjoberg, *The Preindustrial City: Past and Present* (1960).

4   Village studies include Jalal Al-Ahmad, *Owrazan: Topography, Ceremonies and Customs, Folklore, and Dialect* (1954); John Gulick, *Social Structure and Culture Change in a Lebanese Village* (1955); Gavin Maxwell, *People of the Reeds* (1957); Sweet (1960); C. A. O. van Nieuwenhuijze, "The Near Eastern Village: A Profile," *Middle East Journal*, 16 (1962): 295–308; Alberts (1963); John Hanessian "Yosoufabad, an Iranian Village," *American Universities Field Staff Reports, Southwest Asia Series*, Vol. 12 (1963); William Green Miller, "Hosseinabad: A Persian Village," *Middle East Journal*, 18 (1964): 483–98; Paul Stirling, *Turkish Village* (1965).

5   Tribal studies are numerous. Among them are Alois Musil, *The Manners and Customs of the Rwala Bedouins* (1928); C. G. Feilberg, *La Tente noire* (1944); Oliver Garrod, "The Qashqai Tribe of Fars," *Journal of the Royal Central Asian Society*, 33 (1946); 293–306; H. St. John B. Philby, *Arabian Highlands* (1952); Fredrik Barth, *Principles of Social Organization in Southern Kurdistan* (1953); idem, *Nomads of South Persia: The Basseri Tribe of the Khamseh Confederacy* (1961).

6   The problems of thinking in these terms are discussed in Robert Redfield, *Peasant Society and Culture* (1960), pp. 23–39; Gideon Sjoberg, "Folk and Feudal Societies," *American Journal of Sociology*, 58 (1952): 231–39; Horace Miner, "The Folk-Urban Continuum," *American Sociological Review*, 17 (1952): 529–37.

7   Sweet (1960), pp. 228–30.

8   Alberts (1963), p. 1038.

9   Gulick (1955), pp. 56–59.

10   This is not to imply that a geographical approach precludes the study of a single community.

11   The relevance of this to the growing body of literature on central place theory should be noted. See Brian J. L. Berry and Allen Pred, *Central Place Studies: A Bibliography of Theory and Applications* (1965).

12   The terms "landscape" and "cultural landscape" are used here and else-

where in the sense of the appearance of an area (*Landschaftsbild*), not the area itself. See discussion in Philip L. Wagner and Marvin W. Mikesell, eds., *Readings in Cultural Geography* (1961), pp. 9–13.

13 This distinction is fully developed in Sjoberg (1952), pp. 231–39.

14 If true, this supports Bobek's thesis that communal traits in Middle Eastern villages probably originated in the growth of feudalism rather than through the persistence of clan peasantries. Hans Bobek, "Die Hauptstufen der Gesellschafts und Wirtschaftsentfaltung in geographischer Sicht," *Die Erde: Zeitschrift der Gesellschaft für Erdkunde zu Berlin*, 90 (1959): 274–87.

15 Planhol (1959), pp. 2–5.

16 Throughout this study settlement types are defined by size and location. The major categories as presented in Chapter 3 are the city (pop. 60,000), regional subcenters (4,000–6,000), large villages (1,000–2,000), small villages (100–1,000), and hamlets (below 100). There were no settlements in the field area with populations between 6,000 and 60,000; whether this is a local phenomenon or more widespread is uncertain.

17 This correlates with information on economic structure presented in Alberts' study of Davarabad and Gulick's study of Al-Munṣif, though not with that of Sweet's on Tell Ṭoqaan.

18 One reservation should be noted here. All settlements treated in this study lie within forty miles of Kirman City. It seems probable that isolated peasant villages would be more common at greater distances from a city.

19 Though the landed aristocrat who lives luxuriously in the city and has no contact with his farmers is a near-sacred Middle Eastern stereotype, very few landlords in Kirman or for that matter in Iran can afford such a lack of communication with their sources of income.

20 Gulick (1955), pp. 174–77; Alberts (1963), pp. 978–99.

Chapter 1

1 The best physiographic description of Iran is still Raoul Blanchard, "L'Iran," *Géographie universelle*, Vol. 8, *Asie occidentale* (1929), pp. 128–70. Also see F. G. Clapp, "Geology of Eastern Iran," *Bulletin of the Geological Society of America*, 51 (1940): 1–102.

2 Hence, Iranians speak of the people of each city as having a definite personality. Shirazis are described as enlightened and intelligent, Yazdis as phlegmatic but shrewd businessmen, and Kirmanis as lazy, fun-loving, and gregarious.

3 Kirman is the proper name of both city and province. The term "Kirman City" is used to prevent confusion wherever the context is not explicit.

4 Guy Le Strange, "The Cities of Kirmān in the Time of Ḥamd-Allah Mustawfi and Marco Polo," *Journal of the Royal Asiatic Society* (1901), "L'Iran," *Géographie universelle*, Vol. 8, *Asie occidentale* (1929), pp. 299–321.

5 In the past, Kirman and Baluchistan were separate provinces. At present

both areas are included within the same administrative subdivision (*Ustan* 8).

6 More detailed geological information may be found in Philip H. T. Beckett, "The Soils of Kerman, South Persia," *Journal of Soil Science*, 9 (1958): 20–32; Kerman Development Corporation, *Property Report Supplement to Report of Mineral Reconnaissance, Kerman Region, Iran* (1959); A. F. Banfield and V. H. Clarke, "Mineral Resources of the Kirman Region, Iran," *Twenty-First International Geological Congress*, 20 (1960): 74–85.

7 Most passes through this range are noted on the British India Survey maps (with typical English understatement) as being "barely passable by camels."

8 The best general works on the climate of Iran are G. Bauer, "Luftzirkulation und Niederschlagverhältnisse in Vorderasien," *Gerlands Beiträge zur Geophysik*, 35 (1935): 381–548; M. H. Ganji, "The Climates of Iran," *Bulletin de la Société de Géographie d'Égypte*, 28 (1955): 195–299. Other sources may be found in A. D. Peterson, *Bibliography on the Climate of Iran* (1957).

9 Beckett and Gordon calculated potential losses by Thornthwaite's formula (1948) for total evapotranspiration, and by Penman's method (1948) for open water surfaces and for areas completely covered by crops. In each case, the figures clearly showed that all crops must be irrigated, as indeed is the case in Kirman. A figure of 5.89 inches of rainfall was estimated to be the annual average of Kirman City on the basis of data of varying reliability from 1909–52. Philip H. T. Beckett and E. D. Gordon, "The Climate of Kerman, South Persia," *Quarterly Journal of the Royal Meteorological Society*, 82 (1956): 508–9, 512–13.

10 During the period 1951–61 the four months of December, January, February, and March accounted for 67% (5.36 inches) of the average annual precipitation. The months of June, July, August, and September accounted for only 6% (.51 inches) of the total.

11 Beckett and Gordon report that between 1941 and 1952 the absolute maximum and minimum temperatures recorded were 112°F and 3°F. During the period 1955–61 the most extreme temperatures occurred in 1959, with an absolute maximum temperature of 103.6°F in June and an absolute minimum temperature of −3.6°F in December. Iranian Meteorological Department, *Meteorological Yearbook of Iran, 1959* (1962), p. 13.

12 These data were collected by Beckett during three weeks in August 1950. Unfortunately, no other records for comparable elevations are available. Beckett and Gordon (1956), p. 507.

13 On vegetation in Iran see Hans Bobek, "Die natürlichen Wälder und Gehölzfluren Irāns," *Bonner geographische Abhandlungen*, 8 (1951): 1–62; idem, "Die klimaökologische Gliederung von Iran," *Proceedings, International Geographical Union*, VIIIth General Assembly, XVIIth Congress (1952), pp. 244–48; idem, "Klima und Landschaft Irans in

vor- und frühgeschichtlicher Zeit," *Geographischer Jahresbericht aus Österreich*, 25 (1953–54): 1–42; A. Parsa, *Flore de l'Iran* (1952); H. S. Kernan, "Forest Management in Iran," *Middle East Journal*, 11 (1957): 199–202.

14 There are no sacred groves as such, but individual trees can be found. These are covered with various talismans such as brightly colored strips of cloth, locks, keys, and candles.

15 *Tamarisk mannifera* is widespread in Iran, where it is called *gaz mazu*. The Persian word *gaz* refers to the tamarisk itself and to the candy made from its manna. This manna is a raw material for the ancient sugar factories in Yazd and Mashhad.

16 One of the earliest and most eloquent statements concerning the impact of man on the land, particularly his influence on vegetation is George Perkins Marsh's *Man and Nature; or, Physical Geography as Modified by Human Action* (1864). (See also David Lowenthal, *George Perkins Marsh: Versatile Vermonter*, 1958.) For the Middle East, see F. M. Heichelheim, "Effects of Classical Antiquity on the Land," and H. von Wissmann et al, "On the Role of Nature and Man in Changing the Face of the Dry Belt of Asia," pp. 165–82 and 278–303 respectively in *Man's Role in Changing the Face of the Earth*, ed. by William L. Thomas (1956).

17 See endplate map in Bobek (1951).

18 W. D. Shrader, "Report to the Kerman Development Corporation on Agricultural Development of Kerman Region" (MS, 1958), p. 31. Shrader estimates an average carrying capacity of one animal unit (one mature cow, seven sheep, or ten goats) to each 49.4 acres of natural pasture. See also W. D. Shrader, "Agricultural Problems and Potentials in Iran," *Journal of Soil and Water Conservation*, 18 (1962): 23–24.

19 Three major references discussing the use and distribution of these plants are Berthold Laufer, "Sino-Iranica: Chinese Contributions to the History of Civilization in Ancient Iran," *Field Museum of Natural History, Anthropological Series*, 15 (1919): 185–630; David Hooper and Henry Field, "Useful Plants and Drugs of Iran and Iraq," *Field Museum of Natural History, Botanical Series*, 9 (1937): 73–241; Bess Allen Donaldson, *The Wild Rue: A Study of Muhammadan Magic and Folklore in Iran* (1938).

20 For the only published collection of soil profiles from the Kirman Basin see Beckett (1958), pp. 20–32. Details of soil structure mentioned in this section are based on Beckett's data; general observations are based on field work.

21 The cultivated areas around Kirman City, Mahan, and Jupar have been in continuous use for more than 1,500 years.

22 Low nitrogen content is a common characteristic of soils in arid areas with scanty vegetation and high summer soil temperatures. This condition is aggravated in Kirman by such practices as grazing flocks on

crop stubble, failing to plow fallow land, and stripping weeds from fallow and harvested fields for forage or sale.

23 Beckett (1958), pp. 22, 29–30.

24 Philip H. T. Beckett, "Persia's Need for Land Reform," *Fortnightly Review*, 171 (1952): 103–4.

25 Percy M. Sykes, *Ten Thousand Miles in Persia or Eight Years in Iran* (1902), p. 423.

26 The extent of wind erosion is clearly marked at the base of these garden walls by a line separating the tiered layers of adobe mud from the unstructured subsoil beneath. Irrigation channels must be raised several feet above the base of the wall to water the gardens inside.

Chapter 2

1 The earliest sites date from 4,200 to 3,400 B.C., most of them from the first half of the second millennium. L. Vanden Berghe, *Archéologie de l'Irān ancien* (1959), pp. 17–18, 206–7.

2 Bobek believes that sedentary life was more widely spread in early periods and that the Indo-Iranians destroyed and replaced these ways of life with large-scale nomadism. Hans Bobek, "Klima und Landschaft Irans in vor- und frühgeschichtlicher Zeit," *Geographischer Jahresbericht aus Österreich*, 25 (1953–54): 29–40, 42.

3 Aurel Stein, *Archaeological Reconnaissances in North-West India and South-Eastern Irān* (1937), pp. 104–31, 137–56; K. R. Maxwell-Hyslop, "Note on a Shaft-Hole Axe-Pick from Khurab, Makran," *Iraq*, 17 (1955): 161; F. E. Zeuner, "The Identity of the Camel on the Khurab Pick," *Iraq*, 17 (1955): 162–63. Stein dates the Khurab site at 2,900–2,000 B.C.; Maxwell-Hyslop dates it at 2,000–1,800 B.C.

4 Aurel Stein, "Archaeological Reconnaissances in Southern Persia," *Geographical Journal*, 83 (1934): 119–34; idem (1937), pp. 164–69.

5 Stein (1937), Plans 15, 145.

6 Percy M. Sykes, *Ten Thousand Miles in Persia or Eight Years in Iran* (1902), pp. 442–45, 448; idem, *A History of Persia* (1921), 1:184–85.

7 C. Greenwell, "Notes on a Collection of Bronze Weapons, Implements, and Vessels Found at Khinamān," *Journal of the Royal Anthropological Institute*, 37 (1907): 196–200; Sykes (1902), p. 448.

8 The *qal'eh* (or *kala*) as a distinctive Iranian settlement type has been discussed in A. Z. Rosenfeld, "La Kala, type d'établissement fortifié iranien," *Sovietskaïa ethnografia*, 1 (1951): 22–38; Xavier de Planhol, "Les Villages fortifiés en Iran et en Asie Centrale," *Annales de géographie*, 67 (1958): 256–58; idem, *Recherches sur la géographie humaine de l'Iran septentrional* (1964), pp. 9–16.

9 Hans Bobek, "Die natürlichen Wälder und Gehölzfluren Irāns," *Bonner geographische Abhandlungen*, 8 (1951), endplate map.

10 Qanats were used in the ancient cities of Assyria, in Arbil during the reign of Sennacherib (705–681 B.C.), and in the major cities of Iran during the Achaemenian period. Their date and place of origin are still

uncertain; no serious work has ever attempted to document the development and spread of this irrigation system. Cressey has summarized qanat distribution in the Old World, but on their early history simply notes that they are "of Persian origin and date back more than two thousand years." George B. Cressey, "Qanats, Karez, and Foggaras," *Geographical Review*, 48 (1958): 27–44.

The major questions critical to an understanding of the historical development of settlement on the Central Plateau of Iran are (1) when did qanats come into widespread use instead of just serving major cities and (2) through what diffusion processes and at what rates did this occur? Polybius says qanats diffused in Parthian times (248 B.C.–224 A.D.). See Appendix D for further discussion.

11 Polybius, X.28.

12 Herodotus (484–425 B.C.) mentioned the Kirmani (Germanioi) as one of the twelve tribes of Persia. Herodotus, II.438.

13 Lambton goes so far as to state that "the tribal nature of society determined that the village made up of a clan should be the model settlement." Ann K. S. Lambton, *Landlord and Peasant in Persia* (1953), p. 2.

14 Ibid., pp. 7–8.

15 This distribution of power among vassals and lords is an Indo-Iranian trait. The Semites and others concentrated all ownership under a single absolute monarch. J. de Morgan, "Feudalism in Persia: Its Origin, Development, and Present Condition," *Smithsonian Institute Report* (1913), pp. 580–81.

16 Arthur Christensen, *L'Iran sous les Sassanides* (1944), pp. 15–17; Lambton (1953), pp. 11–12.

17 Mazaheri suggests that this social and economic division was quite pervasive, that the upper class was polygamous and the working classes monogamous. Aly-Akbar Mazaheri, *La Famille iranienne aux temps anté-islamiques* (1938), p. 134.

18 *Cambridge Ancient History*, 9: 120.

19 Christensen (1944), pp. 98–99.

20 Reuben Levy, *The Sociology of Islam*, 1 (1931): 34–35, 100–1; Lambton (1953), pp. 13–14.

21 Lambton (1953), pp. 15–16.

22 W. Montgomery Watt, *Islam and the Integration of Society* (1961), pp. 115–16.

23 The origin legend for Kirman City is recited in Sykes (1902), pp. 215–16; Laurence Lockhart, *Persian Cities* (1960), pp. 112–13; Ahmad 'Ali Khan Vaziri, *Tārīkhi Kirmān (Sālārīyeh)* [*History of Kirman*], (1961), ed. by Hafez Farman Farma'ian, pp. 11–12.

24 The reference to Kirman City in Ptolemy (fl. 2nd century) actually refers to modern Sirjan (sometimes called Saidabad); later references in Ammianus Marcellinus (c. 330–395) may refer to either Kirman City or Sirjan. Ptolemy, *Geography*, VI.8; Ammianus Marcellinus, XXIII.6, 48, 80.

25 Vaziri (1961), pp. 10–15.
26 Historically, Azar Mahan is more famous for donating funds to Anu-shiravan the Just to build the "Gate of Gates" dam at modern Darband and the city of Astarabad (Gurgan) in northern Iran. Ibid., pp. 23–24, 25.
27 This settlement process is recited in the oral tradition of the region. Initial settlement by charcoal burners followed by agricultural settle-ment recurs consistently. A similar cycle is in progress in the mountain valleys today.
28 Lambton suggests a different reason for Kirman's lack of communalism. She notes that the explanation is "to be sought in geographical condi-tions. The methods of irrigation owing to the configuration of the ground are such that the settlement of the area may well have been carried out mainly by powerful leaders rather than by groups of joint settlers. Yāqūt records that in Kirmān . . . land was going out of cultivation when he wrote (i.e., in the seventh/thirteenth century). The devastation brought about by Tīmūr at the close of the eighth/fourteenth century may well have accentuated this trend and destroyed the existing basis of village organization, and unfavourable natural conditions may have prevented its revival." Yet unless one assumes a preexisting communalism, there is no need to explain its disappearance. Lambton (1953), p. 8.
29 This theory is presented more fully in Hans Bobek, "Die Hauptstufen der Gesellschafts und Wirtschaftsentfaltung in geographischer Sicht," *Die Erde: Zeitschrift der Gesellschaft für Erdkunde zu Berlin*, 90 (1959): 259–98. Translated as "The Main Stages in Socio-Economic Evolution from a Geographical Point of View," in *Readings in Cultural Geography* (1961), ed. by Philip L. Wagner and Marvin W. Mikesell, pp. 218–47.
30 D. C. Dennett, *Conversion and the Poll Tax in Early Islam* (1950), pp. 28–33.
31 Watt (1961), p. 118.
32 Jehangir B. Sanjana, *Ancient Persia and the Parsis: A Comprehensive History of the Parsis and Their Religion from Primeval Times to Present Age* (1935), pp. 551–54.
33 E. W. West, trans., *Epistles of Manuskihar*, I.iii.11; II.v.14.
34 Watt (1961), pp. 116–19.
35 G. K. Nariman, ed., *The Ahad Nameh* (1925), pp. vii–viii, ix, xv, xviii–xx; Manoutchehr K. Mohebbi, *L'Influence religieuse sur le droit con-stitutionnel de l'Iran* (1958), pp. 49–51.
36 Maneckji N. Dhalla, *History of Zoroastrianism* (1938), p. 439.
37 Lambton (1953), p. 20.
38 Sykes (1921), 1: 530–32.
39 Vaziri (1961), pp. 28–34.
40 The Kharijite movement began in 657 after the murder of the third caliph 'Uthman. These separatists protested that divine law demanded revenge and that war was essential. See G. Levi della Vida, "Khāridjites,"

in *Shorter Encyclopaedia of Islam* (1961), ed. by H. A. R. Gibb and J. H. Kramers, pp. 246–49.

41 Ibid., pp. 246–47.

42 With the exception of Sirjan all of these were small undistinguished towns which now lie well within the hinterland of Kirman City. Sirjan, Jiruft, and Bam are located (from west to east) on a route that lies eighty miles south of modern Kirman. Shahdad is just east of the city on the margins of the Dashti Lut; Ra'in is about forty miles south of Kirman. These and other Abbasid trade routes are reconstructed in Guy Le Strange, *The Lands of the Eastern Caliphate* (1905).

43 This transfer of the seat of government from Sirjan to Kirman is discussed in A. Houtum-Schindler, "Notes on Marco Polo's Itinerary in Southern Persia," *Journal of the Royal Asiatic Society*, New Series, 13 (1881): 490–97; Guy Le Strange, "The Cities of Kirmān in the Time of Ḥamd-Allah Mustawfi and Marco Polo," *Journal of the Royal Asiatic Society* (1901), pp. 281–90; idem (1905), pp. 299–304.

44 Quoted in Le Strange (1905), pp. 303–4, 306–7.

45 Vaziri (1961), pp. 65–66.

46 Quoted in Lambton (1953), p. 8.

47 Marco Polo, *The Book of Ser Marco Polo, the Venetian, concerning the Kingdoms and Marvels of the East* (1921), trans. and ed. by Sir Henry Yule, revised by Henri Cordier. Chap. 17.

48 Le Strange (1901), pp. 287–88; Lockhart (1960), pp. 116–17.

49 Lambton (1953), p. 8.

50 Javad Nurbakhsh Kirmani, *Zindigī va Āṣar Quṭbi Ālmūḥdīn Shāh Ni'matullāh Valī Kirmānī* [*The Life and Writings of Shah Ni'matullah Vali of Kirman*] (1958–59), pp. 1–123.

51 There is no evidence that carpets were woven in Kirman prior to the rise of the Safavid dynasty. Early Muslim geographers made no mention of carpet weaving, nor did Marco Polo find this craft in Kirman during his visit. The earliest mention of carpets in Kirman occurs in a chronicle written during the reign of Shah 'Abbas, when Kirmani carpets were shipped to the court of Akbar the Great in India.

52 John Fryer, *A New Account of East India and Persia, Being Nine Years' Travel: 1672–1681* (1909), ed. by William Crooke, p. 219.

53 Lockhart (1960), pp. 117–18.

54 Sykes (1921), 2: 288.

55 Lambton (1953), pp. 135–37.

56 A. H. Gleadowe-Newcomen, *Report on the British Indian Commercial Mission to South-Eastern Persia during 1904–1905* (1906), p. 49.

57 Ibid., p. 51.

58 Edward Stack, *Six Months in Persia* (1882), 1: 202.

59 Frederic J. Goldsmid, *Telegraph and Travel* (1874), pp. 582–83.

60 Euan Smith, "The Perso-Baluch Frontier Mission, 1870–71," in *Eastern Persia, an Account of the Journeys of the Persian Boundary Commission* (1876), ed. by Frederic J. Goldsmid, 1: 191.

61 Vaziri (1961), pp. 439–41.

62 Euan Smith (1876), pp. 187–88.

63 Stack (1882), 1: 209–11.

64 Sykes (1902), pp. 199–200.

65 Browne mentions a length of three ells (one ell equaling 45 inches). Edward G. Browne, *A Year amongst the Persians* (1950), pp. 482–83.

66 Sykes (1902), p. 200.

67 Kirman wool was so famous for its lightness and fineness that Fath 'Ali Shah tried to introduce Kirmani sheep into other parts of Iran, but the experiment failed.

Chapter 3

1 A number of articles have been written on qanats. Among these are Millard A. Buttler, "Irrigation in Persia by Kanat," *Civil Engineering*, 3 (1933): 69–73; E. Noel, "Qanats," *Journal of the Royal Central Asian Society*, 31 (1944): 191–202; Philip H. T. Beckett, "Waters of Persia," *Geographical Magazine*, 24 (1951): 230–40; idem, "Qanats in Persia," *Journal of the Iran Society*, 1 (1952): 125 et seq.; idem, "Qanats around Kirman," *Journal of the Royal Central Asian Society*, 40 (1953): 47–58; R. L. Fitt, "Irrigation Development in Central Persia," *Journal of the Royal Central Asian Society*, 40 (1953): 124–33; Anthony Smith, *Blind White Fish in Persia* (1953), pp. 72–188; George B. Cressey, "Qanats, Karez, and Foggaras," *Geographical Review*, 48 (1958): 27–44; Farhad Ghahraman, *The Right of Use and Economics of Irrigation Water in Iran* (1958), pp. 43–57, 94–98, 164–70; Henri Goblot, "Le Problème de l'eau en Iran," *Orient*, 23 (1962): 43–60; idem, "Dans l'ancien Iran, les techniques de l'eau et la grande histoire," *Annales: économies-sociétés-civilisations*, 18 (1963): 499–520; Johannes Humlum, "Underjordiske Vandingskanaler: Kareze, Qanat, Foggara," *Skrifter Fra Geografisk Institut* [Ved Århus Universitet], 16 (1965): 81–132.

2 One finds therefore a similarity in settlement patterns in areas such as Yazd, Rafsinjan, and Kirman.

3 The "mother well" of a qanat is that shaft located farthest away from the point where water emerges at the surface. It is important to remember that water is rarely drawn from these shafts. For details see Appendix D.

4 Figure 7 is highly generalized, and only major water-producing qanats are depicted. The real density of qanats in the Kirman Basin is too high to illustrate at such a scale.

5 Counted from aerial photograph.

6 Qanat water law is discussed more fully on pages 103–5 in the context of its role in retarding expansion of the cultivated area in the basin. Also see Appendix D.

7 One qasab roughly equals enough water to flood-irrigate 25 square meters (29.9 sq. yds.) once every 24 hours. This measure is somewhat

nebulous and varies from soil to soil and even from day to day on the same soil. Given the usual 12-day rotation of water, 10–15 qasabs would irrigate less than a tenth of an acre each day (.06–.09) or a total of about an acre (.72–1.08) every 12 days. The total cultivated area in mountain hamlets therefore is usually limited to this amount, which indicates the high population pressure on cultivated land in this area and emphasizes the importance of subsidiary activities in the economy of the region.

8 For water law in Iran see A. Querry, *Recueil des lois concernant les musulmans schytes*, Vol. 2 (1872); Ann K. S. Lambton, *Landlord and Peasant in Persia* (1953), pp. 210–29; Dante Caponera, *Water Laws in Moslem Countries* (1954), pp. 1–52, 124–28.

9 Mentioned by Gardizi in the *Zayn ul-Akhbār*, written in the 11th century A.D.; quoted in Lambton (1953), p. 217.

10 Ibid., p. 199.

11 In the Middle Ages the leading mosque of Kirman was the Masjidi Malik, located south of the bazaar. It was built in the 11th century by the Seljuq ruler, Malik Turan Shah (1084–96). Sir Percy Sykes, British consul in Kirman at the end of the 19th century, discusses its mosques and other public buildings. Figure 11 is based on his map and other descriptions. Percy M. Sykes, *Ten Thousand Miles in Persia or Eight Years in Iran* (1902), pp. 187–201, map facing p. 188.

12 The *badgir* is a square tower with openings at the top. In these openings slats are set, as in a venetian blind but vertically, and manipulated to catch the wind. The offices below these wind towers are 20–30 degrees cooler than other rooms on hot summer days. In Iran badgirs are primarily found in the desert cities of Kirman and Yazd.

13 Listed in Sykes (1902), p. 193.

14 The records of the Zoroastrian community indicate that during the last half of the 19th century there were no municipal planning commissions in Kirman City. The leaders of the Zoroastrian community were completely responsible for construction and repair of buildings, lanes, and streets within their own quarter.

15 Sykes (1902), pp. 196–97, estimated the number of Jews in Kirman City at 70 in 1902. In 1956 there were 568.

16 In Tehran and many other Middle Eastern cities the Jews are wealthy merchants, businessmen, and financiers.

17 The *iwan* is a tunnel-vaulted portico closed on one end and open on the other. Its use in Persia is described in J. H. Iliffe, "Persia and the Ancient World," in *The Legacy of Persia* (1953), ed. by A. J. Arberry, pp. 1–38.

18 These terms are the Persian equivalents for the more familiar Turkish terms *selamlik* (men's quarter) and *harim* (women's quarter).

19 In 1956, 7,027 (56%) of the buildings in Kirman City were owned by their occupants, 44% (5,519) were not. Of the landlord-owned buildings, 53% (2,910) were rented and 47% (2,609) were occupied rent-

free. Government of Iran, *Census District Statistics of the First National Census of Iran, Aban 1335 (November 1956)*, Vol. 17, Part 1 (1960), p. 51.

20 According to Vreeland, "2,500,000 families in the rural areas live in single-room houses." Herbert H. Vreeland, ed., *Iran* (1957), p. 230.

21 See diagram in Jamshid Surushian, *Farhangi Behdīnān* [*Dictionary of the Good People*] (1956), facing p. 142.

22 These details of Zoroastrian life in the desert cities of Kirman and Yazd were noted by many 19th-century travelers. See Edward G. Browne, *A Year amongst the Persians* (1950), pp. 370–71; Sykes (1902), pp. 67, 193, 198; A. V. Williams Jackson, *Persia Past and Present* (1906), pp. 366, 375; Laurence Lockhart, *The Fall of the Ṣafavī Dynasty and the Afghan Occupation of Persia* (1958), pp. 72–73. Concerning the similar but less extreme conditions of the Jews see Walter J. Fischel, "Secret Jews of Persia," *Commentary*, 7 (1949): 28–33; C. L. Lang, "Les Minorités arménienne et juive d'Iran," *Politique étrangère*, 26 (1961): 460–71.

23 Nor is there any record that umbrellas were ever used as parasols. See E. Crawshay Williams, *Across Persia* (1907), p. 202.

24 The records of their council ("Anjumani Zartushtiani Kirman") are still available in Kirman. They are written in Persian script, but the words used are those of the Zoroastrian dialect, "*dari*," which can only be read by the older men of the community.

25 Similar ground plan changes in Mashhad, Shiraz, Abadan, and Tehran are reported in K. Scharlau, "Moderne Umgestaltungen in Grundriss iranischer Stadte," *Erdkunde*, 15 (1961): 180–91; John I. Clarke, *The Iranian City of Shiraz* (1963); Xavier de Planhol, "Abadan: morphologie et fonction du tissu urbain," *Revue géographique de l'Est*, 4 (1964): 338–85; idem, *Recherches sur la géographie humaine de l'Iran septentrional* (1964), pp. 59–76.

26 There is a vague feeling of suspicion about this section of the city — that it is an unhappy place inhabited by spirits. Many of the magicians, sorcerers, and pseudoreligious healers practice their trades in these ruins.

27 For a discussion of the declining role of the church in Iran see R. K. Ramazani, " 'Church' and State in Modernizing Society: The Case of Iran," *American Behavioral Scientist*, 7 (1964): 26–28.

28 Riza Shah favored the Zoroastrians and looked beyond the Arab Conquest back to the ancient glories of Achaemenian and Sassanian Iran. During his rule Zoroastrians from Yazd and Kirman migrated to Tehran. After his abdication (1941), limitations on the Zoroastrians were reimposed in Kirman and Yazd, which intensified emigration to the more cosmopolitan atmosphere of Tehran. In 1956 there were 4,627 Zoroastrians in Tehran. There are now more than 7,000.

29 Each household compound has the right to water its courtyard garden and to utilize the water for domestic purposes.

30 Islamic water law utilizes time shares rather than absolute volume measures to equalize seasonal and diurnal variations in flow.

31 George B. Cressey notes that this is generally true wherever qanats are used for irrigation. This may imply that similar social gradients would also be found elsewhere. Cressey (1958), p. 29.

32 Only water-powered gristmills are located above these homes, usually at the break in slope.

33 In small villages with a single qanat, there is usually only one line of household compounds. In larger places such as Mahan, which has five qanats, rows of houses are aligned along each of the distinct watercourses.

34 See B. J. Spooner, "The Function of Religion in Persian Society," *Iran: Journal of the British Institute of Persian Studies*, 1 (1963): 83–93.

35 A recent description of the Shah Ni'matullah Vali Shrine is presented in Roger Stevens, *The Land of the Great Sophy* (1962), pp. 209–11. For the origin and history of the shrine, see Javad Nurbakhsh Kirmani, *Zindigī va Āṣar Quṭbi Ālmūḥdīn Shāh Ni'matullāh Valī Kirmānī* [*The Life and Writings of Shah Ni'matullah Vali of Kirman*] (1958–59).

36 The Shaykhis are discussed at length in Browne (1950), pp. 509–20, 587–89.

37 The *kadkhuda* of Mahan is the overseer for all villages in the Mahan district (*bakhsh*).

38 On a larger scale, this belief led to the establishment of a local Iranian airline from Isfahan to Karbala in Iraq for the sole purpose of transporting dead bodies to the shrine where Husayn, the grandson of Muhammad, was killed in 680 A.D.

39 The public bathhouse is a central institution in Islamic countries; it was borrowed from the *thermae* of the Mediterranean civilizations by the Sassanians and later by the Muslims. See Xavier de Planhol, *The World of Islam* (1959), pp. 9–10, 23.

40 In Kirman City, the *dalak*s traded on the obnoxiousness (in the eyes of their countrymen) of their profession and demanded double wages. They received the increase since no replacements could be found.

41 The association between walled courtyards and the Muslim religion is clear. Wherever Islam has spread, it has brought this structure with it. In Turkish Croatia, for example, Muslim houses are distinguished from all others by the high wooden fences which enclose their courtyards. See G. Marçais, "Salle-antisalle: recherches sur l'évolution d'un thème de l'architecture domestique en pays l'Islam," *Annales de l'Institut d'Études Orientales*, 10 (1952): 274–301; Phanhol (1959), pp. 23–28.

42 V. Sackville-West, "Persian Gardens," in *The Legacy of Persia* (1953), ed. by A. J. Arberry, pp. 259–91.

43 Sykes called this garden Baghi Farman Farma'ian. A photograph of it at the turn of the 20th century, before it fell into ruins, is included in his book. Sykes (1902), pp. 148–50.

44   *Kur* water has the capacity of cleansing any ritually impure (*najis*) element such as a dish on which a dog or a non-Muslim has eaten. In Mahan, the amount of water needed to make the water "sacred" is equivalent to 128 *mann* (873 lbs.) or a volume measuring $3.5 \times 3.5 \times 3.5$ handbreadths. If the volume of the water is less than this specified amount, the impure item turns the water it is placed in impure.

45   The new land distribution law exempts villages where cash wages are paid from distribution. A few landlords have attempted to change from sharecropping contracts to wages in order to preserve their holdings.

46   Opium cultivation and use were banned in Iran in 1955. The problem of crop replacement has been treated in T. J. Tienstra and N. Strand-kjaer, *Opium Poppy Replacement* (*Ostan IX*) (1958). In Kirman, potatoes and sugar beets have been the major replacement crops.

47   The owners of Toujigun claimed that wet years occurred on an average of once every five years, but that this hillside land (*zar'i*) was cultivated about twice every five years.

Chapter 4

1   This contrasts with Lerner's contention that the bus opened new horizons which did not exist previously in village Turkey, specifically in a village *only* four miles away from Ankara. See Daniel Lerner and L. W. Pevsner, *The Passing of Traditional Society: Modernizing the Middle East* (1958), pp. 19–42.

2   A case could be made for independence in the peasant-owned herding and charcoal-burning hamlets of the Kuhi Jupar which rarely house more than ten or twenty people, but nowhere else.

3   In 1965 these offices were abolished in Iran.

4   These data are based on the 1956 National Census of Iran. An effort was made to check them carefully in the field, but the population of Kirman City was too large and diversified to assure complete reliability. The data for Kirman City, then, are less reliable than those for Mahan, Jupar, and other rural settlements. For Mahan Bakhsh, it was possible to acquire the original IBM cards as well as the original village questionnaires. A more detailed occupation breakdown is presented in Appendix F.

5   The stated figure of about 11% is very conservative because it does not include the myriad of unlicensed hawkers and street vendors who form a goodly percentage of those not reported (9.5%) in the Census.

6   Professional gardening used to be done by the Zoroastrians, and many were transported from Yazd and Kirman to tend the large walled gardens of the upper classes in Tehran. See comments in Ella C. Sykes, *Persia and Its People* (1910), p. 122.

7   Small when compared with the unemployment rates in Mahan and Jupar (12.1% and 11.1% respectively of the heads of households). But these figures are somewhat unreliable; see n. 23 below.

8   For a general discussion of social structure in the preindustrial city see Gideon Sjoberg, *The Preindustrial City: Past and Present* (1960), pp. 108–42.

9   Sjoberg describes a bifurcated social structure in preindustrial cities, comprised of the upper class and the commoner group. The growth of a middle class is a recent phenomenon. Ibid., p. 110. See discussions of modern society in Iran in James A. Bill, "The Social and Economic Foundations of Power in Contemporary Iran," *Middle East Journal*, 17 (1963): 400–18; Reza Arasteh, *Man and Society in Iran* (1964), 112–26; Leonard Binder, *Iran: Political Development in a Changing Society* (1964), pp. 164–65; C. A. O. van Nieuwenhuijze, *Social Stratification and the Middle East* (1965), pp. 1–78.

10   The history of the Gypsies is colorful. In the 8th century these people (called Jatt) were transported from the Indus valley to the banks of the Tigris River by the ruling caliph, Walid I. They revolted after their arrival and successfully controlled the Basra-Baghdad highway for a number of years. After their defeat and surrender in 834 A.D., the Gypsies were exiled to northern Iran and the frontiers of Syria. At some later date they migrated to Khurasan and to Kirman, where they have since resided. Percy M. Sykes, *A History of Persia* (1921), 2: 11.

11   See discussions in Reza Arasteh, *Education and Social Awakening in Iran, 1850–1960* (1962), pp. 5–9; T. Cuyler Young, "Interaction of Islamic and Western Thought in Iran," in *Near Eastern Culture and Society* (1951), ed. by T. Cuyler Young, pp. 130–47.

12   Examples of the former include the 'Amiri family, who are descended from a famous 19th-century governor-general of Kirman; the heirs of Aqa Sayyid Haydayat, who own part of the Vakilabad qanat in Mahan; and the Surushian family, who have been leaders of the Zoroastrian community for more than a century. Among the latter are the builders of the new qanats at Hujatabad, Deh Hunari, and Javadieh. Land ownership is discussed further in Appendix E.

13   The village of Kazimabad in the Tigiran valley exists for this reason. In Kazimabad, water from the Langar qanat is used nine days out of an 18-day rotation. The remaining half of the water flows to Langar and is rented for approximately $1,500 worth of wheat and barley. In a good year, Kazimabad produces less than $1,300 worth of wheat and barley, but the owner still retains it.

14   For more detailed discussion see Raymond D. Gastil, "Iranian General Belief Modes as Found in Middle Class Shiraz" (MS, 1958); idem, "Middle Class Impediments to Iranian Modernization," *Public Opinion Quarterly*, 22 (1958): 325–29; Manfred Halpern, *The Politics of Social Change in the Middle East and North Africa* (1963), pp. 51–78.

15   Interest rates on short-term loans in the bazaar range from 12 to 18%. Landlord profits probably amount to 5 or 10% in an average year.

16   The "House of Strength" (*zurkhana*) is a traditional Iranian athletic institution, whose active membership is largely drawn from the middle

class. See description in Reza Arasteh, "The Social Role of the *Zurkhana* (House of Strength) in Iranian Urban Communities in the Nineteenth Century," *Der Islam*, 37 (1961): 256–59.

17   The middle class shopkeeper's emphasis on religion is pragmatic as well as spiritual. Women do most of the shopping in the bazaar. A man above reproach, who attends all ceremonies and prays faithfully (sometimes ostentatiously), is the tradesman whom husbands will encourage their wives to patronize.

18   A general discussion of the guild in Persian city life may be found in Ann K. S. Lambton, *Islamic Society in Persia* (1954), pp. 17–23.

19   This was also true of the cloth merchants of Qazvin, who had among their number Muslims, Jews, and Zoroastrians. Ibid., p. 23.

20   Among the Zoroastrians, for example, the washers of the dead (*nasasalar*s) are barred from social contact with fellow Zoroastrians. Marriage with them is expressly forbidden.

21   Though weavers live in the villages, they cannot purchase staple foods there. The landlord receives 70% of the grain harvest and transports it immediately to the city. The village is usually drained of any salable surplus.

22   Because domestic animals represent their saving accounts, rural families are most reluctant to discuss the number of animals attached to the household.

23   The Census percentages of unemployed in Mahan (12.1%) and Jupar (11.1%) include an undetermined number of seasonal laborers. Because the Census was taken in November, for example, many men who work during the harvest season were listed as unemployed.

24   In articles such as Douglas D. Crary, "The Villager," in *Social Forces in the Middle East* (1955), ed. by Sydney N. Fisher, pp. 43–59.

25   There are no settlements in the field area with populations between 400 and 1,000. Whether this is a local phenomenon or more widespread is uncertain.

Chapter 5

1   See Stirling's comments on the "urban-rural divorce" in central Turkey. Paul Stirling, *Turkish Village* (1965), pp. 266–67.

2   Hence Bobek's use of the term "rent-capitalism" to describe this economic system. Hans Bobek, "Die Hauptstufen der Gesellschafts und Wirtschaftsentfaltung in geographischer Sicht," *Die Erde: Zeitschrift der Gesellschaft für Erdkunde zu Berlin*, 90 (1959): 279–87.

3   Tenant renters, agricultural laborers, and peasant proprietors are also found in Kirman. The renters pay a fixed sum in money or crops for the right to cultivate irrigated land for a specified period of time. Agricultural laborers are hired on an annual basis for a fixed amount of grain, clothing, and food per month or alternatively are drawn from the ranks of the unemployed on a daily basis.

4   The single exception to this rule is the village of Isma'ilabad, where sum-

mer millet and root beets are divided equally between sharecropper and landlord, the rest of the crops 30–70.

5   As one moves up the Tigiran valley, due south of Mahan, the peasant's share of the harvest is progressively higher. In Husaynabad Mahan and Karimabad, the sharecropper receives 30% of the ground crops and 20% of tree crops. At Kazimabad and Toujigun, 30% of both belongs to the peasant. It is only in the highest mountain hamlets (Baharistan, Chashmeh Kush, and Khankistan) that the peasant receives 50% of all crops.

6   An example of this process was the shift of population of Mah Char in 1960 62, which is described below in Chapter 6.

7   In Chashmeh Kush, for instance, a sharecropper cultivated the land for a period of ten years. Each year he was forced to borrow a small amount of grain from the landlord, so that in the tenth year the entire harvest was owing to the landlord. The landlord did not take the harvest, for to do so would mean starvation for the peasant and his household.

8   Pasture dues are usually 50 rials ($.66) per animal per year plus the manure which they produce.

9   In 1956 more than 13,500 goats and 8,500 sheep were grazed on the northern slopes of the Kuhi Jupar. About a quarter of the residents of mountain villages and hamlets are shepherds. More detail is provided in Appendix C.

10   At the two neighboring villages of Abgarm and Roughanu, for example, local graze and facilities were identical. The shepherd of Abgarm (a man with two children) was paid the equivalent of $40 per year, the shepherd of Roughanu (a man with four children) $50, despite the fact that the former cared for a larger herd of animals.

11   In Qudratabad the shepherd receives two of every fifty lambs born to the flock.

12   The dogs do not herd the flock, they simply protect it from predators. Most of these dogs are ugly, vicious animals whose ears and tails have been clipped to make them "alert and courageous," and to prevent them from being pulled down by wolves.

13   The people of Daristan weave this wool and down into hats, gloves, donkeybags, and stockings.

14   Specifically 900 of 1,250 weavers in Mahan Bakhsh (or about 75% of all weavers) were under contract to carpet factories.

15   See Appendix B for a description of the production of a Kirman carpet.

16   This subsidy (*taqdimeh*) may amount to $250. If the weaver stops working, he must return this sum to the carpet firm. This system, therefore, keeps him in debt.

17   Constant surveillance is absolutely necessary. The weaver may fail to tie the knot in the yarn or may tie a double or *jufti* knot (one around four warp strands instead of two), devices that enable him to weave nearly twice as fast. In the former case the design becomes blurred, though the

carpet remains firm; in the latter, the carpet loses density and wearing qualities.

18   Prices paid to the subcontractor range from 170 to 210 *tumans* ($22.66–$28.00) per *zar* for an 80/40 quality carpet (80 warp strands and 40 knots every 7 cm., or 14.5 × 14.5 knots per square inch). The Kirman zar is a standard measure of area for carpets; it equals 112 × 56 cm., which, on an 80/40 quality carpet, equals 204,800 knots. Four qualities of carpets are woven in Kirman: the 70/35 quality (12.7 × 12.7 knots per square inch) for domestic use; the 80/40 quality mentioned above, which is woven for export to the American market; and two higher density rugs woven only on special order.

19   Photographs of this design may be found in A. Cecil Edwards, *The Persian Carpet: A Survey of the Carpet-Weaving Industry of Persia* (1953), pp. 38–40, Plate 21.

20   In 1958 the owners of the Vakilabad qanat held a meeting because the channel of the qanat had been damaged by winter rains. They voted to tax each share of the qanat and a total fund of $1,200 was collected to pay qanat workers for repair and maintenance work. The fund was administered by the water distributor. By 1962 this repair fund had been exhausted, and another meeting was held and a similar decision reached. Though the elite generally dominate these meetings, local residents participate.

21   For a discussion of the duties and payment of water distributors in other parts of Iran see Ann K. S. Lambton, *Landlord and Peasant in Persia* (1953), pp. 123–24, 220–23.

22   In smaller places, sharecroppers determine the distribution of water without the aid of a water distributor, by casting lots on the autumnal equinox. On this date the sharecroppers and small owners of the village gather at an appointed place. They form a circle and at a signal from the village headman cast out any number of fingers on one or two hands. Starting with one farmer, they count around the circle, until they have reached a number equaling the total number of fingers cast. The person at the end of this count receives water on the first hour of the first day of the water rotation. This lottery continues until each man has a definite time when he will receive water. An adjustment is then made to compensate for evaporation during the daylight hours. Thus, if the first farmer receives two hours of flow on a 12-day rotation system, he gets his water in the first two hours after dawn on the first day, the first two hours after dusk on the 13th day, and so on. Since there is no water distributor, each farmer is responsible for the flow of water and maintenance of channels during the period when he is receiving water.

23   Irrigation ditches crisscross the large communal grainfields to divide them into irrigable plots. There is some attempt at equalizing variations in soil and slope conditions; every sharecropper works several small, widely scattered plots: one near the village, one farther out in the fields, and one at the margin of the cultivated area. Because soils deteriorate

with distance from the village, this system, though inefficient and time-consuming, gives each sharecropper a fair proportion of good and poor quality land. In these settlements there is no annual division of the fields into strips as is common in other parts of Iran and the Middle East.

24 For discussion of the duties and payment of crop-watchers in other parts of Iran see Lambton (1953), pp. 342–45.

25 For other descriptions of guilds see Ann K. S. Lambton, *Islamic Society in Persia* (1954), pp. 12–23; Gideon Sjoberg, *The Preindustrial City: Past and Present* (1960), pp. 187–96.

Chapter 6

1 The evidence from Kirman supports Rhoads Murphey's thesis that the non-Western provincial city has not been a center of change. See Rhoads Murphey, "The City as a Center of Change: Western Europe and China," *Annals of the Association of American Geographers*, 44 (1954): 349–62.

2 The concentration of this group in Tehran is clearly pointed out in James A. Bill, "The Social and Economic Foundations of Power in Contemporary Iran," *Middle East Journal*, 17 (1963): 407–18.

3 Alberts argues persuasively that such changes are occurring in the Garmsar area south of Tehran. Robert C. Alberts, *Social Structure and Culture Change in an Iranian Village* (1963), pp. 946–99.

4 This theme is developed more fully in Paul Ward English, "Culture Change and the Structure of a Persian City," in *The Conflict of Traditionalism and Modernism in the Muslim Middle East*, ed. by Carl Leiden [in press].

5 Julian H. Steward, *Theory of Culture Change* (1955), pp. 36–39.

6 See discussion in Gideon Sjoberg, *The Preindustrial City: Past and Present* (1960), pp. 157–63.

7 B. J. Spooner, "The Function of Religion in Persian Society," *Iran: Journal of the British Institute of Persian Studies*, 1 (1963): 83–93.

8 The *maktab* is discussed more fully in Reza Arasteh, *Education and Social Awakening in Iran, 1850–1960* (1962), pp. 5–7.

9 The impact of these forces on Iranian marriage and kinship patterns is further discussed in Alberts (1963), pp. 964–72; Reza Arasteh, *Man and Society in Iran* (1964), pp. 137–47.

10 Conflict created by this decrease in prestige and power is described in R. K. Ramazani, " 'Church' and State in Modernizing Society: The Case of Iran," *American Behavioral Scientist*, 7 (1964): 26–28.

11 The progress in public health during the reign of Riza Shah is discussed in Amin Banani, *The Modernization of Iran, 1921–1941* (1961), pp. 62–67.

12 Frederic J. Goldsmid, *Telegraph and Travel* (1874), pp. 582–83.

13 A. H. Gleadowe-Newcomen, *Report on the British Indian Commercial Mission to South-Eastern Persia during 1904–1905* (1906), pp. 49–50; E. Fevret, "Le Groupement des centres habités en Perse d'après la nature du sol," *Revue du monde musulman*, 2 (1907): 198.

14 Government of Iran, *First Census of Iran: November 1956* (1961), 1: 252.

15 Gleadowe-Newcomen (1906), p. 149.

16 One-twelfth of the water supply of Shahabad was rented for 40,000 rials ($533.33) a year for a period of eight years.

17 In 1952 Beckett noted that the landlords of Kirman were failing to maintain qanat tunnels and were sending money abroad to guard against a collapse in government. See Philip H. T. Beckett, "Persia's Need for Land Reform," *Fortnightly Review*, 171 (1952): 103.

18 The qualifying adjective "European" is necessary; these windmills are different from the horizontal windmills used in western Afghanistan. Horizontal windmills were used in Kirman, as notations on British India Survey maps and Sykes' map show; but because of light and variable winds in the basin, windmills were not a major source of irrigation water. European windmills were introduced into Kirman after World War II by Jamshid Faruhar, a Zoroastrian landlord of Kirman. See Klaus Ferdinand, "The Horizontal Windmills of Western Afghanistan," *Folk*, 5 (1963): 71–89; Percy M. Sykes, *Ten Thousand Miles in Persia or Eight Years in Iran* (1902), facing p. 188.

19 The comparative advantages and disadvantages of deep well and qanat irrigation are discussed in Overseas Consultants, *Report on the Seven Year Development Plan for the Plan Organization of the Imperial Government of Iran*, 3 (1949): 149–51; US AID/Iran, "Agricultural Feasibility of Deep-Well Irrigation" (MS, 1962), pp. 1–28.

20 It is difficult to evaluate the impact of this exemption. Most local landlords are deeply antagonistic toward the government and suspect the worst. Some believe that the government is attempting to encourage investment in deep wells so that at some later time it can take the land and the well from the owner.

21 Expansion of settlement and increased population pressure on land in the mountains are occurring in other parts of Iran as well. See Xavier de Planhol, "Pressione demografica e vita di montagna nella Persia settentrionale, *Bollettino della Società Geografica Italiana*, 1 (1960): 90–96.

22 Before the revolution of 1906, these hamlets (*mazra'eh*) were taxed as integral parts of parent villages on the plain. See Ann K. S. Lambton, *Landlord and Peasant in Persia* (1953), p. 4, n. 2.

23 The 1956 statistics are from the National Iranian Census, those of 1960 from the Malaria Office survey, and those of 1962 from field notes.

24 Philip H. T. Beckett, "Agriculture in Central Persia," *Tropical Agriculture*, 34 (1957): 21.

25 The impact of the Opium Law on another dry province of the Central Plateau of Iran, Khurasan, is the subject of an FAO report. See T. J. Tienstra and N. Strandkjaer, *Opium Poppy Replacement (Ostan IX)* (1958).

26 Hauser discusses the Afghan plow in these terms. See G. F. Hauser, "Comparison of the Afghan Plough and Tillage Practices with Modern

Implements and Methods," *Empire Journal of Experimental Agriculture*, 23 (1955): 75–80.

27 Undoubtedly pastures were better thirty years ago, but in view of the fact that flocks have been grazing near Mahan and Jupar for some sixteen centuries, this statement seems exaggerated. The villagers insist however that it is true.

28 In 1948 Edwards estimated that half the knots being woven in Kirman were defective. See A. Cecil Edwards, *The Persian Carpet: A Survey of the Carpet-Weaving Industry of Persia* (1953), pp. 210–11.

29 See descriptions for earlier periods in Edward Stack, *Six Months in Persia* (1882), 1: 209–11; Edward G. Browne, *A Year amongst the Persians* (1950), pp. 482–83.

Chapter 7

1 On a broader level, when Coon selects the nine Middle Eastern cities which can be considered "historically and geographically paramount" — Fez, Tunis, Cairo, Istanbul, Damascus, Baghdad, Isfahan, Tabriz, and Mashhad — he notes that all are coordinating centers for major agricultural regions. Carleton S. Coon, *Caravan: The Story of the Middle East* (1958), pp. 230–31.

2 Robert C. Alberts, *Social Structure and Culture Change in an Iranian Village* (1963), p. 1038.

3 John Gulick, *Social Structure and Culture Change in a Lebanese Village* (1955), pp. 56–59.

4 Alberts (1963), pp. 12–14.

5 Robert Redfield, *Peasant Society and Culture* (1960).

6 Ibid., p. 19.

7 A. L. Kroeber, *Anthropology* (1948), p. 284.

8 Also a major characteristic of Syrian villages. See Louise Sweet, *Tell Toqaan: A Syrian Village* (1960), pp. 228–30.

9 Horace Miner, "The Folk-Urban Continuum," *American Sociological Review*, 17 (1952): 529–37; idem, *The Primitive City of Timbuctoo* (1953), pp. 275–80. But see criticisms in George M. Foster, "What is Folk Culture?", *American Anthropologist*, 55 (1953): 159–73; Oscar Lewis and Philip M. Hauser, "The Folk-Urban Ideal Types," in *The Study of Urbanization*, pp. 491–517, ed. by Philip M. Hauser and Leo F. Schnore (1965).

10 See discussion in Raymond D. Gastil, "Iranian General Belief Modes as Found in Middle Class Shiraz" (MS, 1958); idem, "Middle Class Impediments to Iranian Modernization," *Public Opinion Quarterly*, 22 (1958): 325–29; Manfred Halpern, *The Politics of Social Change in the Middle East and North Africa* (1963), pp. 51–78; Morroe Berger, *The Arab World Today* (1964), pp. 249–58; C. A. O. van Nieuwenhuijze, *Social Stratification and the Middle East* (1965), pp. 12–27.

11 Reza Arasteh, *Man and Society in Iran* (1964), pp. 120–26; Leonard Binder, *Iran: Political Development in a Changing Society* (1964), pp. 164–65.

Appendix A

1   The exception is high in the mountains, where small patches of unirrigated land are tilled.

2   This is true of all qanats because they are infiltration systems, but seasonal variation is particularly marked in mountain hamlets, whose qanats tap surface water deposits.

3   W. D. Shrader, "Report to the Kerman Development Corporation on Agricultural Development of Kerman Region" (MS, 1958), pp. 3, 13; Kerman Development Corporation, *Initial Report on a Program for the Economic Development of the Kerman Region* (1959), pp. 13–14.

4   Kevin M. Carroll, "USOM to Iran, Kerman-Baluchistan Provincial Office: Project Accomplishments to January 1957" (MS, 1957), p. 8.

5   The two wheats principally grown in the Kirman Basin are the common breadwheat (*Triticum aestivum*) and durum wheat (*Triticum durum*). The distribution of wheat in Iran is discussed in Hermann Kuckuck, *Distribution and Variation of Cereals in Iran (Including Their Related Wild Species)* (1956), pp. 6–12.

6   These figures refer to the 60-pound bushel which is used for wheat, potatoes, peas, and melons. *Mann/qasab* can be converted to bu./acre by the formula 17.754 mann/qasab equal X bu./acre. Hereafter only the bu./acre figure is noted.

7   Shrader estimates the average wheat yield at 19 bu./acre. Beckett mentions a figure of 700–1,000 lb./acre (12–17 bu./acre). Shrader (1958), p. 11; Philip H. T. Beckett, "Agriculture in Central Persia," *Tropical Agriculture*, 34 (1957): 21.

8   When compared, for example, with Lambton's figures for irrigated wheat in other parts of Iran. Ann K. S. Lambton, *Landlord and Peasant in Persia* (1953), pp. 364–65.

9   The 56-pound bushel is used for barley. Conversion to bushels per acre can be achieved by the formula 19.074 mann/qasab equal X bu./acre. Hereafter only the bu./acre figure is noted.

10   See note 6 above.

11   Theoretically, the price is 1,300 rials ($17.33) per metric ton, but 300 rials ($4) is automatically deducted for transportation costs.

12   A great deal has been written about the nail plow in Iran and other parts of the Middle East. See B. A. Keen, *The Agricultural Development of the Middle East* (1946), pp. 51ff.; A. Muir, "Notes on the Soils of Syria," *Journal of Soil Science*, 2 (1951): 182, Plates II, III, V; G. F. Hauser, "Comparison of the Afghan Plough and Tillage Practices with Modern Implements and Methods," *Empire Journal of Experimental Agriculture*, 23 (1955): 75–80; Beckett, "Agriculture in Central Persia," *Tropical Agriculture*, 34 (1957): 9–28; idem, "Tools and Crafts in South Central Persia," *Man*, 57 (1957): 145–48; Hassan Ali Ronaghy, "Agricultural Problems in Iran" (MS, 1962), pp. 46–47.

13   *Rindeh* literally means "planer" or "grater" and is used locally as a term for both the harrow and a hand-weeding implement.

14 A picture of a *panjeh* in use at the turn of the century can be found in Isaac Adams, *Persia by a Persian* (1900), p. 154.
15 Tractors plow the land to spade depth at a price of $26.67 per hectare. This is so expensive that most tractors plow only to a depth of 12 to 15 inches at a cost of $16 per hectare.
16 Fallow land is colloquially called *"valish kun,"* meaning "we leave it alone."
17 This coincides with Beckett's earlier observation that farmers in Jupar disagreed on whether alfalfa helped or harmed the soil. Beckett, "Agriculture in Central Persia," *Tropical Agriculture,* 34 (1957): 24–25.
18 According to the pharmacist (who was also the fertilizer salesman) in Jupar, 3,000 kg. of chemical fertilizer was sold in Jupar in 1962.
19 Nouredin N. Mohensin, "Mechanization of Agriculture in Iran" (MS, 1953), p. 119; Ronaghy (1962), pp. 63–65.

Appendix B

1 For centuries Kirman Province was the major producer of indigo in Asia, and indigo was exported from the city to India and China for use as a blue dye. Until thirty years ago it was still a major export product of the region. See anonymous, *Ḥudūd al-'Alam (The Regions of the World): A Persian Geography 372 A.H./982 A.D.,* trans. by V. Minorsky (1937), pp. 123–25, 373–76; Berthold Laufer, "Sino-Iranica: Chinese Contributions to the History of Civilization in Ancient Iran," *Field Museum of Natural History, Anthropological Series,* 15 (1919): 370–71.
2 Small quantities of madder are still shipped from Kirman to Shiraz. In the past, madder was exported from Kirman to Russia via Tabriz and to India. A. H. Gleadowe-Newcomen, *Report on the British Indian Commercial Mission to South-Eastern Persia during 1904–1905* (1906), p. 86.
3 In important secondary weaving centers such as Mahan, Jupar, and Ravar, there are entrepreneurs who control varying numbers of spinners in the same fashion as weaving subcontractors.
4 The exchange rate at that time was 55 rials to the dollar. It is now 75. A. Cecil Edwards, *The Persian Carpet: A Survey of the Carpet-Weaving Industry of Persia* (1953), p. 204.
5 In other weaving centers the weavers clip the yarn after each knot is made and thereby save wool. Clipping in one operation after weaving produces a more even pile.

Appendix C

1 In 1956, therefore, most of the estimated 1,100 cattle in the Kuhi Jupar settlements were owned by agriculturalists. All animal statistics in this chapter are based on unpublished materials from the 1956 Census of Iran. Their reliability could not be measured in the field.
2 Castrated cattle are rare in Kirman but are widely used for plowing in

Mashhad. T. J. Tienstra and N. Strandkjaer, *Opium Poppy Replacement (Ostan IX)* (1958), pp. 18–19.

3   For figures on milk production in other parts of Iran see ibid., pp. 18–20; Robert C. Alberts, *Social Structure and Culture Change in an Iranian Village* (1963), pp. 450–57.

4   Donkey meat is eaten by the poorest classes, but it is not favored by anyone. The right side of a donkey, according to Islamic law, may be eaten freely (it is legal or *hallal*). The left side is not eaten by a pious Muslim. Donkey milk is sometimes used unboiled in the villages, but is never sold in the marketplace.

5   In 1956 there were more than 1,800 donkeys on the northern slopes of the Kuhi Jupar. By contrast, only 26 camels, 23 mules, and 12 horses were reported.

6   Cattle and donkeys do not contribute fertilizer. Their dung is collected, molded into cakes, dried in the sun, and burned as cooking fuel.

7   On the northern slopes of the Kuhi Jupar, in 1956, approximately 13,500 goats and 8,500 sheep grazed on local pastures.

8   Among some tribes in the Zagros, suckling is prevented by holding the lamb's or kid's tongue down with a stick rather than by covering the udder. Fredrik Barth, *Nomads of South Persia: The Basseri Tribe of the Khamseh Confederacy* (1961), p. 7.

Appendix D

1   E. Noel, "Qanats," *Journal of the Royal Central Asian Society*, 31 (1944): 192.

2   Farhad Ghahraman, *The Right of Use and Economics of Irrigation Water in Iran* (1958), pp. 44–45; Henri Goblot, "Le Problème de l'eau en Iran" *Orient*, 23 (1962): 50.

3   George B. Cressey, "Qanats, Karez, and Foggaras," *Geographical Review*, 48 (1958): 38–40. An average qanat discharges 20–30 liters per second. The aggregate length estimate includes an additional 8,500 abandoned qanats.

4   The Arabic word qanat means "conduit" or "lance"; it is used in Iran specifically to refer to the subterranean "horizontal wells" described above. *Kariz*, the Persian term, is used throughout Southwest Asia, while in North Africa *foggara* is the most common term.

5   Johannes Humlum, "L'Agriculture par irrigation en Afghanistan," *Comptes rendus du Congrès International de Géographie, Lisbon 1949*, 3 (1951): 318–28.

6   C. W. Carlston, "Irrigation Practices in the Quetta-Pishin District of Baluchistan, Pakistan," *Annals of the Association of American Geographers*, 43 (1953): 160.

7   Aurel Stein, "Note on a Map of the Turfan Basin," *Geographical Journal*, 82 (1933): 236–46; L. W. Golab, "A Study of Irrigation in East Turkestan," *Anthropos*, 46 (1951): 187–99. These qanats are dug only by Turki people, never by Chinese.

8   C. E. N. Bromehead, "The Early History of Water-Supply," *Geographical Journal*, 99 (1942): 195–96.

9   W. A. MacFadyen, "Water Supplies in Iraq," *Iraq Geological Publications*, No. 1 (1938).

10   Cressey (1958), p. 42.

11   The importance of qanat irrigation to the existence of settlement in this area is a dramatic theme in the novel by Hammond Innes, *The Doomed Oasis* (1960).

12   Pierre Troussu, "Les Retharas de Marrakech," *France-Maroc*, 3 (1919): 246–49; P. Fenelon, "L'Irrigation dans le Haouz de Marrakech," *Bulletin de l'Association de Géographes Français*, 18 (1941): 63–70.

13   L. Voinot, "Le Tidikelt: étude sur la géographie, l'histoire, et les moeurs du pays," *Bulletin de la Société de Géographie et d'Archéologie d'Oran*, 29 (1909): 185–216, 311–66, 419–80; C. Lo, "Les Foggaras du Tidikelt," *Travaux de l'Institut des Recherches Sahariennes*, 10 (1953): 139–81; 11 (1954): 49–79.

14   A. T. Olmstead, *History of the Persian Empire* (1948), pp. 223–24.

15   Isaiah Bowman, *Desert Trails of the Atacama* (1924), pp. 19–22. Qanats may have been in the New World in pre-Columbian times; the question merits further study.

16   This process of establishing grade was not observed in the field but has been described in Philip H. T. Beckett, "Qanats around Kirman," *Journal of the Royal Central Asian Society*, 40 (1953): 48.

17   F. H. Kocks K.G., *Rural Development Plan, South Khorassan: Preliminary Study* (1959), p. 29.

18   The laborers receive only 40 rials ($.53) each per day; the remainder goes to the muqanni and his apprentice. All 1962 figures were converted from rials to dollars at the bank rate of 75 to the dollar. A team may be composed of anywhere from four to seven men.

19   Beckett (1953), p. 49.

20   Noel (1944), p. 198. The diagram illustrating this structure has been printed upside down.

Appendix E

1   Land without water has limited value in Kirman; thus ownership of cultivated land is measured in shares of water. Ownership of land and water is indivisible. The share in the water supply, the land on which it is used, and rights derived from ownership (e.g. pasture rights) are all treated as a unit and are written into deeds of ownership. A piece of land or a share in the water supply is rented separately only when a flood or dust storm has ruined one or the other, making it impossible to use them together. Units of measure therefore refer to land and water synonymously.

2   Hasan Arsanjani, "Land Ownership," *Etelaat Havaie*, No. 3660 (1962), p. 1.

3   The term *khurdeh malik* (literally "small owner") is used for small

nonfarmer owners whether resident or nonresident. It excludes peasant proprietors. The term *arbabi* is used for large absentee landlords.

4   These figures are rough averages. It was impossible to determine the total cultivated area in the field.

5   Thus one share of the Vakilabad qanat rents for 225 kg. of wheat and 750 rials ($10) per year, one share of the Tigiran qanat for 240 kg. of wheat, and one share of the Saniabad branch of the Tigiran qanat for 300 kg. of wheat. These rental rates amount to 3–4% of the capital value of each share.

6   Discussion of endowed land elsewhere in Iran and the Middle East can be found in Seymour G. Vesey-FitzGerald, *Muhammadan Law: An Abridgement according to Its Various Schools* (1931), pp. 206 ff.; Ann K. S. Lambton, *Landlord and Peasant in Persia* (1953), pp. 230–37; Asaf A. A. Fyzee, *Outlines of Muhammadan Law* (1955), pp. 231–82.

7   In some cases vaqf properties are devoted to very specific purposes. Carleton Coon mentions some which "are designated for special duties, like the waqf for putting baby storks back in their nests in Turkey, or that for feeding pigeons in Fez — the point being that the pigeons defecate on the university buildings, and the students collect the droppings and sell them to the tanners, this waqf constituting a form of student aid." Carleton S. Coon, *Caravan: The Story of the Middle East* (1958), p. 126.

8   Usually the initiator of the endowment appoints a second official (*nazir izhari*) to oversee the mutavalli and prevent misuse of the resource or embezzlement of its revenues.

9   In 1953 the declared capital value of the vaqf properties administered by the Education Office of Mahan was $117,234. They were rented for a total of $1,992, or 1.7% of the declared capital value. Only $916, then, was actually utilized for the charitable purposes intended by the founders. Figures computed on the basis of the 1951 exchange rate of 32 rials to the dollar.

10 These data on changing ownership in the Kirman Basin were collected in the field.

11 It was impossible to check ownership changes in the towns of Mahan and Jupar; hence these figures are very tentative.

12 Property is distributed among heirs on the basis of blood or for special cause; each male receives two shares, each female of the same degree one.

Bibliography

Adams, Isaac. *Persia by a Persian*. Washington: Privately published, 1900.

Al-Ahmad, Jalal. *Āvrāzān: Vaẓ' Maḥal-Ādāb va Rasūm-Fulklūr-Lahjeh.* (*Owrazan: Topography, Ceremonies and Customs, Folklore, and Dialect.*) Tehran: Danesh Bookstore, 1954.

Alberts, Robert C. *Social Structure and Culture Change in an Iranian Village*. Ann Arbor: University Microfilms, 1963.

Ammianus Marcellinus. *The Roman History of Ammianus Marcellinus*, trans. by C. D. Yonge. London: H. G. Bohn, 1862.

Anonymous. *Ḥudūd al-'Alam (The Regions of the World): A Persian Geography 372 A.H./982 A.D.*, trans. by V. Minorsky. London: Luzac and Co., 1937. (E. J. W. Gibb Memorial, New Series, Vol. 9.)

Arasteh, Reza. "The Social Role of the *Zurkhana* (House of Strength) in Iranian Urban Communities in the Nineteenth Century," *Der Islam*, 37 (1961): 256–59.

————. *Education and Social Awakening in Iran, 1850–1960*. Leiden: E. J. Brill, 1962.

————. *Man and Society in Iran*. Leiden: E. J. Brill, 1964.

Arberry, A. J., ed. *The Legacy of Persia*. Oxford: Clarendon Press, 1953.

Arsanjani, Hasan. "Land Ownership," *Etelaat Havaie*, No. 3660 (1962), pp. 1–2.

Bacon, Elizabeth E. "A Preliminary Attempt to Determine the Culture Areas of Asia," *Southwestern Journal of Anthropology*, 2 (1946): 117–32.

Baer, Gabriel. *Population and Society in the Arab East*. London: Routledge and Kegan Paul, 1964.

Banani, Amin. *The Modernization of Iran, 1921–1941*. Stanford: Stanford University Press, 1961.

Banfield, A. F., and Clarke, V. H. "Mineral Resources of the Kirman Region, Iran," *Twenty-First International Geological Congress*, 20 (1960): 74–85.

Barth, Fredrik. *Principles of Social Organization in Southern Kurdistan*. Oslo: Universitats Etnografiske Museum, 1953.

————. *Nomads of South Persia: The Basseri Tribe of the Khamseh Confederacy*. London: George Allen and Unwin, 1961.

181

Bauer, G. "Luftzirkulation und Niederschlagverhältnisse in Vorderasien," *Gerlands Beiträge zur Geophysik*, 35 (1935): 381–548.

Beckett, Philip H. T. "Waters of Persia," *Geographical Magazine*, 24 (1951): 230–40.

———. "Qanats in Persia," *Journal of the Iran Society*, 1 (1952): 125 et seq.

———. "Persia's Need for Land Reform," *Fortnightly Review*, 171 (1952): 100–104.

———. "Qanats around Kirman," *Journal of the Royal Central Asian Society*, 40 (1953): 47–58.

———. "Agriculture in Central Persia," *Tropical Agriculture*, 34 (1957): 9–28.

———. "Tools and Crafts in South Central Persia," *Man*, 57 (1957): 145–48.

———. "The Soils of Kerman, South Persia," *Journal of Soil Science*, 9 (1958): 20–32.

Beckett, Philip H. T., and Gordon, E. D. "The Climate of Kerman, South Persia," *Quarterly Journal of the Royal Meteorological Society*, 82 (1956): 503–14.

Berger, Morroe, ed. *The New Metropolis in the Arab World*. New Delhi: Allied Publishers, 1963.

———. *The Arab World Today*. Garden City, N.Y.: Doubleday and Co., 1964.

Berry, Brian J. L., and Pred, Allen. *Central Place Studies: A Bibliography of Theory and Applications*. Philadelphia: Regional Science Research Institute, 1965.

Bill, James A. "The Social and Economic Foundations of Power in Contemporary Iran," *Middle East Journal*, 17 (1963): 400–418.

Binder, Leonard. *Iran: Political Development in a Changing Society*. Berkeley and Los Angeles: University of California Press, 1964.

Blanchard, Raoul. "L'Iran," *Géographie universelle*, Vol. 8, *Asie occidentale*. Paris: Librairie Armand Colin, 1929, pp. 128–70.

Bobek, Hans. "Die natürlichen Wälder und Gehölzfluren Irāns," *Bonner geographische Abhandlungen*, 8 (1951): 1–62.

———. "Die klimaökologische Gliederung von Iran," *Proceedings, International Geographical Union*, VIIIth General Assembly, XVIIth Congress, 1952, pp. 244–48.

———. "Klima und Landschaft Irans in vor- und frühgeschichtlicher Zeit," *Geographischer Jahresbericht aus Österreich*, 25 (1953–54): 1–42.

———. "Die Hauptstufen der Gesellschafts und Wirtschaftsentfaltung in geographischer Sicht," *Die Erde: Zeitschrift der Gesellschaft für Erdkunde zu Berlin*, 90 (1959): 259–98. Translated as "The Main Stages in Socio-Economic Evolution from a Geographical Point of View," in *Readings in Cultural Geography*, pp. 218–47, ed. by Philip L. Wagner and Marvin W. Mikesell. Chicago: University of Chicago Press, 1961.

Bowman, Isaiah. *Desert Trails of the Atacama*. New York: American Geographical Society, 1924.

Bromehead, C. E. N. "The Early History of Water-Supply," *Geographical Journal*, 99 (1942): 183–96.

Browne, Edward G. *A Year amongst the Persians: Impressions as to the Life, Character, and Thought of the People of Persia Received during Twelve Months' Residence in That Country in the Years 1887–1888.* London: Adam and Charles Black, 1950.

Buttler, Millard A. "Irrigation in Persia by Kanat," *Civil Engineering*, 3 (1933): 69–73.

Cambridge Ancient History, Vol. 9. Cambridge: University Press, 1932.

Caponera, Dante. *Water Laws in Moslem Countries.* Rome: Food and Agriculture Organization, 1954. (Development Paper No. 43.)

Carlston, C. W. "Irrigation Practices in the Quetta-Pishin District of Baluchistan, Pakistan," *Annals of the Association of American Geographers*, 43 (1953): 160.

Carroll, Kevin M. "USOM to Iran, Kerman-Baluchistan Provincial Office: Project Accomplishments to January 1957." Kerman: Unpublished manuscript, 1957.

Christensen, Arthur. *L'Iran sous les Sassanides.* Copenhagen: Ejnar Munksgaard, 1944.

Clapp, F. G. "Geology of Eastern Iran," *Bulletin of the Geological Society of America*, 51 (1940): 1–102.

Clarke, John I. *The Iranian City of Shiraz.* Durham: Department of Geography, University of Durham, England, 1963. (Research Papers Series, No. 7.)

Coon, Carleton S. *Caravan: The Story of the Middle East.* New York: Henry Holt and Co., 1958.

Crary, Douglas D. "The Villager," in *Social Forces in the Middle East*, pp. 43–59, ed. by Sydney N. Fisher. Ithaca: Cornell University Press, 1955.

Cressey, George B. "Qanats, Karez, and Foggaras," *Geographical Review*, 48 (1958): 27–44.

Cruttenden, Arnold. *Statistical Returns Showing Total Number of Transport Animals Going In and Coming Out of Kerman and Bam, April 1–June 30, 1920.* London: Foreign Office and Board of Trade, Ref. No. D.O.T. 923/FE/20, 1920.

Dennett, D. C. *Conversion and the Poll Tax in Early Islam.* Cambridge: Harvard University Press, 1950. (Harvard Historical Monographs, XXII.)

Dhalla, Maneckji N. *History of Zoroastrianism.* New York: Oxford University Press, 1938.

Donaldson, Bess Allen. *The Wild Rue: A Study of Muhammadan Magic and Folklore in Iran.* London: Luzac and Co., 1938.

Edwards, A. Cecil. *The Persian Carpet: A Survey of the Carpet-Weaving Industry of Persia.* London: G. Duckworth and Co., 1953.

English, Paul Ward. "Culture Change and the Structure of a Persian City," in *The Conflict of Traditionalism and Modernism in the Muslim Middle East*, ed. by Carl Leiden. Austin: University of Texas Press [in press].

Epistles of Manuskihar: see West, E. W., trans.

Feilberg, C. G. *La Tente noire.* Copenhagen: Nationalmuseets København, 1944.

Fenelon, P. "L'Irrigation dans le Haouz de Marrakech," *Bulletin de l'Association de Géographes Français,* 18 (1941): 63–70.

Ferdinand, Klaus. "The Horizontal Windmills of Western Afghanistan," *Folk,* 5 (1963): 71–89.

Fevret, E. "Le Groupement des centres habités en Perse d'après la nature du sol," *Revue du monde musulman,* 2 (1907): 181–98.

F. H. Kocks K.G. *Rural Development Plan, South Khorassan: Preliminary Study.* Tehran: F. H. Kocks K.G., Consulting Engineers, 1959.

Fischel, Walter J. "Secret Jews of Persia," *Commentary,* 7 (1949): 28–33.

Fisher, Sydney N., ed. *Social Forces in the Middle East.* Ithaca: Cornell University Press, 1955.

Fitt, R. L. "Irrigation Development in Central Persia," *Journal of the Royal Central Asian Society,* 40 (1953): 124–33.

Foster, George M. "What Is Folk Culture?" *American Anthropologist,* 55 (1953): 159–73.

Fryer, John. *A New Account of East India and Persia, Being Nine Years' Travel: 1672–1681,* ed. by William Crooke. London: Hakluyt Society, 1909, 1912, 1915. (Hakluyt Society, Second Series, Vols. 19, 20, 39.)

Fyzee, Asaf A. A. *Outlines of Muhammadan Law.* London: Oxford University Press, 1955.

Ganji, M. H. "The Climates of Iran," *Bulletin de la Société de Géographie d'Égypte,* 28 (1955): 195–299.

Garrod, Oliver. "The Qashqai Tribe of Fars," *Journal of the Royal Central Asian Society,* 33 (1946): 293–306.

Gastil, Raymond D. "Iranian General Belief Modes as Found in Middle Class Shiraz." Cambridge: Unpublished Ph.D. dissertation, Harvard University, 1958.

————. "Middle Class Impediments to Iranian Modernization," *Public Opinion Quarterly,* 22 (1958): 325–29.

Ghahraman, Farhad. *The Right of Use and Economics of Irrigation Water in Iran.* Ann Arbor: University Microfilms, 1958.

Gibb, H. A. R., and Kramers, J. H., eds. *Shorter Encyclopaedia of Islam.* London: Luzac and Co., 1961.

Gleadowe-Newcomen, A. H. *Report on the British Indian Commercial Mission to South-Eastern Persia during 1904–1905.* Calcutta: Office of the Superintendent of Government Printing, India, 1906.

Goblot, Henri. "Le Problème de l'eau en Iran," *Orient,* 23 (1962): 43–60.

————. "Dans l'ancien Iran, les techniques de l'eau et la grande histoire," *Annales: économies-sociétés-civilisations,* 18 (1963): 499–520.

Golab, L. W. "A Study of Irrigation in East Turkestan," *Anthropos,* 46 (1951): 187–99.

Goldsmid, Frederic J. *Telegraph and Travel.* London: Macmillan and Co., 1874.

————, ed. *Eastern Persia, an Account of the Journeys of the Persian Boundary Commission*. London: Macmillan and Co., 1876. 2 vols.

Government of Iran. *Census District Statistics of the First National Census of Iran, Aban 1335 (November 1956)*, Vol. 17, *Zarand and Kerman Census Districts*, Part 1, *Kerman*. Tehran: Department of Public Statistics, Ministry of Interior, Government of Iran, 1960.

————. *First Census of Iran: November 1956*, Vol. 1, *Number and Distribution of the Inhabitants for Iran and the Census Provinces*. Tehran: Department of Public Statistics, Ministry of Interior, Government of Iran, 1961.

Greenwell, C. "Notes on a Collection of Bronze Weapons, Implements, and Vessels Found at Khinamān," *Journal of the Royal Anthropological Institute*, 37 (1907): 196–200.

Grunebaum, G. E. von. *Islam: Essays in the Nature and Growth of a Cultural Tradition*. London: Routledge and Kegan Paul, 1955.

Gulick, John. *Social Structure and Culture Change in a Lebanese Village*. New York: Wenner-Gren Foundation, 1955. (Viking Fund Publications in Anthropology, No. 21.)

————, ed. "Dimensions of Cultural Change in the Middle East," *Human Organization*, 24 (1965): 1–104.

Halpern, Manfred. *The Politics of Social Change in the Middle East and North Africa*. Princeton: Princeton University Press, 1963.

Hamdan, G. "The Growth and Functional Structure of Khartoum," *Geographical Review*, 50 (1960): 21–40.

Hanessian, John. "Yosouf-abad, an Iranian Village," *American Universities Field Staff Reports, Southwest Asia Series*, Vol. 12 (1963), Nos. 1–6.

Hauser, G. F. "Comparison of the Afghan Plough and Tillage Practices with Modern Implements and Methods," *Empire Journal of Experimental Agriculture*, 23 (1955): 75–80.

Hauser, Philip M., and Schnore, Leo F., eds. *The Study of Urbanization*. New York: John Wiley and Sons, 1965.

Heichelheim, F. M. "Effects of Classical Antiquity on the Land," in *Man's Role in Changing the Face of Earth*, pp. 165–82, ed. by William L. Thomas. Chicago: University of Chicago Press, 1956.

Herodotus. *The History of Herodotus*, trans. by George Rawlinson and ed. by Manuel Komroff. New York: Tudor Publishing Co., 1956.

Hooper, David, and Field, Henry. "Useful Plants and Drugs of Iran and Iraq," *Field Museum of Natural History, Botanical Series*, 9 (1937): 73–241.

Houtum-Schindler, A. "Notes on Marco Polo's Itinerary in Southern Persia," *Journal of the Royal Asiatic Society*, New Series, 13 (1881): 490–97.

Humlum, Johannes. "L'Agriculture par irrigation en Afghanistan," *Comptes rendus du Congrès International de Géographie, Lisbon 1949*, 3 (1951): 318–28.

————. "Underjordiske Vandingskanaler: Kareze, Qanat, Foggara," *Skrifter Fra Geografisk Institut* [Ved Århus Universitet], 16 (1965): 81–132.

Iliffe, J. H. "Persia and the Ancient World," in *The Legacy of Persia*, pp. 1–38, ed. by A. J. Arberry. Oxford: Clarendon Press, 1953.

Innes, Hammond. *The Doomed Oasis*. New York: Alfred A. Knopf, 1960.

Iranian Meteorological Department. *Meteorological Yearbook of Iran, 1956, 1957, 1958,* and *1959.* Tehran: Climatological Branch, Iranian Meteorological Department, Ministry of Roads, 1958, 1960, 1961, 1962.

Jackson, A. V. Williams. *Persia Past and Present*. New York: Macmillan and Co., 1906.

Jennings, George J. "A Development Project and Culture Change in an Iranian Village," *Proceedings of the Minnesota Academy of Science*, 25–26 (1957–58): 309–25.

———. "Economy and Integration in a Changing Iranian Village," ibid., 28 (1960): 112–19.

Jones, Richard G. "Sheep Industry in Iran." Tehran: Unpublished manuscript [1961].

Keen, B. A. *The Agricultural Development of the Middle East*. London: Her Majesty's Stationery Office, 1946.

Kerman Development Corporation. *Initial Report on a Program for the Economic Development of the Kerman Region*. Tehran: Kerman Development Corporation, 1959.

———. *Property Report Supplement to Report of Mineral Reconnaissance, Kerman Region, Iran*. New York: Behre Dolbear and Co., 1959.

Kernan, H. S. "Forest Management in Iran," *Middle East Journal*, 11 (1957): 199–202.

Kirmani, Javad Nurbakhsh, *Zindigī va Āṣar Quṭbi Ālmūḥdīn Shāh Niʿmatullāh Valī Kirmānī*. [*The Life and Writings of Shah Niʿmatullah Vali of Kirman*.] Tehran: Musui Press, 1958–59.

Kolars, John F. *Tradition, Season, and Change in a Turkish Village*. Chicago: Department of Geography, University of Chicago, 1963. (Research Paper No. 82.)

Kroeber, A. L. *Anthropology*. New York: Harcourt, Brace, and Co., 1948.

Kuckuck, Hermann. *Distribution and Variation of Cereals in Iran* (*Including Their Related Wild Species*). Rome: Food and Agriculture Organization, 1956. (Report No. 517.)

Lambton, Ann K. S. *Landlord and Peasant in Persia*. New York and London: Oxford University Press, 1953.

———. *Islamic Society in Persia*. London: School of Oriental and African Studies, University of London, 1954.

Lang, C. L. "Les Minorités arménienne et juive d'Iran," *Politique étrangère*, 26 (1961): 460–71.

Laufer, Berthold. "Sino-Iranica: Chinese Contributions to the History of Civilization in Ancient Iran," *Field Museum of Natural History, Anthropological Series*, 15 (1919): 185–630.

Leiden, Carl, ed. *The Conflict of Traditionalism and Modernism in the Muslim Middle East*. Austin: University of Texas Press [in press].

Lerner, Daniel, and Pevsner, L. W. *The Passing of Traditional Society: Modernizing the Middle East.* Glencoe, Ill.: Free Press, 1958.

Le Strange, Guy. "The Cities of Kirmān in the Time of Ḥamd-Allah Mustawfi and Marco Polo," *Journal of the Royal Asiatic Society* (1901), pp. 281–90.

———. *The Lands of the Eastern Caliphate.* Cambridge: Cambridge University Press, 1905.

Le Tourneau, Roger. *Fès avant le protectorat.* Casablanca: Institut des Hautes Études Marocaines, 1949.

Levi della Vida, G. "Khāridjites," in *Shorter Encyclopaedia of Islam,* pp. 246–49, ed. by H. A. R. Gibb and J. H. Kramers. London: Luzac and Co., 1961.

Levy, Reuben. *The Sociology of Islam.* London: Williams and Norgate, 1931–33. 2 vols.

Lewis, Oscar, and Hauser, Philip M. "The Folk-Urban Ideal Types," in *The Study of Urbanization,* pp. 491–517, ed. by Philip M. Hauser and Leo F. Schnore. New York: John Wiley and Sons, 1965.

Lo, C. "Les Foggaras du Tidikelt," *Travaux de l'Institut des Recherches Sahariennes,* 10 (1953): 139–81; 11 (1954): 49–79.

Lockhart, Laurence. *The Fall of the Ṣafavī Dynasty and the Afghan Occupation of Persia.* Cambridge: Cambridge University Press, 1958.

———. *Persian Cities.* London: Luzac and Co., 1960.

Lowenthal, David. *George Perkins Marsh: Versatile Vermonter.* New York: Columbia University Press, 1958.

MacFadyen, W. A. "Water Supplies in Iraq," *Iraq Geological Publications,* No. 1, 1938.

Marçais, G. "Salle-antisalle: recherches sur l'évolution d'un thème de l'architecture domestique en pays d'Islam," *Annales de l'Institut d'Études Orientales,* 10 (1952): 274–301.

Marsh, George Perkins. *Man and Nature; or, Physical Geography as Modified by Human Action.* New York: Scribners, 1864.

Maxwell, Gavin. *People of the Reeds.* New York: Harper and Bros., 1957.

Maxwell-Hyslop, K. R. "Note on a Shaft-Hole Axe-Pick from Khurab, Makran," *Iraq,* 17 (1955): 161.

Mazaheri, Aly-Akbar. *La Famille iranienne aux temps anté-islamiques.* Paris: Librairie Orientale et Américaine, 1938.

Miller, William Green. "Hosseinabad: A Persian Village," *Middle East Journal,* 18 (1964): 483–98.

Miner, Horace. "The Folk-Urban Continuum," *American Sociological Review,* 17 (1952): 529–37.

———. *The Primitive City of Timbuctoo.* Princeton: Princeton University Press, 1953.

Mohebbi, Manoutchehr K. *L'Influence religieuse sur le droit constitutionnel de l'Iran.* Tehran: Imprimerie Taban, 1958.

Mohensin, Nouredin N. "Mechanization of Agriculture in Iran." East Lansing, Mich.: Unpublished M.A. thesis, Michigan State University, 1953.

Morgan, J. de. "Feudalism in Persia: Its Origin, Development, and Present Condition," *Smithsonian Institute Report* (1913), pp. 579–606.

Muir, A. "Notes on the Soils of Syria," *Journal of Soil Science*, 2 (1951): 163–82.

Murphey, Rhoads. "The City as a Center of Change: Western Europe and China," *Annals of the Association of American Geographers*, 44 (1954): 349–62.

Musil, Alois. *The Manners and Customs of the Rwala Bedouins.* New York: American Geographical Society, 1928. (Oriental Explorations and Studies, No. 6.)

Nader, Laura. "Communication between Village and City in the Modern Middle East, *Human Organization*, 24 (1965): 18–24.

Nariman, G. K., ed. *The Ahad Nameh.* Bombay: Iran League, 1925.

Nieuwenhuijze, C. A. O. van. "The Near Eastern Village: A Profile," *Middle East Journal*, 16 (1962): 295–308.

———. *Social Stratification and the Middle East.* Leiden: E. J. Brill, 1965.

Noel, E. "Qanats," *Journal of the Royal Central Asian Society*, 31 (1944): 191–202.

Olmstead, A. T. *History of the Persian Empire.* Chicago: University of Chicago Press, 1948. (Phoenix edition.)

Overseas Consultants. *Report on the Seven Year Development Plan for the Plan Organization of the Imperial Government of Iran.* Vol. 3. New York: Overseas Consultants, 1949.

Parsa, A. *Flore de l'Iran.* Tehran: Ministry of Education, Government of Iran, 1952. 5 vols.

Patai, Raphael. "Nomadism: Middle Eastern and Central Asian," *Southwestern Journal of Anthropology*, 7 (1951): 401–14.

———. "The Middle East as a Culture Area," *Middle East Journal*, 6 (1952): 1–21.

Peterson, A. D. *Bibliography on the Climate of Iran.* Washington, D.C.: United States Weather Bureau, 1957.

Philby, H. St. John B. *Arabian Highlands.* Ithaca: Cornell University Press, 1952.

Planhol, Xavier de. "Les Villages fortifiés en Iran et en Asie Centrale," *Annales de géographie*, 67 (1958): 256–58.

———. *The World of Islam.* Ithaca: Cornell University Press, 1959.

———. "Pressione demografica e vita di montagna nella Persia settentrionale," *Bollettino della Società Geografica Italiana*, 1 (1960): 90–96.

———. "Abadan: morphologie et fonction du tissu urbain," *Revue géographique de l'Est*, 4 (1964): 338–85.

———. *Recherches sur la géographie humaine de l'Iran septentrional.* Paris: Centre de Recherches et Documentation Cartographiques et Géographiques, 1964. (Mémoires et documents, Vol. 9.)

Polo, Marco. *The Book of Ser Marco Polo, the Venetian, concerning the Kingdoms and Marvels of the East,* trans. and ed. by Sir Henry Yule, revised by Henri Cordier. London: J. Murray, 1921. 2 vols.

Polybius. *The Histories of Polybius*, trans. by Evelyn S. Shuckburgh. London and New York: Macmillan and Co., 1889.

Ptolemy, Claudius. *Geography of Claudius Ptolemy*, trans. and ed. by E. L. Stevenson. New York: New York Public Library, 1932.

Querry, A. *Recueil des lois concernant les musulmans schytes*. Paris: Imprimerie nationale, 1871–72. 2 vols.

Ramazani, R. K. " 'Church' and State in Modernizing Society: The Case of Iran," *American Behavioral Scientist*, 7 (1964): 26–28.

Redfield, Robert. *Peasant Society and Culture*. Chicago: University of Chicago Press, 1960. (Phoenix edition.)

Rivlin, Benjamin, and Szyliowicz, Joseph S., eds. *The Contemporary Middle East: Tradition and Innovation*. New York: Random House, 1965.

Ronaghy, Hassan Ali. "Agricultural Problems in Iran." Carbondale, Ill.: Unpublished M.A. thesis, Southern Illinois University, 1962.

Rosenfeld, A. Z. "La Kala, type d'établissement fortifié iranien," *Sovietskaïa ethnografia*, 1 (1951): 22–38.

Sackville-West, V. "Persian Gardens," in *The Legacy of Persia*, pp. 259–91, ed. by A. J. Arberry. Oxford: Clarendon Press, 1953.

Sanjana, Jehangir B. *Ancient Persia and the Parsis: A Comprehensive History of the Parsis and Their Religion from Primeval Times to Present Age*. Bombay: Privately published, 1935.

Scharlau, K. "Moderne Umgestaltungen in Grundriss iranischer Stadte," *Erdkunde*, 15 (1961): 180–91.

Shrader, W. D. "Report to the Kerman Development Corporation on Agricultural Development of Kerman Region." Tehran: Unpublished manuscript, 1958.

————. "Agricultural Problems and Potentials in Iran," *Journal of Soil and Water Conservation*, 18 (1962): 23–24.

Sjoberg, Gideon. "Folk and Feudal Societies," *American Journal of Sociology*, 58 (1952): 231–39.

————. "The Preindustrial City," ibid., 61 (1955): 438–45.

————. *The Preindustrial City: Past and Present*. Glencoe, Ill.: Free Press, 1960.

Smith, Anthony. *Blind White Fish in Persia*. London: George Allen and Unwin, 1953.

Smith, Euan. "The Perso-Baluch Frontier Mission, 1870–71," in *Eastern Persia, an Account of the Journeys of the Persian Boundary Commission*, 1: 143–224, ed. by Frederic J. Goldsmid. London: Macmillan and Co., 1876.

Spooner, B. J. "The Function of Religion in Persian Society," *Iran: Journal of the British Institute of Persian Studies*, 1 (1963): 83–93.

Stack, Edward. *Six Months in Persia*. London: Sampson Low, Marston, Searle, and Rivington, 1882. 2 vols.

Stein, Aurel. "Note on a Map of the Turfan Basin," *Geographical Journal*, 82 (1933): 236–46.

————. "Archaeological Reconnaissances in Southern Persia," ibid., 83 (1934): 119–34.

————. *Archaeological Reconnaissances in North-West India and South-Eastern Irān.* London: Macmillan and Co., 1937.

Stevens, Roger. *The Land of the Great Sophy.* London: Methuen and Co., 1962.

Steward, Julian H. *Theory of Culture Change.* Urbana, Ill.: University of Illinois Press, 1955.

Stirling, Paul. *Turkish Village.* London: Weidenfeld and Nicolson, 1965.

Strabo, Gnaeus Pompeius. *The Geography of Strabo,* trans. by H. C. Hamilton and W. Falconer. London: Henry G. Bohn, 1854. 3 vols.

Stratil-Sauer, G. "Beobachtungen zur Sommerwitterung einer südpersichen Höhenstation (Ra'in)," *Gerlands Beiträge zur Geophysik,* 41 (1941): 193–225.

Surushian, Jamshid. *Farhangi Behdīnān [Dictionary of the Good People].* Tehran: J. S. Surushian, 1956.

Sweet, Louise, *Tell Ṭoqaan: A Syrian Village.* Ann Arbor: University of Michigan Press, 1960. (University of Michigan, Museum of Anthropology, Anthropological Papers, No. 14.)

Sykes, Ella C. *Persia and Its People.* London: Methuen and Co., 1910.

Sykes, Percy M. *Ten Thousand Miles in Persia or Eight Years in Iran.* London: John Murray, 1902.

————. *A History of Persia.* London: Macmillan and Co., 1921. 2 vols.

Thomas, William L., ed. *Man's Role in Changing the Face of the Earth.* Chicago: University of Chicago Press, 1956.

Tienstra, T. J., and Strandkjaer, N. *Opium Poppy Replacement (Ostan IX).* Rome: Food and Agriculture Organization, 1958. (Report No. 963 and No. 58/9/7221.)

Troussu, Pierre. "Les Retharas de Marrakech," *France-Maroc,* 3 (1919): 246–49.

United Nations Report. "Changing Socio-Economic Patterns in the Middle East," in *The Contemporary Middle East: Tradition and Innovation,* pp. 299–313, ed. by Benjamin Rivlin and Joseph S. Szyliowicz. New York: Random House, 1965.

US AID/Iran. "Agricultural Feasibility of Deep-Well Irrigation: A Typical Deep-Well Pumping Plant, Karaj, Gazvin, and Zanjan Area, Iran, Pumping Plant A." Tehran: Unpublished manuscript, 1962.

Vanden Berghe, L. *Archéologie de l'Irān ancien.* Leiden: E. J. Brill, 1959.

Vaziri, Ahmad 'Ali Khan. *Tārīkhi Kirmān (Sālārīyeh) [History of Kirman],* ed. by Hafez Farman Farma'ian. Tehran: Persian Book Co., 1961.

Vesey-FitzGerald, Seymour G. *Muhammadan Law: An Abridgement according to Its Various Schools.* London: Oxford University Press, 1931.

Violich, Francis. "Evolution of the Spanish City," *Journal of the American Institute of Planners,* 28 (1962): 170–79.

Voinot, L. "Le Tidikelt: étude sur la géographie, l'histoire, et les moeurs du pays," *Bulletin de la Société de Géographie et d'Archéologie d'Oran,* 29 (1909): 185–216, 311–66, 419–80.

Vreeland, Herbert H., ed. *Iran.* New Haven: Human Relations Area Files, 1957.

Wagner, Philip L., and Mikesell, Marvin W., eds. *Readings in Cultural Geography.* Chicago: University of Chicago Press, 1961.

Watt, W. Montgomery. *Islam and the Integration of Society.* London: Routledge and Kegan Paul, 1961.

West, E. W., trans. "Epistles of Manuskihar," in *The Sacred Books of the East,* 18: 279–366, ed. by F. Max Müller. Oxford: Clarendon Press, 1882.

Weulersse, Jacques. "Antioche, essai de géographie urbaine," *Bulletin d'études orientales,* 4 (1934): 27–79.

———. *Paysans de Syrie et du Proche-Orient.* Paris: Gallimard, 1946.

Williams, E. Crawshay. *Across Persia.* London: Edward Arnold, 1907.

Wissmann, H. von, et al. "On the Role of Nature and Man in Changing the Face of the Dry Belt of Asia," in *Man's Role in Changing the Face of the Earth,* pp. 278–303, ed. by William L. Thomas. Chicago: University of Chicago Press, 1956.

Young, T. Cuyler. "Interaction of Islamic and Western Thought in Iran," in *Near Eastern Culture and Society,* pp. 130–47, ed. by T. Cuyler Young. Princeton: Princeton University Press, 1951.

———, ed. *Near Eastern Culture and Society.* Princeton: Princeton University Press, 1951.

Zeuner, F. E. "The Identity of the Camel on the Khurab Pick," *Iraq,* 17 (1955): 162–63.

Index

Abadan, 4
Abbasids, 25
'Abdul Hamid Mirza, 58
'Abdullahabad, 36–37, 56, 64, 142
Abgarm, 36–37, 138, 171n10
Ab Kush *qanat*, 34, 138
Achaemenians, 20, 136, 166n28
Afghanistan, 3, 27, 136, 174n18
Afghans: attack Kirman, 27, 44–45
Africa, 21
Agriculture: organization of, 21, 69, 88–90, 113, 141–46, 170n3; in villages, 54, 59–60, 83–84, 85–86, 151–54 *passim*; in mountains, 61–64; in city, 70–71, 77, 148; in regional subcenters, 79–83, 150, 151; change in, 102, 105–7; crops, 117–20; tools, 120–21; techniques, 121–24; role of animals in, 128–34. *See also* Crops
Ahmadabad Dogu, 36–37, 68
Ahura Mazda, 19
Ahwaz, 4
'Aishabad, 36–37
Akbar the Great, 163n51
Alberts, Robert C., 112–13, 173n3
Alfalfa: as fodder crop, 105–6, 107–8, 131; yields, 120; mentioned, 59, 64, 82, 177n17
Algeria, 136
'Aliabad, 36–37, 142, 145
Al Kharj, 136
Alluvial fans: soils of, 14–16; settlement of, 19–20, 22, 49–60, 135
Almond, 13, 59, 108, 120
Al-Munṣif, xviii, 113
Al Qatif, 136

Alum, 125, 126
Amirabad, 36, 68, 121, 142
'Amiri family, 169n12
Amritsar, 28
Anahita, 22
Anar, 3, 4
Anaristan, 33
Animals: ownership of, 56, 82, 91–92, 107–8; shelters for, 62; population in Kirman Basin, 88–89, 128–34, 170n22, 178n5, 178n7; and overgrazing, 107–8, 159n18
Ankara, 168n1
Anushiravan the Just, 21, 162n26
Apple, 59, 120
Apricot, 59, 108, 120
Aqa Sayyid Haydayat, 169n12
'Arababad, 142
Arab conquest, 23–25, 166n28
Arabia, 7, 136
Arbabi (large landowners), 88, 179–80n3
Arbil, 136, 160n10
Ardashir I, 21
Ardistan, 4
Arg. See Citadel
Artisans: in city, 39, 41–42, 74–76, 148; in regional subcenters, 68–69, 79, 81–82, 149, 150–51; in villages, 132, 143, 151–54 *passim*; mentioned, 70, 71. *See also* Craftsmen
Asafoetida (*Ferula alliacea, F. persica*), 14, 27
Ash, 59
Asiab 'Abd ul-Hasan, 36–37
Asiab Kaleh, 36–37

Asiatic plane, 58, 59
Assyria, 160n10
Astarabad (Gurgan), 162n26
Astragalus (*Astragalus echidnae formis, A. gossypinus*), 12, 13, 14
Atacama, 136
Atlas Mountains, 136
Azar Mahan, 162n26

Bab, 56
Baghdad, 42, 169n10, 175n1
Baghin, 5, 12, 15, 16, 33, 38
Bagh Sayyid Husayn, 36–37
Bagh Shahzadeh, 36–37, 58–59
Baharistan, 36–37, 61, 118, 120, 142, 171n5
Baker, 41, 68, 69, 70, 81, 149–52 *passim*
Bakhsh, 79, 146, 167n37
Bakhshdar, viii, 57, 65
Baluchi sheep, 131, 133
Baluchistan: tribes of, 66, 125; migration from, 123, 128; mentioned, 5, 22, 91, 136, 157–58n5
Bam, 4, 5, 25, 28, 35, 66, 136, 163n42
Bampur, 18
Bandar 'Abbas, 4, 27
Band gav, 120
Banker, 69, 80, 81
Barber: traveling, 68, 85; guild, 76; mentioned, 70, 149–53 *passim*
Bardsir: Arab name for Kirman City, 25
Bardsir (Mashiz): sugar beet mill at, 60, 105, 106, 117, 119
Barley: and climate, 9; types and yields, 117, 118–19; sour, 118, 131; cultivation techniques, 121–24; mentioned, 54, 64, 69, 106
Basra, 169n10
Bath: in Kirman City, 28, 39, 41; in villages, 56, 57; origin of, 167n39; mentioned, 53, 82, 83, 144
Bathkeeper, 68, 70, 75, 76, 89, 149–53 *passim*
Batmann, 125
Bazaar: of Kirman City, 39, 41, 46, 66, 84; moneylenders of, 67; traditional retail merchants of, 74–76. *See also* Vakil Bazaar
Beckett, Philip H. T., 17, 139, 177n17
Beef, 128
Beggar, 54, 69, 82, 99

Bibigrami, 36–37, 56–57
Birjand, 4, 7–8, 135, 136
Birkand, 62
Blacksmith, 41, 68, 70, 75, 76, 78, 81, 89, 149–54 *passim*
Bobek, Hans, 13, 157n14, 160n2
Breadwheat (*Triticum aestivum*), 176n5
British: in Kirman, 27–28
British East India Company, 26
Bulbulu, 33
Butcher, 78
Butter, 129, 133
Buwayhid dynasty, 3, 25
Byzantium, 21

Cabbage, 120
Cairo, 175n1
Camel, 122, 129, 178n5
Camelthorn (*Alhagi camelorum*), 12–13, 14
Cantaloupe (*Kharbuzeh*), 119
Caravanserais: in Kirman, 28, 39, 41
Caraway (*Carum carui*), 14
Carpenter, 41, 68, 70, 75, 76, 78, 81, 89, 149–54 *passim*
Carpet merchant, 39, 41, 88, 91–92, 98, 107, 111, 132. *See also* Merchant
Carpet weaver: contracts of, 70, 92–94; conditions of, 80–81, 110, 132; in villages, 83, 84, 151–53 *passim*
Carpet weaving: historical development of, 26, 27–29, 163n51; production process of, 67, 109, 125–27, 171–72n17, 172n18, 175n28; contracts in, 70, 92–94; in Kirman City, 70, 92–94; in villages, 83, 84, 151–53 *passim*; change in, 102, 109–10
Cash crops, 54, 105–6, 117, 119–20, 122–23. *See also* Crops
Castor bean, 14, 120
Cathay, 26
Cattle, 82, 107–8, 120, 122, 123, 128–30, 177n1, 177–78n2, 178n6
Cemetery, 44, 45–46, 57
Census, First Iranian (1956), vii, viii, 147
Central Asia, 7, 19, 136
Central Plateau: historical development in, 18–19, 161n10; agriculture of, 117, 118, 131
Chahar ayish, 122

Change: in Iran, xx, 173*n1*, 173*n3*; social, in Kirman, xx, 74–76, 78, 98–110; economic, in Kirman, xx, 102, 105–10, 145, 146. *See also* Modernization

Charcoal: burners, 22, 85, 104, 107–8, 149, 151, 154, 162*n27*; burning, 38, 61, 68; sellers, 41; mentioned, 86, 129

Char-Khanu, 12

Chashmeh Kush, 36–37, 38, 61, 62, 104, 143, 171*n5*, 171*n7*

Chashmeh Shaghin, 36–37, 64

Chatrud, 29

Cheese, 128, 133

Cherry, 59

Chicken, 82

Chicory (*Cichorium intybus*), 14

Chile, 136

China, 21, 136, 177*n1*

Chinese Turkestan (Sinkiang), 136

Circumcision, 57

Citadel: of Kirman City, 25, 39, 40, 46, 47

Citrus fruit, 10

City: Middle Eastern, xvii, 111–12, 175*n1*; Iranian, 21, 65–69, 157*n2*; Kirman, 39–45; planning, 42, 45–46, 165*n14*. *See also* Kirman City; Urban dominance

Clan villages, xix, 22–23, 161*n13*. *See also* Communalism; Villages

Clay hoops, 139, 140

Clerk, 69, 70, 74, 147

Climate: of Iran, 7–8; of Kirman, 7–12; houses and, 61. *See also* Rainfall; Temperature

Clipping: of carpets, 127, 177*n5*

Cloth: sellers, 39, 41, 75, 76; guild, 170*n19*; mentioned, 27, 67, 74, 129

Cochineal, 125, 126

Commerce. *See* Trade

Commoner class: in Iran, 21, 169*n9*; in Kirman City, 44, 71, 76–79, 99–100; in villages, 54, 81–83, 161*n17*

Communalism: little, in Kirman, xix, 20, 22–23, 157*n14*,162*n28*; in Islamic law, 24; in grainfields, 82, 172–73*n23*. *See also* Clan villages; Villages

Communications: in Iran, 3; in Kirman Basin, 65–69, 99, 112–13; clerical control of, broken, 72–73, 100–101

Contract system: in agriculture, 66–67, 143; in herding, 67; in weaving, 67; mentioned, 69, 113. *See also* Carpet weaving; Herding; Sharecroppers

Coon, Carleton S., 175*n1*, 180*n7*

Coppersmith, 39, 41, 68, 75, 76

Coriander (*Coriandrum sativum*), 14

Cotton, 117

Craftsmen: in Kirman City, 39, 41, 70, 71, 74–76, 148; in regional subcenters, 79, 81–83, 149, 150–51; in villages, 132, 143, 151–54 *passim*. *See also* Artisans

Cressey, George B., 161*n10*

Croatia, 167*n41*

Crops: rotation of, 16, 62, 94–95, 117, 122; grown in Kirman Basin, 64, 95, 107–8, 117–20; division of, 85, 88–90, 106, 124, 170–71*n4*, 171*n5*. *See also* Agriculture

Crop-watcher, 89, 94–95, 150–54 *passim*

Cross-cousin marriage, 100, 101

Cucumbers, 119, 122, 123

Cummin (*Cuminum cyminum*), 14, 105–6

Cypress, 58–59

Cyprus, 136

Cyrus, 19

Dagh Razin, 36–37, 38

Dalak, 167*n40*

Damascus, 175*n1*

Damghan, 3, 4

Dang, 145

Darband, 162*n26*

Dareh Gaz, 36–37, 61, 142

Dareh Hasani, 36–37, 64

Dari, 166*n24*

Darlstan, 36, 38, 61, 62, 92, 103, 142, 145, 171*n13*

Darius, 19, 136

Darsinuieh, 33

Darvish, 56, 76

Dashti, 123

Dashti Kavir, 3, 4

Dashti Lut, 3, 4, 5, 25, 163*n42*

Dates, 10

Davarabad, xviii, 113

Debt: of villagers, 67, 90, 141, 171*n7*; interest rates on, 169*n15*

Deep well, 103–4, 107, 175*n20*

Deh Hunari, 36–37, 103, 139, 141, 169*n12*
Dehlalu, 33
Dhahran, 136
Digging stick, 122
Dihistan, 57, 79
Dihqan, 21, 24
District head (*bakhshdar*), viii, 57, 65
Division of crop. *See* Crops
Division of labor. *See* Labor, division of
Do ayish, 122
Doctor, 65, 70, 80, 149, 150
Dog, 168*n44*, 171*n12*
Donkey: uses of, 120, 123, 128; dung, 122, 178*n6*; population in Kirman, 129–31, 178*n5*; mentioned, 82, 107–8, 178*n4*
Donkeyman, 71, 78, 129
Down, 26, 28, 131, 133, 171*n13*
Dues, 84–85, 89
Dum Dahaneh Zahrud, 36–37, 64
Dung, 122–23, 178*n6*
Durum wheat (*Triticum durum*), 176*n5*
Dutch East India Company, 26
Dye-houses, 88, 92–93, 125
Dyer's weed, 126
Dyes: plants used for, 14, 125–26, 177*n1*; mentioned, 75, 81, 92–93, 109, 125–26. *See also* Carpet weaving

Economy: of Kirman City, xix, 69–72, 75–76, 100–101, 102; of villages, 38, 56–60, 61–62, 64, 83–86; regional organization of, 65–69, 87–97, 111–13; of regional subcenters, 79–83; change in, 101–10, 113–14
Education: and social status, 80–81, 99, 101; and religion, 100, 101, 144; mentioned, 72–73, 74
Eggplant, 119
Egypt, 136
Elburz Mountains, 3, 4
Elite. *See* Upper class
Elm, 59
Embroidery, 26
Endowed land. *See Vaqf*
Entrepreneurs: in carpet weaving, 93, 177*n3*
Environment: of Kirman, xx, 3–17, 30, 60, 87; and economy, 3–17 *passim*, 94, 105, 118, 131, 135, 143–44. *See also* Climate; Soils; Topography; Vegetation
Evil eye, 58, 82
Extended family. *See* Family

Fallowing, 119, 122, 159–60*n22*, 177*n16*
Familles souches, 100
Family: changing role of, 80, 99–100, 101, 113–14; as economic unit, 82, 110, 146
Farizan *qanat*, 34, 35
Farmitan *qanat*, 34
Fars, 3, 25
Farsi knot, 127
Faruhar, Jamshid, 174*n18*
Fath 'Ali Shah, 164*n67*
Fennel (*Foeniculum vulgare*), 14
Fenugreek (*Trigonella foenumgraecum*), 14
Fertilizer: use of chemical, 16, 106, 107, 122–23, 144, 177*n18*; practices, 66, 120, 122–23, 143; mentioned, 62, 73, 88, 133, 178*n6*. *See also* Dung; Manure; Night soil
Feudal system: historical, 20–23, 157*n14*; persistence of, 56–59, 113–14
Fez, 175*n1*, 180*n7*
Field patterns, 50, 54, 59–60, 62–64. *See also* Agriculture
Fig, 120
Fire-temple, 21, 25, 49
Flocks. *See* Goats; Sheep
Fodder crops, 107–8, 118, 120, 131. *See also* Crops
Foggara. *See Qanat*
Folk society, xvii, xviii, xx, 80–81, 85–86, 112–13. *See also* Peasantry; Peasant society
Folk-urban continuum, 113
Food: habits, 118, 128–29, 133; and religion, 144, 178*n4*
Fragmentation, 50, 56, 60, 143–44, 146
Fruit trees, 59, 82, 89, 108, 120
Fuel: collectors, 22, 38, 53–54, 61, 85–86, 104; problem of, 107–8, 112, 178*n6*

Ganj 'Ali Khan, 39
Garden: household, 50, 54, 76, 82, 120; Persian, 58–59, 71, 168*n6*
Garlic, 59, 120

Garmsar, 173*n3*
Gav ahan, 120
Gaz. See Tamarisk
Ghalzai, 27
Ghasalkhaneh, 57
Ghazban ibn Qab'siri, 25
Ghuzz Turks, 26
Goats: in Kirman Basin, 13, 131–34, 171*n9*, 178*n7*; ownership of, 61, 62, 67; overgrazing of, 107–8; mentioned, 9, 12, 82, 88, 91–92. *See also* Animals; Kashmir goats; Ra'in goats
Goldsmith, 69
Grocer, 41, 75
Guild, 75–76, 96–97
Gujgin, 33
Gulick, John, xx, 113
Gum tragacanth, 13, 14, 27
Gypsies, 72, 78, 126, 169*n10*

Hadhramaut, 136
Hafiz, 59
Hakimabad, 36–37, 142
Halil Rud, 18
Hallaj (hand-carder of wool), 126
Hallal, 178*n4*
Hamadan, 4, 135
Hamlets: regional function of, 60–64, 108; economy of, 85–86, 118, 129–34 *passim*, 153–54, 176*n2*; mentioned, xix, 113, 174*n22*. *See also* Settlement; Villages
Hanak Bala, 36–37, 61, 92, 103, 142, 145, 146
Hanak Pa'yin, 36–37, 92, 142, 145, 146
Hanak valley, 86, 92, 105, 108, 121–22, 146
Harim, 38–39, 42, 165*n18*
Harrow, 121–22, 176*n13*
Hasanabad, 36–37, 142
Hasanabad Kupang, 36–37
Hawkers, 69, 76–77, 168*n5*
Hazelnut, 120
Henna (*Lawsonia inermis*), 14, 120, 125, 126
Herbs, 14, 54, 59, 82, 120
Herding: in mountains, 38, 61–62, 64, 132–33; contracts in, 67, 69, 88, 91–92, 97, 171*n10*, 171*n11*; in regional subcenters, 79, 150, 151; change in, 102, 107–8; in villages, 151–54 *passim*

Herodotus, 161*n12*
Hinaman, 33
Hinterland: of Kirman City, 49–50, 67, 111–12
Honeydew melon (*garmak*), 119
Horse, 129, 178*n5*
Hound's tongue (*Cynoglossum officinale*), 14
House of Strength (*zurkhana*), 75, 169–70*n16*
Houses: in Kirman City, 41–44, 165*n19*; in villages, 53–54, 57–59, 61–62, 166*n20*, 167*n41*
Hujatabad, 36–37, 53, 92, 103, 139, 145, 169*n12*
Husayn, 56, 144, 167*n38*
Husaynabad, 36–37
Husaynabad Akhlaqi, 36–37, 142
Husaynabad Mahan, 36–37, 171*n5*
Husaynabad Mahdi Quli, 36, 142

Ice factory, 46, 75, 102
Ikhtiarabad, 12, 33
Ilyas, Abu 'Ali ibn, 25
Imam (religious leader), 24, 72–73
India, 3, 5, 21, 26, 56, 103, 126, 177*n1*, 177*n2*
Indigo, 14, 125–26, 177*n1*
Indo-Iranians, 18–20, 160*n2*, 161*n15*
Indus valley, 169*n10*
Infant mortality, 102–3
Inheritance, 145, 146, 180*n12*
Insaba, 89
Insecurity: in villages, 90, 95
Iquique, 136
Iran: topography of, 3–5; historical development of, 18–20, 23–25; agriculture in, 38–39, 113–14, 117, 118, 135–36, 141, 172–73*n23*; mentioned, xx, 26, 59, 65, 87, 165*n12*, 169*n10*
Iraq, 23–24, 56, 136
Irrigation: in Kirman, 18–19, 87; practices, 50–55, 105, 106, 117–23 *passim*, 135. *See also* Qanat; Water supply
Isfahan, 3, 4, 5, 7–8, 23, 103, 111, 117, 125, 167*n38*, 175*n1*
Islam: historical, 23–27; water law in, 38–39; in villages, 56–57, 58; mentioned, 42, 167*n41*. *See also* Religion; *Shari'a*
Isma'ilabad, 33, 36, 68, 142, 170–71

Isparak. See Dyer's-weed
Istakhr, 19
Istanbul, 28, 29, 175n1
Iwan, 43, 165n17

Janiabad, 33
Javadieh, 17, 36–37, 103, 139–40, 141, 169n12
Jewish Quarter, 40, 41, 42–43, 47
Jews: of Kirman, 42–43, 46, 49, 71–72, 76, 165n15; mentioned, 165n16; 170n19
Jiruft, 18, 25, 163n42
Job's-tears (*Coix lacryma-jobi*), 14
Jordan, 136
Judas tree, 58
Jufti knot, 94, 109, 171–72n17, 175n28
Ju Muiidi, 40, 41, 44
Jupar: carpet weaving in, 29, 96, 177n3; *qanat*s in, 34, 35, 137–38; agriculture in, 58–59, 119, 120, 122–23, 130, 131, 146, 178n18; herding in, 61, 91, 128, 129–34 *passim*, 175n27; social structure of, 65, 79–80, 80–83, 112, 150–51; regional functions of, 66, 67, 68–69; mentioned, viii, 12, 15, 16, 33, 38, 49, 56–57, 84, 94, 103, 108, 139, 142, 168n7, 170n23, 177n12. *See also* Regional subcenter

Kadkhuda, viii, 57, 65, 167n37. *See also* Village headman
Kafeh Bala Mahan, 36–37
Kafeh Sehkunj, 36–37
Kahnu, 33
Kahnuj, 33, 35, 36, 61, 142
Karbala, 167n38
Karimabad, 36–37, 171n5
Karimabad (Jupar), 36–37, 142
Karimabad Haji 'Ali, 36–37, 62, 142, 145
Karimabad Sardar, 36–37, 142, 145, 146
Kariz. See Qanat
Kashan, 3, 4, 135
Kashmir goats, 26, 28, 82, 131
Kazimabad, 36–37, 68, 104, 118, 142, 169n13, 171n5
Khabis, 25
Khankistan, 36–37, 61, 143, 171n5
Kharga, 136

Kharijites, 25, 162n40
Khinaman, 19
Khur, 123
Khurasan, 23–24, 128, 138, 169n10, 174n25
Khurdeh malik, 141, 143–44, 179–80n3. *See also* Landlord
Khurramshahr, 127
Khushnishin ("new settlers"), 81
Kinship, 99–100
Kirkuk, 136
Kirman Basin: environment of, 5–17; historical development of, 20–27; settlements of, 30–39 *passim*, 49–50, 65–69; urban dominance in, 61, 65–69, 87–97, 111–14; change in, 98–110; agriculture in, 117–24, 141–46, 176n5; herding in, 128–34; *qanat*s in, 135, 137–40, 164n4
Kirman City: history of, xix, 3, 5, 21–22, 24–25, 87; change in, xx, 98–110; climate of, 7–12; in nineteenth century, 27–29, 39–45; carpet weaving in, 28–29, 39, 41–42, 75–76, 92–93, 109–10, 125–27, 178n18; *qanat*s of, 32, 35, 135, 137–38, 140; modern, 45–49, 102–3, 165n19; regional functions of, 49–50, 65–72, 80–81, 84, 111–12, 147–49; social structure of, 76–79; agriculture in, 77, 103–4, 120, 124; mentioned, viii, 33, 166n28. *See also* City; Urban dominance
Kirman Province, 5, 18–29, 157–58n5, 177n1
Kirmanshah, 4, 9, 125
Kitābi Qanī (Book of Qanats), 38
Kousar Riz, 28, 33, 34, 36, 49, 51, 68, 103, 118, 119, 138, 142
Kroeber, A. L., 113
Kuhan Chinar, 36–37, 119
Kuhi Badaman, 5, 6, 12, 15, 19, 32, 33
Kuhi Darmanu, 5, 6, 15, 32, 33, 35
Kuhi Dukhtar, 5, 6, 15, 32, 33
Kuhi Jupar: settlements of, 16, 49–50, 60–64, 79–85, 104–5, 168n2; herding in, 108, 177n1, 178n5, 179n9; *qanat*s of, 34, 135, 137–39; mentioned, 5, 6, 15, 17, 32–36 *passim*, 56–57, 90
Kuhi Sehkunj, 5, 6, 15, 32, 33, 34, 36
Kuh Paiyeh, 5, 6, 15, 32, 33, 35

Kupang, 36–37, 92
Kur, 59, 168*n44*
Kutbabad, 40, 41

Labor, division of: in Kirman City, 69–72; in regional subcenters, 79–80, 83; in villages, 83–86. *See also* Occupations
Laborer, 70, 77–78, 81, 149–54 *passim*
Lalehzar River, 19
Lambton, Ann K. S., 161*n13*, 162*n28*
Land: as status symbol, 73, 141, 143, 169*n13*, 169*n15*; preparation of, 122–23; mentioned, 56, 88–89, 144, 179*n1*
Land distribution, 88, 103, 143, 168*n45*, 174*n20*
Landlord: in villages, 51, 53–54, 91–92, 118, 174*n17*; relations with peasants, 59–60, 66–67, 88–90, 132, 141, 143–44; characteristics of, 66–70, 71, 72–73, 141, 143–44, 150–54 *passim*, 157*n19*; and change, 98, 104, 105–7
Land ownership: historical, 20–21, 23, 24; types of, 141–46, 179*n1*; change in, 145–46
Land redistribution, 90, 172–73*n23*
Land reform. *See* Land distribution
Landscape, xviii, 156–57*n12*
Land tenure, 22–23, 88–90, 106, 113, 141–46
Land use, 49–60, 60–64, 95
Langar: economy of, 67, 83–85, 112, 151–52; animals in, 128–34 *passim*; mentioned, 17, 33, 36, 56, 64, 66, 68, 69, 80, 94, 103, 122–23, 138, 142, 145, 146, 169*n13*
Laurel, 12
Law, 70, 72–73, 100, 101. *See also* *Shari'a*
League of Nations, 110
Leek (*Allium porrum*), 14
Legumes, 122, 177*n17*
Lentils, 54, 64, 119
Lerner, Daniel, 74–75, 168*n1*
Lettuce, 120
Levant, 136
Linseed, 120
Locusts, 119
Looms, 92–94, 126–27
Lower class: in villages, 54, 81–83,

161*n17*; in Kirman City, 44, 71, 76–79. *See also* Commoner class
Lutf 'Ali Khan, 27

Madder (*Rubia tinctorum*), 14, 125–26, 177*n2*
Mahan: historical, 22, 25, 26, 56–57, 103; carpet weaving in, 29, 96–97, 171*n14*, 177*n3*; *qanat*s of, 34, 35, 50, 52, 94, 137–38; agriculture in, 58–59, 105, 119–24 *passim*, 146, 167*n37*, 180*n9*; herding in, 61, 91, 92, 128–34 *passim*, 175*n27*; social structure of, 65, 79–80, 80–83, 112, 149–50, 168*n7*, 170*n23*; regional functions of, 66, 67, 68–69; mentioned, viii, 15, 16, 17, 33, 38, 49, 84, 102, 108, 142. *See also* Regional subcenter
Mahan, Azar, 22
Mahani, 40, 41, 44, 46
Mah Char, 36, 61, 68, 105, 122, 138, 142, 171*n6*
Mah Char *qanat*, 34, 138
Mahdiabad, 36–37, 143
Maidani Qal'eh, 40, 41
Makkran, 25
Maktab (religious elementary school), 72, 100
Malaria, vii–viii, 103
Malik Turan Shah, 165*n11*
Mandrake (*Mandragora officinarum*), 14
Mann, 89, 118, 119, 168*n44*, 176*n6*, 176*n9*
Manna, 13
Manure, 16, 64, 122–23
Marco Polo, 26, 163*n51*
Marrakech, 136
Marriage, 100, 101, 170*n20*
Mashhad, 3, 4, 13, 56, 111, 125, 159*n15*, 175*n1*, 177–78*n2*
Mashiz. *See* Bardsir (Mashiz)
Masileh, 4
Masjidi Jami', 39
Masjidi Malik, 165*n11*
Mat, woolen (*jajim*), 69, 81, 82, 84, 126
Mayor. *See* Shahrdar
Mazaheri, A. A., 161*n17*
Mazra'eh, 68, 174*n22*
Mazra'eh Shur, 16, 36–37, 104

Mechanization: in carpet weaving, 109–10, 126

Mediterranean, 7, 9

Melon, 54, 59, 117, 119, 122, 123

Men's quarter (*birun*), 44. *See also* Selamlik

Merchant, 39, 41, 69, 70, 74, 101. *See also* Carpet merchant

Mesopotamia, 3, 21, 136

Mexico, 126, 136

Middle class, 71, 74–76, 80–81, 98–99, 169*n9*, 170*n17*, 173*n2*. *See also* Professional class

Middle East: society in, xvii, 155*n2*; villages of, xviii–xix, 23, 112–13, 172–73*n23*; cities of, xx, 39, 111–12, 175*n1*; change in, xx, 113–14, 168*n1*; landlords of, 73, 157*n19*; mentioned, 19, 26

Midwife, 68, 76

Migration: to Kirman City, 46, 70, 100, 101; to Tehran, 49, 73, 98, 103, 109, 166*n28*, 168*n6*, 173*n2*; intervillage, 82–83, 105, 146; mentioned, 136, 169*n10*

Milk, 82, 91–92, 128–29, 132–33, 178*n4*

Mill, 69, 83, 124, 144, 167*n32*

Millet, 122, 170–71*n4*

Minal, 89

Miner, Horace, 113

Mirab. See Water distributor

Mir 'Alamdar Shrine, 56–57

Modernization: economic, in Kirman, 29, 45–49, 75–76, 105–10, 113–14, 168*n1*; social, in Kirman, 45–49, 72–76, 98–110. *See also* Change

Moldboard plow, 106–7

Moneylender, 67, 75, 90

Mongols, 26

Mosque, 39, 41, 46, 53, 56–57, 75–76, 100

Mother well (*madiri chah*), 137

Mountains: settlements in, 33, 35, 36, 37, 104–5, 174*n21*; herding in, 108, 129–34 *passim*; agriculture in, 118, 121, 122, 171*n5*, 176*n1*; mentioned, 135, 142–46 *passim*. *See also* Kuhi Jupar

Mubashir (intermediary), 69, 141

Mubashiri ab, 95. *See also* Water distributor

Muhallab, 25

Muhammad, 56, 167*n38*

Muharram, 97, 100, 144

Muhiabad: economy of, 59–60, 83–85, 152–53; animals in, 128–34 *passim*; mentioned, 33, 36, 49, 51, 56, 66, 68, 69, 80, 103, 138, 142

Mulberry, 59, 108, 120

Mule, 120, 129, 178*n5*

Mulla (Muslim religious leader), 49, 69, 72–73, 80, 149–52 *passim*

Muqaddasi, 25

Muqanni (*qanat* digger), 136–37, 138–39, 149–54 *passim*, 179*n18*

Murtazi Quli Khan, 28

Mustard, wild (*Brassica alba, B. nigra*), 14, 59

Mutavalli (official), 144, 145, 146, 180*n8*

Nadir Shah, 27

Nail plow, 106–7, 120–21, 121–22

Na'in, 3, 4, 136

Najis, 168*n44*

Napoleonic Code, 101

Narmakan, 36–37, 105, 142

Narmashir, 123

Nasasalar (washer of the dead), 170*n20*

Nay. See Clay hoops

Nayshapur, 24

Nazimabad, 36–37

Nazir izhari (official), 180*n8*

Night soil, 16, 78, 122–23

Nihavand, 23

Ni'matabad, 36–37, 64

Ni'matabad Toujigun, 36–37, 61, 143

Nomads: Middle Eastern, xvii; in Kirman, 19–20

Noria (*na'ura*), 135

North Africa, 136

Nouveaux riches, 72, 73, 141, 143

Nuts, 74, 111

Oak, 12, 13

Occupations: in regional subcenters, 68–69, 79–83, 149–51; in Kirman City, 69–72, 147–49; in villages, 83–85, 112–13, 151–54; in hamlets, 85–86, 153–54; and social status, 99, 100. *See also* Labor, division of

Oleander, 12

Oman, 136

Onion, 59, 120, 123

Opium, 59, 103, 105–6, 119–20, 168*n46*, 174*n25*

Orchard, 44, 53, 54, 59, 62, 82, 89, 108, 117, 120

Overgrazing, 107–8, 175*n27*

Ownership: of houses, 4, 165–66*n19*; in agriculture, 59–60, 95, 141–46; and social status, 72–74, 88–97; of animals, 91–92, 107–8, 129–34, 177*n1*

Paisley shawls, 28

Panjeh, 121, 122, 123, 177*n14*

Parsis, 27

Parthians, 19, 20, 88

Pasture dues, 23, 62, 91, 171*n8*

Pea, 54, 64, 117, 119, 122

Peach, 59, 120

Pear, 59, 120

Peasant proprietors: as farmers, 106, 118, 121–22, 143–44, 146; distribution of, 105, 150–54 *passim*, 170*n3*; mentioned, 59, 69, 81, 85, 132, 145

Peasantry: relations with urbanites, 65–67, 67–68, 85–86, 87–88, 113, 157*n14*; conditions of, 88–90, 118, 128, 129–30, 133. *See also* Sharecroppers

Peasant society, xviii, xx, 112–13. *See also* Folk society

Peddler, 68, 85

Pennyroyal (*Mentha pulegium*), 14, 59

Persepolis, 19

Persia. *See* Iran

Persian Gulf, 23, 71

Persian knot, 127

Peru, 136

Pesticides, 107, 120

Pharmacist, 68, 102, 177*n18*

Pica, 136

Pine, 58, 59

Pistachio, 13, 117, 120, 123

Plow. *See* Nail plow; Moldboard plow; Tractor

Plowing: methods of, 95, 106–7, 121–22; of crops, 118, 119–20; animals used, 128, 177–78*n2*; mentioned, 64, 177*n15*

Plum, 120

Poll tax (*jizya*), 23, 45

Polybius, 161*n10*

Pomegranate, 58, 59, 120, 125, 126

Poplar, 58, 59, 108

Population: historical, 18–29, 100; growth in Kirman, 45–46, 102–5; in mountains, 60–61, 104–5, 174*n21*

Potato, 54, 105–6, 119, 122, 123

Potter, 41, 75, 76

Poverty, 54, 82–83, 89–90, 110, 118

Professional class: in villages, 65, 151, 152, 153; in Kirman City, 69–70, 147; in regional subcenters, 74, 149, 150. *See also* Middle class

Ptolemy, 161*n24*

Qadirabad, 36–37, 118, 119, 142, 145, 146

Qajars, 27

Qalatu, 36–37, 142, 145

Qal'eh (fortress), 19

Qal'ehi Ardashir, 21, 25, 40, 46, 47

Qal'ehi Dukhtar, 22, 25, 40, 46, 47

Qal'ehi Shur, 16

Qanaghistan: economy of, 67, 83–85, 112, 122–23, 152; animals in, 128–34 *passim*; mentioned, 17, 26, 33, 36, 49, 64, 66, 68, 69, 80, 103, 142

Qanat: and settlement, 18–19, 32–39, 49–55, 103–4, 112, 164*n4*, 167*n31*, 180*n5*; historical, 19, 21, 22, 26, 27, 135–36, 160–61*n10*, 178*n7*, 179*n15*; nature of, 30–31, 94–95, 123, 135–40, 164*n3*, 172*n20*, 174*n16*, 176*n2*, 178*n3*; mentioned, xix, 9, 60, 82, 145, 174*n17*, 178*n4*. *See also* Irrigation; Water supply

Qanat builders. *See* Muqanni

Qandahar, 27, 136

Qasab, 38, 50, 118, 119, 164–65*n7*, 176*n6*, 176*n9*

Qatlagah, 56

Qazvin, 3, 4, 103, 135, 170*n19*

Qubbai Sabz, 26

Qudratabad, 36–37, 68, 142, 145, 146, 171*n11*

Quercus persica, 13

Quetta, 136

Quince, 59, 120

Qumm, 3, 4, 56

Qutlugh Beg, 26

Rafsinjan, 4, 117, 120, 136, 164*n2*

Rahimabad, 36–37, 68
Ra'in, 25, 163*n42*
Rainfall, xix, 9, 10, 117, 158*n9*, 158*n10*. *See also* Climate
Ra'in goats, 131, 133
Ramazan, 100
Rasht, 4
Ravar, 5, 66, 177*n3*
Redfield, Robert, 113
Region: as unit of study, xviii, 113; in Middle East, 111–12, 112–13
Regional subcenter: economy of, 68–69, 79–83, 149–51; social structure of, 80–83; mentioned, 65, 112, 168*n7*, 170*n23*. *See also* Jupar; Mahan
Religion: and segregation, 42–43, 44–45; opposition to change, 45–46, 72–73, 99–101, 113–14; traditional role of, 56–57, 75–76, 80, 96–97, 100, 170*n17*, 178*n4*. *See also* Islam; Zoroastrians
Renting: of land, 143–44, 170*n3*; of houses, 165–66*n19*; of water, 180*n5*
Reservoirs (*ambars*), 41
Resources: urban control of, 66–69
Ribat, xix
Rice, 74
Ricinus communis, 14
Rindeh. See Harrow
Rish safid (elders), 75
Riyadh, 136
Riza Shah, 49, 98–99, 144, 166*n28*, 173*n11*
Romans, 21, 136
Root beet, 120, 123, 131, 170–71*n4*
Rose, wild, 12, 13
Rotation: of crops, 16, 62, 94–95, 117, 122; of water, 94–95, 123, 172*n22*
Roughanu, 36–37, 138, 142, 145, 171*n10*
Rudi Lalehzar, 19
Rue (*Ruta graveolens*), 13, 14, 82, 123
Rug (*gilim*), 82, 126
Russia, 177*n2*

Sa'adi (poet), 58
Sa'adi (village), 33
Sabzavar, 4, 7–8
Sad nishan, 93
Safavids, 26–27, 163*n51*
Saffron, 105–6, 120
Sagebrush, 12, 13
Sahni Atabak, 58

Salt, 67
Salvia spp., 13
Samanids, 25
Sand dune: encroachment of, 12, 16–17; distribution of, 33, 34
Saniabad, 180*n5*
Sarasiab, 33
Sar Asiab Khirandish, 36–37
Sar Asiab Sayyid Husayn, 36–37
Sarkar Aqa, 56
Sassanians, xix, 20–23, 87, 88, 136, 166*n28*, 167*n39*
Saudi Arabia, 7, 136
Saveh, 135
Sayyid 'Ali Muhammad (Bab), 56
Sayyid Taghi, 36–37
Secularism: rise in Kirman, 46, 49, 72–73, 101. *See also* Religion
Seed: and sharecropping contracts, 88–89, 143; amount sown, 121, 122
Segregation: religious, 42–43, 44–45, 46, 48, 49
Sehkunj: economy of, 52–54, 96, 122, 124; historical development, 53–54, 55, 57; mentioned, 33, 34, 36, 49, 103, 119, 139, 142
Selamlik (men's quarter), 165*n18*
Seljuq Turks, 26
Sennacherib, 160*n10*
Senneh knot, 127
Servants, 70, 71, 73, 76, 78
Service occupations: in Kirman City, 70, 148; in regional subcenters, 149, 150; in villages, 151, 152, 153
Sesame (*Sesamum indicum*), 14, 59, 120
Settlement: pattern of Kirman Basin, xix, 30, 33, 35, 36–37, 38–39, 87–88, 94–97, 102–5, 111–12, 137–38, 164*n2*; expansion of, 13–14, 103–5, 162*n27*, 174*n21*; and environment, 17, 49–55, 64, 137–38; historical development of, 18–29, 161*n10*; types in Kirman Basin, 49–50, 60–64, 65–69, 112–13, 157*n16*. *See also* Hamlets; Villages
Shaduf, 135
Shahabad, 33, 36, 68, 103, 140, 142, 174*n16*
Shah 'Abbas, 26, 163*n51*
Shah 'Adil, 40, 41
Shahdad, 13, 25, 28, 77, 163*n42*
Shah Ni'matullah Vali, 26

Shah Ni'matullah Vali Shrine, viii, 56–57, 58–59, 79
Shahr, 40, 41
Shahrdar (mayor), viii, 65
Sharecroppers: conditions of, 53–54, 59–60, 106, 123, 132, 141, 150–54 *passim*; contracts with landlords, 69, 77, 88–90, 141, 143–44, 168*n45*, 171*n5*; mentioned, 76, 81, 84, 85. *See also* Peasantry
Shari'a, 38–39, 101
Shawls, 25, 26, 27, 28–29, 76, 111
Shaykh 'Ali Baba Shrine, 53, 55, 57
Shaykhi sect, 56, 83
Sheep: in Kirman Basin, 13, 91–92, 107–8, 131–33, 171*n9*, 178*n7*; ownership of, 61, 62, 67; mentioned, 82, 125. *See also* Animals
Shelters, underground, 62
Shepherds: conditions of, 53–54, 132–33, 150–54 *passim*, 171*n9*; contracts of, 91–92, 171*n10*, 171*n11*; mentioned, 9, 22, 69, 108. *See also* Herding
Shikarpur Hindus, 27
Shiraz, 4, 9, 135, 157*n2*, 177*n2*
Shoemaker, 41, 75, 81, 149–53 *passim*
Shopkeeper, 43, 68, 74, 75, 79, 80–81, 98, 143, 149–53 *passim*
Shrines, viii, 41, 46, 53, 55, 56–57, 58–59, 79, 83, 100
Shurabad, 16, 36–37, 142
Shurdar, 16
Sickle, 121
Silversmith, 75
Sinbad, 24
Sind, 7
Sinkiang, 136
Sirjan, 3, 4, 22, 24, 25, 28, 161*n34*, 163*n42*
Sistan, 58
Sjoberg, Gideon, 169*n9*
Social mobility, 78–79, 83, 99, 100, 101
Social status, 72–74, 78, 80–81, 99, 100
Social structure: in Kirman City, 71–79, 98–101, 169*n9*; in regional subcenters, 80–83; in villages, 83–86; regional organization, 112–13; change in, 113–14; mentioned, 20–21, 49–55, 155*n2*. *See also* Lower class; Middle class; Upper class

Soils, xix, 14–17, 95, 107, 122, 139, 144, 159–60*n22*, 172–73*n23*, 177*n17*
South America, 136
Sowing, 94–95, 118, 119–20, 121–22
Spade, 118, 120, 121–22, 123
Spain, 136
Spices, 28, 54, 59, 111, 120
Spinning, 96, 109–10, 126, 177*n3*
Squash, 59, 120, 122
Stack, Edward, 28
Stein, Sir Aurel, 18
Steward, Julian H., 99
Straw, 89, 124, 131
Street pattern: of Kirman City, 41–46
Sufis, 26, 56
Sugar, 27, 67, 74, 129
Sugar beet, 54, 59–60, 105–6, 119, 122, 123
Sugar beet mill, 60, 105, 106, 117, 119
Sulaymaniyah, 136
Summer crops, 117, 119–20, 122–23. *See also* Crops
Surushian family, 169*n12*
Sweep, counterpoised. *See Shaduf*
Sweet, Louise, xviii
Sykes, Sir Percy, 17, 19, 28
Syria, 136, 169*n10*

Tabaristan, 24
Tabriz, 4, 27–29, 56, 111, 135, 175*n1*, 177*n2*
Tademait plateau, 136
Tailor, 39, 70, 75, 81, 149–53 *passim*
Tajir, 74
Takhteh, 121
Talli Iblis, 18–19
Tamarisk (*Tamarisk gallica, T. mannifera*), 12, 13, 159*n15*
Tanner, 68, 75, 78, 81
Taqdimeh (subsidy), 171*n16*
Tea, 27, 67, 74, 83, 129
Teacher, 65, 69, 80, 85, 147–53 *passim*. *See also* Education
Technology: impact of modern, 98–99, 101–2, 113–14, 120–21
Tehran: environment, 7–8, 9; migration to, 49, 98, 103, 166*n28*; as center of change, 72, 98–99, 173*n1*; mentioned, 3, 4, 5, 56, 73, 111, 127, 135, 141, 165*n16*, 168*n6*
Tell Toqaan, xviii

Temperature: at Kirman City, 10–11, 12, 158*n11*. *See also* Climate
Thermae, 167*n39*
Thistle shrubs (*Artemesia absinthium*), 13
Thresher, wooden (*garjin*), 121, 123
Threshing, 121, 123–24, 128
Tidikelt, 136
Tigiran *qanat*, 34, 180*n5*
Tigiran valley, 68, 83, 108, 169*n13*, 171*n5*
Tigris River, 169*n10*
Timur, 26, 162*n28*
Tinsmith, 81, 149–54 *passim*
Tomato, 54, 117, 119, 122, 123
Topography, 3–5, 95, 135
Toujigun, 36–37, 62–64, 68, 104, 142, 145, 146, 168*n47*, 171*n5*
Tractor, 66, 73, 98, 106, 107, 118, 121–22, 144, 177*n15*
Trade: routes of, 3–5, 25, 26–27, 163*n42*; in Kirman City, 39, 41, 74, 111–12, 148, 169*n15*; historical development of, 21, 25, 26–27, 27–29, 103, 177*n1*; mentioned, 125, 127, 177*n2*
Transportation, 99, 101, 129
Trees, 13–14, 58–59, 107–8, 159*n14*
Tribes: Middle Eastern, xvii; in Kirman, 19–20
Tuberculosis: in cows, 129
Tunis, 175*n1*
Turbati Haydari, 138
Turfan Basin, 136
Turkey, 168*n1*, 180*n7*
Turkhan Khatun, 26
Turki, 178*n7*
Turnip, 123

'Umar I, 24
'Umar II, 24
Underground shelters, 62, 108, 133
Unemployment: in Kirman City, 71, 78, 90, 149, 168*n7*; in regional subcenters, 79, 82–83, 150, 151, 168*n7*, 170*n23*; in villages, 83, 84, 151–54 *passim*
United States, 29, 127
Upper class: historical, 39, 99–100, 161*n17*, 169*n9*; in Kirman City, 44, 71, 72–74, 169*n12*; in villages, 53,

80–81; role of, 88, 98–99, 113–14
Urban dominance: concept of, xviii, xix, xx, 111–14; in Kirman Basin, 56, 66–69, 80–81, 85–86, 87–97; and economy, 88–90, 91–94, 94–97, 132; and change, 98–99, 113–14. *See also* City; Kirman City
Ustan, 158*n5*
'Uthman, 162*n40*

Vakilabad *qanat*, 28, 34, 50, 169*n12*, 172*n20*, 180*n5*
Vakil Bazaar, 39, 40, 41, 47, 75–76, 78. *See also* Bazaar
Vakil-ul-mulk, Muhammad Isma'il Khan, 28, 39
Vaqf (religious endowment), 100, 101, 144–45, 146, 180*n7*, 180*n9*
Vegetation: of Kirman, xix, 12–14; destruction of, 13–14, 61, 107–8, 159*n18*, 175*n27*
Vendors, 76–77, 168*n5*
Vertical mobility, 78–79, 83, 99, 100, 101
Vetches, milk-producing (*Hedysarum alhagi, Astragalus gossypinus, A. echidnaeformis*), 12
Village headman, viii, 57, 65, 80, 89, 125, 126, 167*n37*. *See also* Dihqan
Villages: regional function of, xvii, 67–68, 83, 88, 94–97, 112–13, 170*n21*; organization of, 49–60, 60–64, 90, 94–97, 161*n13*, 166*n20*; economy of, 68, 83–86, 107–8, 117–20, 126–27, 129–34 *passim*, 141–46, 151–54. *See also* Clan villages; Communalism; Settlement

Walid I, 169*n10*
Walnut, 59, 120, 125, 126
Warp (*tun*), 126
Water, sacred. *See Kur*
Water distributor, 89, 94–95, 96, 123, 150–54 *passim*, 172*n22*
Water law, 35, 38–39, 167*n30*
Watermelon (*hindavaneh*), 119
Water supply: and settlement location, xviii, 18–19, 30, 32, 34, 35, 38–39, 68, 112, 176*n2*; social adjustment to, 49–55, 96, 105, 167*n31*; distribution of, 51, 53–54, 94–96, 172*n22*; and

economy, 88–89, 94–95, 117, 119, 122, 179*n1*, 180*n5*; *qanat*, 103–4, 135–40. *See also* Irrigation; *Qanat*
Waterwheel (*dulab*), 135
Weaning, 132, 178*n8*
Weaver. *See* Carpet weaver
Weaving. *See* Carpet weaving
Weft (*putun*), 126
Weld (*Reseda luteola*), 14, 125, 126
Wells, 19–20, 35, 44, 68. *See also* Deep well
Westernization. *See* Change; Modernization
Wheat: and climate, 9; cultivation techniques, 59–60, 121–24; types and yields, 117–18, 176*n5*, 176*n7*; mentioned, 54, 64, 69, 86, 106
Willow, 59
Windmill, 103, 174*n18*
Wind tower (*badgir*), 41, 165*n12*
Winnowing: fork, 121, 123; method of, 123–24
Women: social role of, 58, 77, 170*n17*; economic role of, 82, 126
Women's quarter (*andarun*), 44. *See also Harim*
Wool: of Kirman, 26, 74, 125, 164*n27*; in carpet weaving, 29, 92–93, 125–26; in villages, 91–92, 171*n13*; mentioned, 81, 82, 86, 131, 133

Wormwood, 12

Yaqut, 26, 162*n28*
Yazd, 3, 4, 5, 7–8, 13, 20, 42, 66, 91, 125, 128, 135, 136, 139, 157*n2*, 159*n15*, 164*n2*, 165*n12*, 166*n28*, 168*n6*
Yemen, 136
Yoghurt, 129, 133

Zagros Mountains, 3, 4, 7, 23, 136, 178*n8*
Zahidan, 4, 5, 7–8
Zahrud, 36–37, 142, 145
Zands, 27
Zangiabad, 12, 33
Zar, 172*n18*
Zarand, 13
Zar'i (hillside land), 168*n47*
Zarkuh, 36–37, 68, 143
Zinilabad, 36, 142
Zoroastrian quarter, 27, 40, 41, 44–45, 46, 47, 48, 165*n14*
Zoroastrians: historical treatment of, 21, 24–25, 27, 44–45; in modern Kirman, 46, 48, 49, 71–72, 76, 166*n28*; dialect of, 166*n24*; mentioned, 166*n24*, 168*n6*, 170*n19*, 170*n20*. *See also* Religion
Zurkhana. See House of Strength